Creative Subversions

Creative Subversions
Whiteness, Indigeneity, and the National Imaginary

Margot Francis

UBCPress · Vancouver · Toronto

20 19 18 17 16 15 14 13 12 11   5 4 3 2 1

Printed in Canada on FSC-certified ancient-forest-free paper (100% post-consumer recycled) that is processed chlorine- and acid-free.

Library and Archives Canada Cataloguing in Publication

Francis, Margot
Creative subversions : whiteness, indigeneity and the national imaginary / Margot Francis.

Includes bibliographical references and index.
Issued also in electronic format.
ISBN 978-0-7748-2025-7 (bound); ISBN 978-0-7748- 2026-4 (pbk.)

1. Nationalism – Canada. 2. Patriotism – Canada.
3. National characteristics, Canadian. 4. Emblems, National – Canada.
5. Canada – Symbolic representation. 6. Native peoples – Canada.
I. Title.

FC97.F73 2011   971.07   C2011-906621-1

Canadä

UBC Press gratefully acknowledges the financial support for our publishing program of the Government of Canada (through the Canada Book Fund), the Canada Council for the Arts, and the British Columbia Arts Council.

This book has been published with the help of a grant from the Canadian Federation for the Humanities and Social Sciences, through the Aid to Scholarly Publications Program, using funds provided by the Social Sciences and Humanities Research Council of Canada.

Printed and bound in Canada by Friesens
Set in Hypatia Sans and Warnock by Artegraphica Design Co. Ltd.
Text design: Irma Rodriguez
Copy editor: Joanne Richardson
Proofreader and indexer: Dianne Tiefensee

UBC Press
The University of British Columbia
2029 West Mall
Vancouver, BC V6T 1Z2
www.ubcpress.ca

Contents

Illustrations

Figures

Plates (after page 94)

Preface

By most accounts, the second decade of the twenty-first century has opened with rarely before seen displays of a "new Canadian patriotism."[1] And yet two very different stories about this surge of national sentiment emerged from the Winter Olympics and the mass protests at the G20 Toronto Summit (2010). At the Olympics, pundits, ranging from John Honderich (former publisher of the *Toronto Star*) to Mullkam Samint (on his Vancouver Ethiopian Blog) suggested that "finally, Canadians have shown their patriotic side,"[2] making these games a "coming of age moment" for the entire country.[3] Honderich was a "lucky spectator" at the Montreal (1976), Calgary (1988), and Vancouver (2010) Olympics and suggests that there was a "total difference" in Vancouver, where "the explosion of passion, patriotism and deep emotion about country were nothing short of extraordinary."[4] During the same year, mass protests against the G20 Summit also prompted an outpouring of national passion. In contrast to the self-congratulatory commentary on offer during the Olympics, however, protesters used nationalist images for more uncommon ends. Here commentators like Margaret Atwood, in an article for the *Globe and Mail,* highlighted the emergence of a "new Canada" by drawing attention to the militarization of public space, breaches of protesters' right to peaceful assembly, and mass arrests of over a thousand people – the largest mass arrests in Canadian history.[5] And, in the weeks after the G20 Summit, as thousands of people gathered to demand a public inquiry, many continued to invoke ideas of the nation by carrying or wrapping themselves in the Canadian flag, while others spontaneously sang the national anthem while facing down riot police.[6]

These dramatically different examples of nationalist sentiment nevertheless hold in common important ideas about Canadianness. First, many of the images of Canada on display at both the G20 protests and the Winter Olympics link Canadianness with "doing good." The very "Canadian" idea of a normally benign and compassionate nation was evident in the signature

Figure 0.1 **"Canada Get Well Soon."**
Flag carried by a protester at Canada
Day protest, 2010 Photograph by
Mitchel Raphael

Figure 0.2 **Flag tattoo inspired by**
2010 Olympics patriotism Amazing Ink,
Edmonton, AB. Courtesy of Edmonton CTV

image chosen by *Maclean's* in its coverage of the Canada Day protest in
Toronto, where thousands gathered at the Ontario legislature to demand a
public inquiry into police tactics at the G20 protests (Figure 0.1).[7] Here a
Canadian flag carried by a protester has graffiti, which reads "Canada: get
well soon," drawn over the maple leaf. The graffiti bemoans a temporary illness associated with extraordinary events and hopes for a return to a well-
adjusted normality. Similarly, the Winter Olympics also highlighted the
connection between Canadianness and goodness. As CTV News reported
in March 2010, this inspired a rash of Canadiana-related consumerism, including specialty tattoos from Amazing Ink, an Edmonton-based tattoo
shop. An interview with Mike Henderson, the "man behind the needles,"
who had just applied a Canadian flag to a customer's arm (Figure 0.2), suggests why he thinks business will continue to be brisk. The Canadian flag

makes a great tattoo, Henderson commented, because: "(a) We do good. (b) We're proud of our country. And (c) We're proud of our freakin' country."[8]

In addition to the implicit and explicit connections between Canadianness and goodness, both Olympics organizers and G20 protesters shared a commitment to highlight Indigenous people as central icons in their events.[9] From the "unprecedented inclusion" offered Indigenous people that signed on as co-hosts to the Olympics to the first demonstration to take to the streets at the G20 telling the world about Canada's violations of Indigenous rights,[10] images of Indigenous people were key to how each group positioned itself on the global stage.[11] Further, of the astonishing 15.5 million Canadians who watched the "Aboriginal-inspired" opening of the Olympics, 66 percent "agreed that the opening ceremonies 'reflected Canada' as they know it."[12]

The "new patriotism" highlighted here rests, however, on a much older foundation, for if overt expressions of nationalist sentiment are to be described as "new," they must be contrasted with a much more common set of assumptions, including the sense that Canadianness can only be covertly known – indeed, that it is often undefinable. The actor Mike Myers has pithily described this as "the essence of not being. Not English, not American. It is the mathematic of not being."[13] In a front-page article in the *Globe and Mail* on Canada Day, 2010, Patrick Brethour put it a little differently. He argued that, despite the recent displays of nationalist fervour, Canadians continue to "take delight" in "not demanding plaudits, indeed in not being noticed at all."[14]

So are Canadians "secretly nationalistic"? And, if so, what does this actually mean? And if many people across the political spectrum from Olympics fans to G20 protesters think we live in a compassionate and moral nation (which, from time to time, sickens and loses its way), then why are we so persistently ill at ease with nationalist emotions? And finally, how does our attachment to images of Indigeneity as emblematic of the nation co-exist with a continuing antipathy towards actual Indigenous people – the only group in Canada who continue to live in "Third World" conditions in a country that consistently rates among the top ten in the United Nations Human Development Index?[15]

This book takes up these contradictions by exploring how some of Canada's most recognizable national icons can illuminate the puzzles associated with nationalist attachments. If most Canadians believe that the core of Canadianness is "fairness,"[16] as does James Orbinski, the long-serving head of Doctors without Borders, then how do commonplace and even kitschy symbols articulate Canadianness through implicitly white concepts of justice and evenhandedness? I investigate this question by examining historic and contemporary discourses – about beavers, railways, Banff National Park, and "Indians" – in order to understand how taken-for-granted emblems can also be deeply suggestive artefacts of a national culture. To do this, I employ the theoretical work of Michael Billig to reflect on what I take to be one of Canadian nationalism's most salient features: its banality.

In addition, I explore the persistence of the idea that Canadians, while passionately nationalistic, nevertheless prefer to be "not noticed at all." Here the work of Indigenous writers and scholars has been crucial to my investigation as they point to aspects of the national psyche that are experienced as shadowy or even beyond words. Métis activist and author Maria Campbell, writing in *The Book of Jessica,* says: "Using the word ghost is good because that's what the old people say when they talk about white people in this country: 'Ghosts trying to find their clothes.'"[17] I highlight Campbell's assessment as I am interested in employing the predictable emblems of national purpose in order to explore the ghosting of national identity and the spectres haunting the Canadian imaginary. In sketching out how ideas about haunting link significant themes in Canadian visual culture, I also highlight the potential of select artists to befriend and reimagine Canada's troubled inheritance as they take up its banal symbols and give them new, suggestive meanings. My objective is to engage with what Jacqui Alexander calls "different kinds of remembering" that invite new forms of struggle and, thereby, articulate possibilities for different collectivities and different selves within and beyond the Canadian nation.[18]

Yet this research did not begin with banal objects or ghosts; rather, like many other intuitively grasped projects, I began with what I loved: namely, the work of select Canadian artists who have presented radical, if ephemeral, challenges to Canadianness. Having begun to write about artists, however, I became curious about the connections between seemingly disparate projects. Consequently, my research methodology itself became haunted as visual and artistic texts returned me to questions regarding the material and historic conditions of nation building, and the work of contemporary artists took me back to explore how national symbols had come to serve as points of condensation for a host of contradictory meanings. Thus, I began to investigate how the most predictable objects might still invite a self-reflexive engagement through the displacing image of art.[19] In each of the following chapters, then, I highlight the contradictory meanings implicit in historic images and contemporary artistic work, and invite viewers to reconsider taken-for-granted ideas about power, memory, and national identity.

This book, then, emerged at the juncture of two divergent but inter-secting questions. I wanted to explore the ways in which cultural analysis and artistic engagement can serve as contrapuntal methods for reimagining white, Anglo-Canadian historical memory. And here the use of "contrapun-tal" refers to both the contrapuntal perspective developed in postcolonial theory (which challenges myths of cultural purity to trace how imperial identity has been furnished by non-Western difference)[20] and contrapuntal music (which proceeds with several simultaneous and contrasting mel-odies).[21] Thus, the following chapters investigate banal objects of national purpose in order to explore how, with regard to the past, they offer the pos-sibility of moving from unproblematized possession to imaginative reconsideration.[22]

Acknowledgments

The ideas in this book have taken many years to develop, so I have incurred many debts. First thanks go to colleagues and friends who supported the intuitive process that allowed me to write. In an academic context, Kari Delhi proved a remarkable mentor and friend, while providing cogent feedback on early drafts of this material contained in a thesis; and, in my personal life, I have been extremely fortunate to have been nourished over many years by the friendship and smarts of Hershel Russell. I also owe thanks to faculty at OISE/UT, who assisted with the early development of this work, including Kathleen Rockhill, Roger Simon, Rinaldo Walcott, Sherene Razack, Kathleen Gallagher, and David Levine.

For the sections of the book that deal with the history of Hiawatha performances, I extend my thanks to Karl Hele, director of First People's Studies at Concordia. Thanks are also extended to Clarence Boyer from Batchewana First Nation, whose exhibit of archival photographs on Hiawatha performances at the Art Gallery of Algoma first inspired my curiosity; to my colleagues at Algoma University, Linda Savory-Gordon and Jan Clarke, whose commitment to research allowed me the time to write; to Don Jackson, Alice Corbiere, Alanna Jones, and Gail Broad, who facilitated my connections with Garden River and Batchewana First Nations; and to Jean Pine, Alice Corbiere, Joe Corbiere, Betty Grawbarger, Lana Grawbarger, and Angela Neveau, who graciously participated in interviews. Most significantly, I want to thank Alice Corbiere and Joe Corbiere for commenting on my writing about the Hiawatha legacy and Joe for organizing an interview slide-show – with remarkable results. Thanks also go to all of the artists who graciously allowed me to interview them about their work, particularly those who became friends during the process of writing, including Jeff Thomas, Richard Fung, and Wendy Coburn.

Friends, family, and colleagues also inspired my love, curiosity, and intellectual engagement with art, history, and the difficult politics of race, gender, sex, and the Canadian nation. For this, I want to thank a wide circle of people who made comments on early drafts and provided intellectual, emotional, and material support in ways too numerous to mention. I hope each of you know what you have offered: Fernanda Faria, Shohini Ghosh, Shani Mootoo, Anna Lathrop, Nance Dodington, and Joe Hermer; my sisters, Ailsa and Michele Francis; and my colleagues in Women's Studies/Sociology/Social Justice and Equity Studies at Brock University, in particular, Janet Conway, Nancy Cook, Hijin Park, Christine Daigle, Jessie Short, Caleb Nault, Sue Spearey, Rebecca Raby, Ebru Ustundag; in northern Ontario, Joe Corbiere, Sue Barber, Jeff and Juanita Arbus, and Joahnna Berti; and Sarita Srivastava, Jennifer Stephen, Andrea Fatona, Krys Verrall, Janice Hladki, Sue Guttenstein, Victoria Freeman, Ali Kazimi, Sartaj Kaur, Alanis King, Darlene Lawson, Susanne Luhmann, Minelle Mahtani, Laura Mitchell, Mary Jo Nadeau, Cynthia Wright, Farzana Doctor, Judith Nicolson, Moon Joyce, Robert Wallace, and Lisa Taylor.

A number of archives have supported my research, including Library and Archives Canada, Canadian Pacific Archives, and the Whyte Museum of Banff. I am grateful also for the financial support of doctoral and postdoctoral fellowships from the Social Sciences and Humanities Research Council; doctoral fellowships from OISE/UT and Ontario Graduate Scholarships; and for support from my parents, Jack and Patricia Francis, whose generous belief in me enabled me to pursue my own path. For support to publish the colour images in this book I thank Brock University. I also want to acknowledge the vibrant arts scene that showcased some of the work written about in the following pages and that continues to teach me about the role of art in remaking the imagination, in particular the Centre for Media and Culture in Education at the Ontario Institute for Studies in Education, University of Toronto; the imagineNative Film + Media Arts Festival; the Inside Out Lesbian and Gay Film Festival; the Images Media Arts Festival, Debajehmujig Theatre Group and New Traditions Media Arts.

A host of artists, cartoonists, galleries, and visual arts distributors have helped me to obtain the fabulous images included here, and many have waived their fees in light of the lack of funding provided for scholarly publishing. For their generosity I thank Jeff Thomas, Wendy Coburn, Rebecca Belmore, Jim-me Yoon, Richard Fung, Shawna Dempsey, Lorri Millan, and Kent Monkman; Marnie Flemming at the Oakville Gallery; Bill Quackenbush at the Barkerville Museum; Vtape Media Arts; the Hamilton Art Gallery, the Ontario Art Gallery, the Catriona Jeffries Gallery, and the National Gallery of Canada; cartoonists Adrian Raeside, Vance Rodewalt,

Karl MacKeeman, Dan Murphy, Margaret Pritchard; and the estate of Ed Franklin.

My oldest friend, Yolande Mennie, edited the manuscript and, more than that, provided intellectual advice and support at key moments during revisions. This book, literally, would not have been possible without her remarkable spirit, intelligence, and detailed attention. The two anonymous reviewers at UBC Press provided stellar intellectual guidance, which made the review process extraordinarily useful. Darcy Cullen, my editor at the Press, and Holly Keller, the production manager, have both provided thoughtful and detailed support for the text and images throughout.

Earlier portions of some chapters have been published in the *Journal of Historical Sociology* 17, 2-3 (2004); the *Canadian Journal of Film Studies/ Revue Canadienne d'études cinématographiques* 10, 1 (2001); *Canadian Woman Studies/Les cahiers de la femme* 20, 2 (2000); and in Deborah Brock, Rebecca Raby, and Mark P. Thomas, eds., *Power and Everyday Practices* (Nelson, 2011). I thank all involved for their comments.

When I first started this book, I had little real sense of how my own family history intersected with my research; however, over the course of the writing, I became aware of a myriad number of connections. I learned that the most common occupation listed in our family Bible was "hatter," so some of my ancestors might have made beaver hats; that a bachelor uncle worked for many years on the railway; and that my Fife ancestors were responsible for bringing Red Fife wheat to Canada. Red Fife wheat has a short growing season and enabled farming in previously inhospitable areas of Ontario and the Prairies, helping to make Canada the "Granary of the Empire" while also displacing Indigenous communities from their lands and livelihoods. I have learned this history in conversation with my father, who is the family genealogist, and I thank him for his work to preserve these stories. While these connections highlight my familial implication in colonialism, I hope this book can be one step in the long project of imagining and acting otherwise.

In recognition of their very different forms of courage, I dedicate this book to my parents, Jack and Patricia Francis.

Creative Subversions

1

Introduction
"Ghosts Trying to Find Their Clothes"

> Using the word ghost is good because that's what the old
> people say when they talk about white people in this country:
> "Ghosts trying to find their clothes."[1]
>
> – Maria Campbell, *The Book of Jessica*

An Auto-Ethnographic Story

Although the intellectual work of this project led, on its own account, to a consideration of haunting, the material conditions of writing offered a parallel process, one that also invited me to consider how the experience of ghosts is implicated in the everyday geography of Canadianness. Much of my writing on spectres was done after working at Algoma University College (AUC) in Sault Ste. Marie, an institution built, literally, from the bricks and mortar of the now (in)famous Shingwauk Indian Residential School.[2] As I had spent many summers canoeing in the Fox Islands in Georgian Bay, I decided when I accepted the position at AUC that I wanted to live with a view of Lake Huron. With the help of my new colleagues I was able to rent a small house in Bruce Mines, a historic village of six hundred, east of the Sault, which, in the late 1800s, had been a thriving mining town and the second largest community in Ontario. The house was built in 1854 and has large picture windows that provide a view of the water and the twin industries that fuel the local economy: tourism (at the thriving local marina) and resource extraction (as signalled by the huge barges hauling their cargo across the open mouth of the bay).

One of the first things I learned when I moved to AUC was that members of the two nearest Anishinaabek communities, Garden River First Nation and Batchewana First Nation, had, from 1900 through to 1968, been internationally famous for their performance of a play based on Henry

Longfellow's epic poem *Song of Hiawatha*. Longfellow based this poem on ethnographic writings about the Anishinaabek mythology originating from precisely this region of the upper Great Lakes. In Chapter 5, entitled "Playing Indian," I assess the multiple meanings associated with these historic performances. And, in a research project begun while I lived in Bruce Mines, I explore the Garden River First Nation's current re-engagement with this legacy through a series of new productions that reimagine community theatre from contemporary Anishinaabek perspectives.

In order to understand the background for this long-running series of theatre performances, I began to investigate the history of Garden River First Nation and, by extension, my own village of Bruce Mines. Janet Chute's fascinating history of Anishinaabek leadership in Garden River tells us that the copper mining that provided the rationale for Euro-Canadian settlement in this region originated from the work of Anishinaabek prospectors who had, from the early 1840s, brought samples of copper, gold, silver, and iron to local government agents and private entrepreneurs. The purpose of their proactive work in identifying the mineral resources of that territory was to lobby for Anishinaabek proprietorship. More specifically, they wanted a system of leases and royalties to ensure they gained a share in potential profits from mining on their land. And their concern in mounting this lobby was well founded, as, by 1849, the Montreal Mining Company sank some of the first shafts to search for copper in Bruce Mines.[3]

The company's initiative to capitalize on these resources suggests an assumption that the issue of Anishinaabek land claims would, if ignored, simply disappear. And this is not surprising, as, by the late 1840s, the Indian Department had already begun to pressure Anishinaabek communities to relocate from the area under development. Nevertheless, Chief Shingwaukonse, working with other community leaders, prepared a petition to be sent to the Indian Department, which declared their commitment to remain. The petition provided a scathing assessment of Euro-Canadian/Anishinaabek relations:

> Already has the white man licked clean up from our lands the whole means of our subsistence, and now they commence to make us worse off. They take everything from us ... I call God to witness in the beginning and do so now again and say that it was false that the land is not ours, it is ours.[4]

As Chute notes, their letter received no reply.

During the same period, there was a run on the sale of additional mining sites, located along the north shore of Lake Huron and Lake Superior, that were in competition with those held by the existing companies. These included claims in Garden River and in the adjacent town of Bruce Mines. In response, the Anishinaabek lobby intensified: Shingwaukonse and several other elders made further petitions, participated in a controversial and dangerous blockade to stop operations in Mica Bay (a mining operation on Lake Superior), travelled to Montreal to lobby the corporations and government directly, made a presentation to the governor general (the text of which was published in the *Montreal Gazette* and widely praised), and gave numerous public interviews.[5]

The following spring, the government initiated treaty negotiations with all the communities of the North Shore region. According to Chute, negotiators for Upper Canada used the tactics of divide and rule to separate Shingwaukonse from his allies in neighbouring communities. The result was a treaty in which Indigenous petitions for a share in the royalties from mining operations were unequivocally rejected. Indeed, according to government officials at that time, the Anishinaabek people, by definition, could not hold title to territory or resources, and no Indigenous leader had ever exercised the authority to transfer land to a Western power. This treaty (which provided the template for all others in that region), at one and the same time granted the Anishinaabek little autonomous decision-making power in the governance of their own territory and withdrew most substantive opportunities for economic self-sufficiency. Indeed, "Indians" could only be imagined as those who were due a generalized form of annuity or allowance, which essentially meant they could only exist as "dependants" of the state.[6]

I read this history while at my desk, looking out the picture windows of my house in Bruce Mines. I had always known that this house was built in 1854, but I do not remember at what point I learned that it had been built by the Montreal Mining Company, the very same enterprise that sank early shafts to search for copper in that community.[7] I do, however, remember the moment, near the end of my research, when I read who the colonial government had appointed to negotiate on its behalf. His name was William B. Robinson. The name meant nothing to me until I learned why he had been considered a "clever political appointment." In the late 1840s, William B. Robinson had been the manager of the Montreal Mining Company in Bruce Mines, and, thus, he was familiar with the territory and the people of the North Shore region.

Thus, the government of Upper Canada had sent, as its representative, the former manager of one of the mining companies that stood to benefit from resource extraction in the very territory contested by the treaty-making process. It was this man who would negotiate the Robinson-Huron Treaty, a document that ensured the Anishinaabek people would have access to *none* of the revenues from the mines. And I was reading this history while living in a house built, possibly as an operational headquarters, by that same company.

To put the matter plainly: I was living in that house in the company of ghosts. And all of them, from the early Anishinaabek prospectors to the Montreal Mining Company employees, had offered me both hospitality and stories.[8] So the next question seemed to be: how would I respond?

The cultural theorist Kathleen Brogan argues that one of the most frightening aspects of being haunted is its involuntary nature: we cannot choose our ghosts.[9] Nor do we choose the open secrets of Canadianness. But these "secrets" can provide a way into thinking through what Robert Jay Lifton calls "the potentially transformative influence of death on theory."[10] For histories of death and dispossession through the consolidation of Canadian nation building are far from exemplary. On the contrary, the story I have just recounted is noteworthy precisely because histories of this nature are both little acknowledged and ubiquitous. As scholars such as Bonita Lawrence and Victoria Freeman argue, an investigation into the history of Indigenous/Anglo-Canadian relations in southern Ontario, where I now live, would reveal very similar themes.[11] So while it was the Anishinaabek reappropriation of Hiawatha that led me to investigate the history of Bruce Mines, this "background" research soon became a history of my own country and people – and our continuing implication in the secrets of Canadianness.

How, then, to understand this notion of histories that are implicitly known and, at the same time, frequently denied? Here I turn to Michael Taussig's notion of the "public secret," which provides an evocative framework for my exploration. Taussig describes public secrets as a form of knowledge that is generally known but that, for one reason or another, cannot be articulated.[12] Consequently, the secretiveness of the public secret is constituted through a whole set of "strategic absences" that ensure that most citizens know "what not to know" through an active "not seeing," a process that is often accomplished without the slightest conscious engagement.[13] In this context, I ask: when banal emblems of national belonging convey a knowledge that is both articulated and refused, what might this

4

teach us? To address this query I assess how, in a Canadian context, the "regime of the open secret" operates through images and discourses of national belonging.

If public secrets are one of the most powerful undercurrents of our collective consciousness, then, as Susanne Luhmann asserts, they are also an animating force for cultural production.[14] Indeed, I would argue that the everyday iconography of Canadianness is itself a form of cultural work through which Anglo-Canadian settlers have engaged with the symbolic inheritance of these traumatic legacies. My work is intended to contribute to mapping the affective processes through which spectres are both remembered and refused within the national consciousness. I to do this through case studies that investigate how nationalist emblems construct banal and nostalgic versions of a past that cannot be expelled or assimilated. The irony, however, is that, insofar as Canadians consume versions of a past that do not nourish, the living can themselves become ghostly. Indeed, drawing on the work of Kathleen Brogan, I argue that nationalist emblems often memorialize the past as a form of banal possession, with the result that the present continues, as a failure of memory, to render history useable.[15] Thus, the traumatic ordeals of nation building continue to haunt both those excluded or dispossessed of the full benefits of national belonging *and* those who are at the very centre of a particularly Canadian hegemony.

In the conclusion to *Specters of Marx*, Derrida turns to the theme of the links between power and haunting, suggesting that "the intellectual ... if he loves justice at least" should learn from ghosts, talk to them, "even if it [the ghost] is in oneself, in the other, in the other in oneself. They are always there, spectres ... [and] they give us to rethink the 'there' as soon as we open our mouths."[16] But how might one learn from ghosts? Walter Benjamin offers a few thoughts on this dilemma. The problem, he suggests, with "outing" a ghost, or with revealing a public secret, is that the act of exposure often threatens to distort the inner content of that which has been hidden and to appropriate its energy rather than to undertake a revelation that does it justice. Taussig, reflecting on Benjamin, notes that "the whole problem lies in the ease with which the secret invites injustice, an invitation [the] Enlightenment cannot easily resist in its unappeasable hunger for the raw energy provided by demystification."[17] Thus, both scholars highlight the importance of self-reflexive engagements with secrets and ghosts. The point is not simply to demystify the public secrets that shape a national consciousness, a project that they suggest is tantamount to wanting the power of mystery without the mystery;[18] rather, it is to engage in a drama of re-enchanting the world, or revealing a secret, but only through a "transgressive uncovering" of what is already "secretly familiar."[19]

Throughout this book I explore how select Canadian artists have taken up the task of uncovering the secretly familiar and consider their efforts to re-enchant a banal nationalist imaginary. I start this process through auto-ethnography as a way into sketching out a politics of "locatedness." But I hope the various methods of "storying-in-and-against colonial legacies"[20] provided throughout this text allow for multiple entry points for considering Benjamin's reflection: that the "truth is not a matter of exposure which destroys the secret, but a revelation which does justice to it."[21]

Material and Spectral Exclusions

This book traces a double haunting: mapping how whiteness and Indigeneity are both occluded and conjured up in the visual emblems of Canadian social life. If the trauma of nation building cuts both ways, to haunt both those excluded from national belonging and those at the centre of nationalist hegemonies – though in very different ways – then it would seem useful to begin this exploration of haunting, public secrets, and national belonging with a brief tour through the contradictory meanings associated with spectrality. I start with the *Oxford Encyclopedia of Theatre and Performance*, which highlights how spectral presences return to disturb the present, representing those excluded from power and demanding retribution for a past wrong. Some of the earliest examples of this come from early modern stage figures associated with revenge tragedy.[22] In Victorian England, those groups most identified with having access to the spectral realm were women and the working classes – an unsurprising coincidence as haunting has traditionally been associated with those who were outside the rationalist modes of thought associated with the Enlightenment.[23] However, Renee L. Bergland argues, that after the Enlightenment, ghost belief shifted, with communal phantoms growing more significant as "enlightened" people began to speak more about the ghosts that haunted national rather than familial communities. In Europe this was the ghost of communism, and in North America it was the spectral return of slaves and Indigenous peoples.[24] Ghosts have also always been connected to issues of law and justice, with the question of land and ownership having a central place in this legacy. Patricia Williams articulates the connections between these different threads when she describes her search for traces of her great-great-great-grandmother, a slave, and her great-great-great-grandfather, Austin Miller, a slave owner. Here spectral exclusions are hinged at the intersection of the meanings associated with family, property, and ideologies defining progress.[25]

Freud's essay "The Uncanny" also makes reference to the intersection of haunting and property through analyzing how the meanings associated with two seemingly opposite terms actually circulate through each other.[26] These two terms are *heimlich* (the homely, the familiar) and *unheimlich* (the uncanny, the strange, and the hidden). Freud argues that an experience of the uncanny can emerge when the place one considers home is somehow rendered unfamiliar, so that one is pressed into a sense of being "in place and 'out of place' simultaneously."[27] Julia Kristeva's book, *Strangers to Ourselves*, takes this paradox further by reflecting on the difficulties of disentangling what is considered home from what is considered foreign or strange. Here the notion of the uncanny speaks to anxieties that afflict home directly:

> Freud wanted to demonstrate at the outset, on the basis of a semantic study of the German adjective *Heimlich* and its antonym *unheimlich,* that a negative meaning close to that of the antonym is already tied to the positive term *Heimlich,* "friendly, comfortable," which would also signify "concealed, kept from sight," "deceitful and malicious," "behind someone's back." Thus, in the very word *Heimlich,* the familiar and intimate are reversed into their opposites, brought together with the contrary meaning of "uncanny strangeness" harboured in *unheimlich.*[28]

Kristeva's strategy for dealing with the ambivalence at the heart of the "home" is to individuate it, exploring how we come to terms with the "stranger in ourselves." My interest is to take this notion in a slightly different direction, namely, to explore the ways in which the uncanny intrudes on the Anglo-Canadian historical and cultural (un)conscious. Like Avery Gordon, then, I am interested in reflecting on "the political status and function of systemic hauntings" and the ways in which collective ghosts "conjure up social life."[29]

Jo-Ann Episkenew's study of Indigenous cultural production in Canada also highlights stories of cultural haunting and explores the role of literature in reimagining histories of colonization and displacement. Her study traces the ways in which the literature of cultural haunting can lead to an awareness of how collective stories continue to inform, sometimes even possess, the living. Yet Episkenew's reading of these spectral themes suggests that they can also provide a necessary and even positive introjection. In looking at Maria Campbell's autobiography *Halfbreed,* for example, Episkenew explores how Campbell, as someone haunted by the traumatic legacies of racism and dispossession, writes about her Métis family and community.[30] It is only through writing a testimony of her experiences, reconfigured from a Métis perspective, that Campbell can begin to decolonize that story and so escape the self-loathing that distorted her familial and community history. Thus, Campbell's book attempts to move from haunting as "deathly possession" to haunting that enlarges her sense of self by contesting the violence of colonial relations.[31] In this context, stories of cultural haunting can be read as a record of the struggle to gain enough distance from the past to move from memory as traumatic possession to a place where one can re-narrativize those memories in ways that allow for revision. In Episkenew's analysis, then, Indigenous literature about cultural haunting serves to emphasize the importance of calling into question nationalist narratives that signal a failure of memory and thus to render history useable. For Euro-Canadian readers, in particular, this analysis invites us to confront national myths as a nostalgic flight from history, where alternative voices nevertheless reassert themselves, much like the return of the repressed. Thus, the disparate implications associated with ghostliness highlight the ways that spectral tropes have ambiguous meanings: signifying the perils of unresolved wrongs and the phantasmal as sources of nourishment and life. An engagement with ghosts, then, while hazardous, can also be the occasion for necessary and even positive introjection.

How might these analyses of spectrality influence our exploration of Canadianness? And what are the links between haunting and the narratives of Anglo-Canadian nation building? G. Turcotte suggests that our national literature is resonant with numerous examples of the uncanny precisely because these enable the articulation of fears that are, in other circumstances, unmentionable – fears of dispossession, miscegenation, and contamination.[32] Historically, one can trace a terror of the nameless "other" by examining the charts available to early explorers of the Americas. As Margaret Turner notes, when the adventurers dared to go beyond the circumference of the known world, their maps warned them what to expect: "Here there be monsters."[33] And, while these "monsters" could be understood as the "fantastical beasts" thought to inhabit the new continent, they also served as metaphors for the anxiety emerging from the confrontation with new philosophies and peoples. Thus, the very conception of Canadian space within the European imagination, Edwards argues, "invoke[d] a crisis of selfhood that continues to move like a spectre within Canada's borders."[34] And, lest we assume that these spectres are only a historical phenomenon, in a recent special issue of the *University of Toronto Quarterly* (2006), the editors argue that much of the work being produced by contemporary Canadian authors, artists, and filmmakers indicates that many seem "obsessed with ghosts and haunting."[35]

In this context, I believe Taussig's notion of the open secret provides a useful framework for exploring one of the most obvious, and yet frequently occluded, contradictions shaping Canadian identity: namely, our history as a country founded on a commitment to democratic forms of order and good government for some, while, at the same time, endorsing devastating forms of legal exclusion, forced assimilation, and mass death for others. In an international context, John Eddy and Deryck Schreuder argue that *all* settler colonies enshrined a democratic system for "citizens" and an exclusionist set of laws and regulations for Indigenous peoples and multiple groups of racialized "others." Their account does not fully trace the ways that access to the political benefits of citizenship were not only racialized but also hetero-masculinist and restricted to those with access to capital and property. They do highlight, however, how the "colonial nationalism" of settler countries was based on a sense of ideal citizenship that was inclusionist in its popu-lism while being exclusionist in relation to Indigenous peoples and to all those immigrants racialized as "not white" – a form of ethnocentrism and racism that was legitimized by state immigration policies.[36] As Sunera Thobani summarizes, in Canada this resulted in a "world divided: on the one side, a world of law, privilege, access to wealth, status, and power for the settler; on the other, a world defined *in law* as ... a world of poverty, squalor, and death for the native."[37]

Ann Laura Stoler argues that narratives of colonial authority in many European settler outposts were built on an overarching premise, namely, "the notion that Europeans in the colonies made up an easily identifiable and discrete biological and social entity – a 'natural' community of common ... racial attributes and political affinities so that lines separating colonizer from colonized were thus self-evident and easily drawn."[38] But as in most colonial contexts, including Canada, this premise did not hold. Indeed, as Renisa Mawani has argued for British Columbia, the "colonial contact zone" was "a space of racial intermixture" that reconstituted the terrain of racial power as Europeans, Indigenous peoples, and racialized migrants came into frequent and sometimes unexpected contact.[39] Thus, Canada's far-flung and often far from respectable settler outposts were formed through diverse ra-cial intimacies.[40] Further, by the turn of the twentieth century, there was even more intermixture as 800,000 of the 3 million immigrants who arrived in the major wave of in-migration between 1896 and 1914 were from the non-Anglo-Saxon world.[41] In this context, a heterogeneous mix of "state racisms" determined the politics of life and death, particularly for Indigenous peoples and racialized newcomers.[42]

However, the most shattering impact of Euro-Canadian settlement was felt in Indigenous communities. While it is not possible to review the details of this history here, Canada's role in this process proceeded through a host of different actions: from the unchecked and sometimes deliberate spread of disease, which resulted in the deaths of between 70 and 95 percent of the original Indigenous population, to attempted physical extermination (as among the Beothuk and Odawa), to brutal armed conflict, to the practice of eugenics and forced sterilization.[43] In 1876, the Indian Act provided a coercive and patriarchal set of cradle-to-grave directives governing Indigenous culture and education, while also setting arbitrary and gendered standards for who was, and was not, a status Indian. This legislation began a process that continues to profoundly undermine local self-governance, in particular women's spheres of authority within communities.[44] Further, the imperial ideology governing treaty agreements and the seizure of huge tracts of non-treaty land, along with the marginalization of the remaining Indigenous communities to reserves, deprived them of a sustainable economic and political base. They were also barred from the federal franchise until 1960.[45] On the cultural front, the state outlawed Indigenous religions, cultural practices, and languages, and profoundly distorted the integrity of familial and community structures by removing generations of children to residential schools, where, until the end of the Second World War, up to 50 percent of them died.[46] As Stasiulis and Jhappan conclude, "taken together, these and other measures denied Indigenous people access to legal or political forums and betrayed a clear and plain intent to destroy their cultures and economies and indigenous forms of female autonomy, as well as to abrogate their citizenship and democratic rights."[47]

Yet, while the United Nations Department of Economic and Social Affairs noted in 2006 that the situation of Indigenous peoples remains "the most pressing human rights issue facing Canadians" in the new millennium, there is still only the barest public acknowledgment of this crisis.[48] Indeed, despite Prime Minister Stephen Harper's widely praised apology for the government's role in residential schools (2008) and Canada's recent decision to sign the United Nations Declaration on the Rights of Indigenous Peoples (2010), profound inequities remain. Just one example highlights the disparity: contrary to the idea that Indigenous people get "special privileges," the average Canadian receives government services at a rate almost two-and-a-half times greater than that received by Indigenous citizens.[49] In other words, Indigenous people are the most disenfranchised citizens in their own land. In this context, it is important to note a recent survey by the Coalition for the Advancement of Aboriginal Studies in collaboration with the Canadian Race Relations Foundation (2000-1), which found that 80 percent of first-year university and college students had gained little exposure to Indigenous issues, while those in secondary school said the information that is available left them unprepared to address contemporary conflicts between Indigenous and non-Indigenous peoples.[50]

How then might one understand the work of nationalism, public secrets, and ghosts in this context? And what role do seemingly banal national emblems serve in the reproduction of the affective ties through which Canadians continue to identify themselves as, by and large, a benign and moral nation? National symbols are, at root, metaphors, and the logic of the metaphor is that it can provide an image through which people distance themselves from those things that are closest to them.[51] As many scholars have already noted, this process of "distancing from that which is closest" has profoundly shaped popular representations of the "noble savage." For it was only after the long period of intense conflict over land and resources was substantively over that those people once described as "savages" could become "noble." Ernest Renan notes that most nations, once they are established, depend on a general amnesia about the often brutal methods through which unity has been established.[52] However, this process does not consist of a simple loss of memory; rather, it consists of a dialectical movement in which conscious remembering and forgetting are not, in fact, polar opposites. Just as most of life follows established traditions through which actions transmit past grammars and semantics, so national traditions can be simultaneously present and absent – available in everyday objects in ways that preserve collective memory without the conscious activity of individuals remembering.[53] Thus, banal forms of commemoration also function as forms of haunting – for they are the affective process through which the ghosts of memory adhere within a popular consciousness. Or, to use a different metaphor, they can be understood through Pierre Bourdieu's notion of "habitus": the dispositions and practices that constitute the "second nature" in the routines of daily life. These also emphasize remembering and forgetting, so that habitus – or embodied history – is internalized as a second nature and thus forgotten as history.[54]

Michael Billig's exploration of banal nationalism is useful in precisely this context for his analysis attempts to grapple with the continuing reproduction of nationalist sentiments that are present when a country becomes an established homeland. He argues that the "metonymic image of banal nationalism is not a flag which is being consciously waved with fervent passion: it is the flag hanging unnoticed on the building."[55] Similarly, the ordinary signifiers of Canadian identity – from the ubiquitous beaver to wilderness parks to canoes and railways – all serve to turn background space into a very specific "homeland space." But this does not mean that any of these serve as a magnet for intense national feeling. Quite the reverse, for all these reminders of national belonging are habitually discounted and overlooked in the routines of a place marked as "home." At the same time, these images do tell a story of "our" people and homeland, and define the borders that distinguish us from them. Thus, Billig argues that seemingly innocent narratives can also prompt powerful forms of affective nationalist sentiment – just like the seemingly hot mass movements fuelled by overt emotion. Indeed, one of the ways established nations, like Canada, normalize and legitimate their own passionate and patriotic sentiments is through identifying nationalism as something surplus and alien: as something other people have. Thus, our patriotism is presented as banal, invisible, and benign, whereas their nationalism is presented as the dangerous property of irrational others.[56]

Building on Billig's analysis, then, I explore how the Canadian cultural imaginary is constructed through objects whose very banality belies their crucial role in rendering both the crisis of national identity and its reproduction. Perhaps it is their very ordinariness that ought to make us suspicious for, in the following chapters, I show how Canadian emblems have articulated elements of an ideological struggle between European settlers and those who were marginalized from the nation-building project. Indeed, as Eva Mackey argues, these images have constructed a variety of others in central narratives of Canadianness at the same time as they have produced the investments that fashion an unmarked yet dominant national identity.[57]

While all settlers who were racialized as not-white were excluded, in different ways, from the rewards of citizenship, the legacy of settler colonialism and its impact on Indigenous peoples constitutes the most profound spectre to hover over the banal images explored in the following chapters. I suggest that these ghostly Indians, who are both acknowledged and refused in the Canadian imaginary, also impinge on the present, or move from one present to another and, in so doing, are paradigmatic of the public secrets that continue to haunt Canadianness.[58]

One of the most thoughtful explorations of this Indigenous absent presence comes from the Sioux cultural critic Philip Deloria. He argues that ideas about American truth and freedom have rested on the United States' ability to "wield power against Indians – social, military, economic, and political – *while simultaneously drawing power from them*" (emphasis added).[59]

Deloria's language here is unsettling as his illustration turns the spectral Indian on its head and like the quote by Maria Campbell at the start of this chapter focuses attention back on white settler colonialists. The classic biological image of an organism that draws its life power from another is the parasite. According to the *Canadian Oxford Dictionary*, "parasite" comes from the Greek *parasitos*, "one who eats at another's table."[60] Interestingly, the force of this naming seems, inexorably, to lead to another because, if we carry the allusion to its conclusion, the figure that lives by drawing out the life (blood) of another is the vampire. And, perhaps not surprisingly, this chain of associations returns us to the ghost: for a vampire is defined as a "ghost" who "preys ruthlessly on others."[61]

If Deloria's observation originated in an exploration of the American experience, what is distinctive about the force of the public secrets embedded in the settler colonial relationship to Indigenous peoples in Canada? This legacy has often been encapsulated in stories related to what Eva Mackey calls the "benevolent Mountie myth." The narrative relies on the idea that Canadian expansion proceeded with a benevolent gentleness that was a result of the naturally superior forms of British justice.[62] Scholars have written about the ways in which this myth misrepresents the encounter between cultures and the brutal history of conquest and cultural genocide upon which Canada was founded.[63] Yet these critiques have done little to lessen the affectionate sentiment that accrues to this iconic figure. In the United States, by contrast, the violence of western settlement is widely acknowledged. Indeed, the American experience of conquering the frontier has been mythologized as foundational to the national character through what Richard Slotkin aptly terms "regeneration through violence." Here a whole host of public discourses has valorized early settlers' racial aggression as a kind of heroic ideal, with public memorials to countless battles, from the Seminole Wars to the Battle of Little Big Horn. And, in the twentieth century, we have the spectacle of Hollywood's version of the Wild West.[64] While Canada's history with regard to Indigenous populations must be distinguished from that of the United States, the effects here were also ruinous.[65] Indeed, the Indo-Canadian filmmaker Ali Kazimi has described this distinction with the pithy phrase "genocide through bureaucracy."[66]

If the force of the cultural haunting associated with Euro-Canadians' parasitic relationship to Indigenous peoples has had different symbolic consequences than has the bloody history glorified in the United States, how might one encapsulate this distinction? I argue that the "Indians" who are both acknowledged and refused in Canadian national symbols do not mythologize a national character forged through violent struggle; instead, they

Figure 1.1   Indian sculpted into the stonework over entrance to the Department of Justice building, Ottawa, 1936   Photograph by Jeff Thomas

reinscribe Canada's peculiarly benign self-image. We can see this process at work directly in figures that range from the "noble Indian" sculpted over the entrance to the Department of Justice on Parliament Hill in 1936 (Figure 1.1) to the Indigenous-inspired Olympic mascots (Miga the sea bear, Quatchi the sasquatch, and the hybrid animal spirit Sumi) developed for the Vancouver-based 2010 Olympic Games.[67] Here, as in most other official representations, noble and even kitschy images of Indianness have served a richly metaphoric purpose. They signify Canada's commitment to the values of justice and racial harmony, and, consequently, they assist primarily white Canadians, as well as a wide range of others, to bask in the warm glow of being from a nice country that is innately given to tolerance and civility.[68] Throughout the following chapters I argue that these images also contribute to cleansing the national memory. For, insofar as Canadians avoid examining the relationship between banal symbols of national purpose and the ways a nation forgets its own complicity in a deeply racialized legacy, we ourselves become ghostly.

A "Subject without Properties"

While one thread in this book traces the simultaneous erasure and spectacularization of Indigenous peoples through emblems of Canadianness, another looks at the ways that national emblems construct a seemingly benign and yet hard to define national self-image. Perhaps the deeply contradictory nature of this process can best be introduced through a consideration of how clichéd national images – hard-working beavers, an enterprising railway, and the towering mountains of Banff National Park – might be seen in dialogue with our national literature. Put simply, on the one side we have banal symbols that articulate tropes of an enterprising and heroic masculinity, while on the other side we have our national literature, which has traditionally presented precisely the opposite – namely, anti-heroes just barely clinging to survival. To illustrate: A.A. Den Otter highlights how the Canadian Pacific Railway has most often been seen to embody the hopes of a "young and virile country," where the "vacant" and "boundless" plains were imagined as crying out "come and till me, come and reap me!"[69] And the railway answered with a "ribbon of steel" thrust across the west signifying imperial speed, mastery, and control.[70] Here the tropes of an implicitly white masculine vigour and feminine fertility ventriloquize the imperial and patriarchal values imposed on a wilderness that was seemingly just waiting to be "taken." Yet, in our national literature, Margaret Atwood highlights a distinctly anti-heroic aesthetics. Her 1972 book *Survival* argues that, if the definitive American symbol is the Frontier, the Canadian equivalent is the struggle for survival. This could mean a preoccupation with the bleak physical challenges of the land and climate or a more internal set of terrors.[71] While Atwood's focus is on Canadians' self-image as "born losers," Gaile McGregor, writing in the mid-1980s, highlights Canadians' fascination with and awe of nature. She argues that Canadian literature and painting present the natural world as a gothic symbol of chaos and indifference.[72] Thus, both these influential authors present a national psyche grappling for survival in the face of chaotic challenges.

The past three decades have witnessed the development of a considerable body of literature that challenges these early nationalist representations. Yet this same tendency to picture white Anglo-Canadians as representative of a benign country in a struggle for survival has continued as a prominent strain in the nationalist imaginary. To take just two examples: we continue to see these themes in multimedia heritage programming in public school curricula and in English-language print media responses to the events of 11 September 2001. Katarzyna Rukszto assesses the salience of these trends in Heritage Minutes, a series of sixty-second dramatizations of important Canadian events aired on television and incorporated into the public education system. As her analysis of the visual and curricular aspects of this project demonstrates, the cultural "DNA of our nationalist discourse as represented in the Heritage Minutes is quite racially specific," so that white Canadian heritage survives as exemplary of the Canadian spirit, while "'diversity' is managed as folkloric, and conflicts, historical grievances, and inequality are excluded, contained or disavowed."[73]

And these splits between "us" and "them" – terms which, tellingly, never seem to need definition – have become substantively worse since the events of 9/11.[74] As a recent manifesto on the "War on Terror" written by twenty-one Canadian academics and activists notes, the "clash-of-civilizations" discourse, which is frequently invoked in contemporary debates on multi-culturalism and "reasonable accommodation,"[75] continues to reify the idea that Canada is emblematic of a decent and tolerant nation struggling for survival. At the same time, this discourse avoids responsibility for exclusion-ary immigration policies, escalating anti-Muslim and anti-Arab discourse in civil society, anti-terrorist legislation, the use of security certificates, and other limitations on civil liberties.[76]

Thus, it seems that significant strains in contemporary popular dis-course continue early literary themes in their representation of white Anglo-Canadians engaged in a struggle for survival while under siege.[77] However, the emblems of identity explored in the following chapters suggest precisely the reverse. Here we see triumphal narratives articulated through images of an enterprising and resilient hetero-masculinity. Yet perhaps this binary ac-tually suggests two sides of the same coin. On the one hand, we have banal national emblems: the hard-working beaver, the enterprising railway, the majestic mountains – all of which present the values, technologies, and land-scapes of white enterprise and manly accomplishment. On the other hand, we have a national literature and popular discourse that suggest we couldn't possibly be associated with the more rapacious aspects of imperialist ad-venture because the Canadian character is best expressed by anti-heroes absorbed in a struggle for survival. Might these seemingly oppositional im-ages express the state of play between the renewed respectability of an in-nocent white Anglo-Canadian identity versus our fear of annihilation? And is the outcome of this tension a sense of Canadianness so riven by contra-diction as to be a blank and formless void?

Interestingly, both sides of this dilemma remove us from the actual traumas of our colonial history of nation building *and* from the contem-porary contradictions of a multiracial globalizing economy. In other words, both the discourse of heroic innocence and the discourse of the fear of annihilation function as decoys. For while most representations of Can-adianness are neither heroic Mounties who sort out other people's prob-lems nor anti-heroes who survive despite the assault of the wilderness or the demands of unruly others, these extreme images do have an important function. As Richard Dyer argues, it is over and against these extremes that ordinary whiteness *becomes* ordinary. In his words:

> The extreme image of whiteness acts as a distraction ... Extreme whiteness is, precisely, extreme. If in certain periods of derangement – the empires at their height [for example, the British Empire], the Fascist eras – white people have seen themselves in these images, they can take comfort from the fact that for most of the time they haven't. Whites can thus believe that they are nothing in particular [and thus maintain the elision of their own history] because the white particularities on offer are so obviously not them. Extreme whiteness leaves a residue, a way of being that is not marked as white, in which white people can see themselves. This residue is non-particularity, the space of ordinariness. The combination of extreme whiteness with plain, unwhite whiteness means that white people can both lay claim to the spirit that aspires to the heights of humanity and yet supposedly speak and act disinterestedly as humanity's most average and unremarkable representatives.[78]

And so it is that images of Canadianness vacillate between the hero and the anti-hero – for it is in the residue of such representations that the unremarkable and banal ties to national belonging take shape.

David Lloyd argues that one of the key philosophical underpinnings of colonial expansion is the idea of the white European as a "subject without properties," by which he means someone with the capacity to attain a position of disinterest, abstraction, distance, separation, and objectivity, all as a mark of what is necessary to create a civilized public sphere.[79] In contrast, non-white peoples are presumed to be still, and perhaps forever, bound by the local, the particular, the raced, and as not having made the move to disinterested subjecthood. In this context, he argues that the "global ubiquity" of the white European becomes almost "self-legitimating since the capacity to be everywhere present becomes an historical manifestation of the white man's gradual approximation to the universality he everywhere represents."[80] Lloyd's discussion suggests the extent to which whiteness is associated with pure spirit or disembodiedness. These connections are echoed by the anthropologist Ruth Frankenberg in her study of white identity, which highlights white people's own affective descriptions of "race." She notes that many of the women she interviewed talked about the sense of "formlessness" they associated with being white.[81] Similarly, Richard Dyer, in his cultural studies analysis of the ways in which whiteness is embodied, notes how

Christian beliefs, along with ideologies of race and imperialism, all emphasize the paradoxical struggle between the body and the spirit, which is central to white representation.[82]

Throughout the following chapters, I explore how the troubling formlessness attributed, in particular, to white, Anglo-Canadian identity might
be linked to a set of visual and discursive practices through which this same
group has imagined itself as the most civilized, peaceful, and benign of nations. Here classic images of national purpose have articulated masculinity,
enterprise, and racial purity as "authentic" aspects of the Canadian ethos.
In the late nineteenth and early twentieth centuries this process was, as
Benedict Anderson argues, often expressed through a paradoxical binary:
"On the one side, the hunt was on for 'authenticity,' 'roots,' 'originality,' and
'history,' as nationalism's historically new consciousness created a radical
break with the past. On the other side, nations were everywhere understood
as 'gliding into a limitless future,' developing in perfect synchrony with the
breakneck speed of Progress."[83] I investigate how this process took shape
through a very ordinary, even banal, set of images that allowed specific national emblems to articulate an imagined set of "roots" that would enable
"the short tight skin of the nation [to be] stretched over the old, gigantic,
transcontinental body of the empire."[84]

My intent throughout this analysis is not simply to debunk the romantic
narratives usually associated with national belonging; rather, I trace how the
visual and discursive meanings associated with national emblems take shape
through the process of nation formation. The struggle over the meanings
associated with national symbols has also been a historical contest over the
building of communities and political participation.[85] Consequently, I explore how the categories of meaning relating, for example, to racial purity
and sexual respectability, were constructed in and through national images
in order to decontaminate a mongrel nation.[86] The common starting point
in all these analyses is a focus on how language both constructs and reflects
meaning, and an understanding of discourse that allows the old split between the material and the ideological to be abandoned in favour of a concept that embraces both ideas and practices.[87] Here the dialectical and
relational character of nation formation is always its most fundamental
characteristic. As Homi Bhabha notes, in democratic and political contests
"the question of identification is never the affirmation of a pre-given identity, never a self-fulfilling prophecy – it is always the production of an image
of identity and the transformation of the subject in assuming that image."[88]
Consequently, I inquire into how ideas about Canadianness have been
transformed through particular emblems that signify national purpose and,

conversely, how, over time, those same images have been reimagined in ways that often serve dominant versions of nation building.

Befriending Ghosts: The Politics of Art and Secrets

How, then, might contemporary artistic work prompt questions about the nature of Canadian benevolence while also articulating alternative visions of the ties that bind in this deeply contested nation? The artists profiled here engage this task through critical and aesthetic strategies that exploit the creative contradictions that are the very precondition of the Canadian nation. These interventions appeal to me, in part, because of the possibilities they offer for complementing critique with other practices that may not be so "sure of themselves."[89] Indeed, in a context in which the exercise of state and corporate power is deeply tied to affect, Brian Massumi argues that alternative forms of agency must learn to meet "affective modulation with ... abductive participation" and thus engage the "performative" in politics.[90] This is not to say that energy should not continue to be directed towards the detailed and difficult negotiations for structural and systemic change – these are desperately necessary. But attention must also be paid to a range of ethico-political practices that enlarge the possibilities for new forms of memory, analysis, and activism. And, in this process of re-enchantment suggested by Benjamin, the legacy of trauma and the sparks of playfulness both have a crucial role.

The artistic work profiled in the following chapters includes a diverse range of media, from video to photography, from performance and sculpture to painting. It ranges from the wildly humorous appropriations of Banff National Park by Shawna Dempsey and Lorri Millan in *Lesbian National Parks and Services* (1997); to Jin-me Yoon's postcard series *Souvenirs of the Self* (Banff Park Museum), 1991-2000, which presents a wry confrontation with taxidermic museum display practices in relation to beavers as emblems of the Canadian nation; to Richard Fung's video *Dirty Laundry* (1996), which deftly reimagines the Chinese workers on the Canadian Pacific Railway; to the Cree painter Kent Monkman, whose series The Moral Landscape (2003) smartly reconfigures issues of power and sexuality in relation to the colonial legacy. Indigenous artists make up the largest group within this mix, an unsurprising fact given that many are responding to white imaginings of Indianness.

The force of all these works can be seen in the performative use of language and the body in ways that deliberately cannibalize Canadian culture. As Kobena Mercer argues, these practices of counter-appropriation exemplify the critical work of art insofar as they are self-consciously aware that, to quote Bakhtin:

> The word in language is half someone else's. It becomes "one's own" only when ... the speaker appropriates the word, adapting it to his own semantic and expressive intention. Prior to this moment of appropriation the word does not exist in a neutral or impersonal language ... but rather it exists in other people's mouths, serving other people's intentions: it is from there that one must take the word and make it one's own.[91]

But "making the word one's own" involves a paradoxical process as minoritized artists have had to identify with emblems that exclude them – and it is this process of identification gone awry that has most interested me. For, as Ella Shohat and Robert Stam argue, nationalism's potentially regressive "ideological effects" can *also* open up opportunities for utopian imagining.[92] So while the process of responding to visual texts is, at one level, "structured and determined," it is also possible to read images against the grain for their unexpected and polymorphous possibilities.[93] The artists included here have read themselves and their own life narratives into particular kinds of objects or moments, with which they were not supposed to connect.[94] Of course, this strategy is risky, for artists can be implicated within the terms of the very discourse they seek to assess and subvert. Monika Kin Gagnon succinctly describes this predicament in relation to "race": "naming racism's operations means racializing oneself and others within the very terms and operations that have historically enabled racist discourse to proliferate."[95] Nevertheless, these tactics can also allow for the articulation of multiple kinds of resistance amidst the contradictory eddies of power. And these tools also provide an opportunity, as José Esteban Muñoz suggests, to "breathe new life into old situations," allowing a "suturing of different lives and reanimating through repetition with a difference, a lost country that is relished and loved."[96]

Now what might it mean to speak of "love" as I draw these introductory comments to a close? I use Muñoz's words here to signify something other than the "love of country" that one might typically assume. Indeed, this alternative form of love rejects the exclusivity associated with the Aristotelian model of *philia*, wherein the bonds of responsibility are usually directed towards fellow citizens. Instead, it draws on models of affiliation that were first articulated by early challengers to Aristotle at a time when friendship was understood "as philoxenia, or a love for guests, strangers, and foreigners."[97] So while the polis defined exclusion as the principle origin for that "city of men," there are other ways of imagining the bonds of alliance. And I argue that it is these alternative forms of love that bind together the artistic works included here.

In this regard, I draw on Leela Gandhi's work on the politics of love and friendship, for, taken as a whole, the artists whose work I consider do not simply propose alternative models of national belonging; rather, they *play with and against* the very notion of belonging as it has been organized through nationalist ideas of affiliation. Thus, the political potential of these artistic challenges can be seen in how they introduce the profoundly disruptive categories of *risk* and *doubt* into otherwise banal and heroic narratives. Gandhi elaborates this alternative through positing the twinned tropes of hospitality and guest friendship, which suggest the risk of

> becoming strange or guestlike in [one's] own domain, whether this be home, nation, community, race, gender, sex, skin, or species. So too, the open house of hospitality or the open heart of friendship can never know guests-friends in advance, as one might a fellow citizen, sister, or comrade. Such sociality might take the form of Judith Butler's coalition, "an emerging and unpredictable assemblage of positions." Or it might arrive in the form of Donna Haraway's fabulist cyborg community, "permanently partial ... monstrous and illegitimate."[98]

In this spirit I suggest that the artistic works explored in the following chapters promote doubt about banal nationalist fantasies of security and point instead towards an unknown set of alternatives. Just as nationalist images "gather up ... the residues of the past, recontextualize ... and re-presence them,"[99] so do the artists included here reiterate familiar symbols whose etiology is contested or forgotten. These counter-narratives work in the space between memory and forgetfulness to address the continuing traumas of nation building. Thus, the following chapters attempt a number of risky tasks. The first is to reimagine the secretly familiar phantoms that shape Canadianness. The second is to fashion tactics of demystification that memorialize the nation according to a different set of terms – terms that admit the doubts that follow from acknowledging the incommensurability of different historical moments and competing interpretive frameworks. And, finally, they attempt to sketch out multiple ways of responding to Walter Benjamin's invocation to engage in a drama of re-enchanting the world through a "transgressive uncovering" of what is already "secretly familiar."[100]

2

The Strange Career of the Beaver
Anthropomorphic Discourses and Imperial History

The strange career of Canada's national rodent is a journey that takes us on an unlikely route from the early beaver images in the natural history maps of European explorers to the more secretive language of sexual slang. Images of the beaver in contemporary popular culture range from reruns of the American television sitcom *Leave It to Beaver* to Canadian political cartoons that portray the beaver with bemused affection or faint ridicule to Bell Canada's advertising campaign, with Frank and Gordon as two animated "hoser" beavers (2005-08).[1] Like these contemporary images, the historic discourses associated with the beaver suggest a startlingly conflicted legacy. Indeed, predominant beaver representations highlight important social territories (like the norms of industry, bodily decorum, sexual respectability, and racial progress), while less "legitimate" ones inhabit the subterranean language of sexual slang. The first half of this chapter considers the shifts and continuities in these beaver representations, while the second analyzes how select Canadian artists have reworked many beaver narratives to re-imagine the most taken-for-granted image in the Canadian visual lexicon.

Castor Canadensis

In *Images du castor canadien: XVIe-XVIIe siècles*, François-Marc Gagnon provides a fascinating examination of the "bestiary" of Lower Canada.[2] Beavers were the most frequently represented of all animals in New France, and the author takes these images from maps, illustrations, and engravings, examining them as original historical sources rather than simply as images that corroborate the written word. Following Foucault, he argues that natural history texts were a privileged site for the new world of ideas in French society.[3] I draw from Gagnon's work to investigate the meanings associated with the beaver in the earliest writings from New France – meanings to which I return later in this chapter, when I explore how representations from popular culture and contemporary arts reconfigure these early narratives.

The central theme emerging from the discourse of natural history is an interest in "beaver society." In "The Description and Natural History of the Coasts of North America" (1672), Nicholas Denys asserts that the beaver was most remarkable for its "laborious and disciplinable nature, its industry and its obedience in work."[4] Denys considered the beaver "first among animals," and his descriptions of beaver society are striking for their anthropomorphic characterizations, which reflect his own decidedly monarchical tendencies. In his elaborate vision, beavers are said to gather in groups of up to four hundred animals led by an "architect," while "commanders" direct a host of manual workers who are chastised and beaten to ensure that the lazy work.[5] In 1698, Nicolas Guérard, an engraver for "Carte murale des deux Amériques," produced an enormously influential illustration of beavers at work – clearly inspired by Denys' text. Guérard identifies no fewer than seven categories of worker-beavers, including "lumberjacks," "carpenters," "carriers," those who make mortar, those who dragged mortar on their tails, those who hit the masonry with their tails to harden it, and the masons who are responsible for actually building the embankment (Plate 1). All these are supervised by an architect and an "inspector of the disabled." Gagnon notes that the engraving's representation of dam construction as involving the activity of hundreds of workers in a hierarchically structured setting actually mirrors a building site at Versailles under Louis XIV.[6] Needless to say, the illustration portrays a very different environment than one would encounter should one observe beavers in the wild, where the animals live in colonies of one adult pair and several progeny (averaging three to eight beavers per site), with the occasional transient beaver.[7] Nevertheless, Guérard's emphasis on a beaver society characterized by large hierarchical colonies and a punishing work regimen was reproduced in countless natural history texts.[8]

Future writers continued to focus on representing a "beaver society," and most displayed similarly anthropomorphic tendencies, although these varied according to the political winds of the time. In "Mémoires de l'Amérique Septentrionale" (1705), Baron de Lahontan proposes a new analogy through which hierarchy is replaced with exchange and cooperation in a "beaver republic." Here the system rests on the virtue of its members, and, while the concept of order is still important, it no longer depends on hierarchy or duty but, rather, on virtuous individuals' sacrificing their interests for the common good. In this society, beavers are said to speak and reason together in "assemblies," where they consult on how to maintain the lodges, dikes, and lakes of the lands they hold in common.[9] In "elation du voyage du Port Royal, de l'Acadie ou de la Nouvelle-France" (1708), Dièreville replaces Lahontan's democratic republic with an aristocratic one, in which an elder presides over community affairs and discipline comes from peer beavers.[10] However, Dièreville's peers seem remarkably invested in their disciplinary role. He notes: "There are some beavers called Runaways, who can be found wandering everywhere without living in lodges like the others, and these beavers are vagabonds only because, as they did not want to work, they were beaten and chased away by the sedentary ones."[11] In "Histoire de l'Amérique Septentrionale" (1722) by Bacqueville de la Potherie, the focus is on the "familial" social organization of beavers, with the stigmatization of "vagabond" or single beavers existing in a direct relationship with the valorization of this animal's supposedly ideal family arrangements. Early naturalists observed that beavers are monogamous and mate for life; however, they also assumed that male beavers were the sternest of patriarchs. Indeed, Potherie describes the animals as follows: "His house is so admirable that one can recognize in him the authority of an absolute master, the true character of the family Father, and the genius of a skilled architect."[12] Here the values of industry and patriarchy are joined together in an overlord and architect, while the single or vagabond beavers are assumed to be both unfit to lead and unproductive.

In contrast to these early naturalists, contemporary scientific research provides alternative information about our national rodents: namely, that the majority of "male" beavers have a uterus-like structure that has led to their biological classification as pseudo-hermaphrodites, or intersexed.[13] Beavers also have an egalitarian family structure, with both genders involved in cutting trees, building and maintaining lodges and dams, provisioning the winter food cache, marking and defending territory, and caring for the young. Indeed, it is almost impossible to tell male and female beavers apart except when one can see the nipples of a lactating female. Thus, as Quebec biologist Jacques Bovet puts it, "it can be safely said that the industrious [and] ... patriarchal beavers ... are as likely to be females as they are to be males."[14]

Nevertheless, narratives about beavers as intelligent and paternal overlords in large hierarchically organized communities survived over several centuries and constituted a collective image, not one that was simply touted by eccentric or isolated writers. Gagnon notes that what is striking about these texts is how the image of social organization projected onto beaver society is so often despotic, conceiving of order among the workers only through the intervention of the police, or fellow workers, who castigate the lazy and remind them of their duty.[15] Similarly, beaver society is characterized by distinctly eighteenth-century norms regarding the paternal organization of the family unit. These texts also display considerable anxiety about older, single, or disabled beavers, who are reduced to the status of wheelbarrows whose bodies are used to carry earth. Indeed, it is these beavers who are chased away from the larger society and condemned to become vagrants because they might bring on the degeneration of the race. When these narratives are transposed onto human society, they are not encouraging regarding the fate reserved for older, disabled, or single workers or, indeed, for anyone else who fails to conform to the social regimes that characterized New France. Indeed, the image of social organization that emerges from this zoological discourse, when seen as a projection, is far more repressive than narratives about the Enlightenment as a period of learning, culture, and refinement might lead us to believe.[16] Yet this unassuming literary genre called natural history – through which illustrations of the beaver made their way into so many early texts – provides an important introduction to the strange contradictions that haunt the beaver image.

These early representations of beaver society suggest a masculine contest of the will. This seems evident whether the contesting parties are the beaver and the fur trader or the architects and patriarchs at the top of the beaver hierarchy and the workers at the bottom. And this theme of masculine contest continues from the narratives of natural history to the tales told by early traders and explorers. As Elizabeth Vibert notes, many traders professed a deep respect for the beaver, an animal whose slaughter provided their livelihood.[17] David Thompson and Pierre-Esprit Radisson both marvelled not only at the feats of engineering and the skills of social organization that enabled the beavers to build winter lodges but also at the animal's ability to change the natural landscape.[18] Others, like Ross Cox, who travelled to the northwest plateau in the early 1800s, echoed the natural history writers' comments on the social organization of beavers: "it is no unusual sight to see them beating those who exhibit any symptoms of laziness. Should, however, any fellow be incorrigible ... he is driven unanimously by the whole tribe to seek shelter and provisions elsewhere."[19]

However, the most interesting aspect of traders' perceptions of beavers is how these narratives were racialized and then transposed back onto human society. As Elizabeth Vibert notes, this discourse was implicitly directed at Indigenous peoples:

> The traits celebrated in the beaver, industry and providence, are the very ones traders considered to be lacking in the Indigenous peoples of the region ... The central paradox is that the traders' admiration for the

beaver coexisted with – one might even say masked – the most predatory intentions. [And this] paradox is emblematic of the contradictions
that characterized traders' responses to the land.[20]

Indeed, an important theme of the colonial encounter, particularly during
the later stages of the fur trade, was that Indigenous hunters were wasteful,
lazy, and far from manly – unlike the beavers. This is not to say that European
discourses about the wide variety of communities they encountered were
intractable; indeed, there were many shifts and contradictions in what was
"known" about Indigenous peoples.[21] However, the public discourse about
beaver society and images of the local bestiary reproduced remarkably
European norms over and against Indigenous peoples, whose mixed farming, hunting, and gathering way of life was characterized as "backward."[22] As
the colonizer and colonized came into more intense competition for land,
wildlife, and resources, these opinions on the part of European settlers
hardened. The communities in which these designations were most often
mitigated were those of the Plains and Plateau hunters who tracked the "big
game" buffalo. These men were cast as "brave, industrious, stoic – in a word,
manly,"[23] quite unlike those who trapped the much admired colonial emblem, the beaver.

The Choreography of Gender and Empire

The projection of laudatory representations of the beaver onto the contested
terrain of European/Indigenous relations is not the only narrative associated with this animal. Discourses relating to the fashionable beaver hat are
also an unharmonious chronicle in the theatre of racial and gendered distinctions in early settlement life. During the contemporary period, it is
taken as axiomatic that the fur market (for fur coats and fashion in general)
is primarily feminine while the hard and economically profitable work of
the fur trade is unquestionably masculine. Yet it was men's extraordinary
attentiveness to the dictates of fashion that fuelled three hundred years of a
cataclysmic European fur trade in North America.[24]

   In the premodern period, shifts in fashion were connected with muta-
tions in political power and prestige, and, consequently, it was men who
most often initiated basic changes in style and dress. The rise of the beaver
hat was associated with the Swedish cavalier's hat, which gained popularity
across Europe after Sweden's victories in the Thirty Years War (1618-48) and
its rise to "great power" status.[25] Beaver fur has the unique ability to hold
its shape through felting, and its resilience allowed for the development of

Figure 2.1 **Drawing of a cavalier hat in England at the time of Charles I** From Hilda Amphlett, *Hats: A History of Fashion in Headwear* (London: Richard Sadler Ltd., 1974), 106

particularly fine quality wide-brimmed hats. However, by the early 1600s, beaver had been virtually trapped out in England and most of Europe, and the process of making hats with fur imported from Russia or North America was extraordinarily long and costly. Thus, beaver hats were a prestigious luxury reserved for the aristocracy and wealthy merchants, though a thriving trade in second-hand hats allowed some dispersion to a wider populace.

As Mertes and others argue, the display of luxury was an important means through which premodern political authority was manifested and reproduced.[26] While fur has always had a role in establishing the status of its wearers, by the seventeenth century, scarcity and cost equated it with sumptuous display. In this context, the beaver hat and other luxurious fashions were evidence of the "honourably futile existence" accorded the wealthy (Figure 2.1).[27] However, early men of fashion did not simply mobilize their privilege over a mute and obliging populace. The extravagance in hat styles was a favourite subject for caricaturists and spoof conduct guides. For instance, Samuel Butler describes the mid-seventeenth-century "modish man" as "keen to see and be seen,"[28] and men of leisure were often ridiculed as self-indulgent and exhibitionist. Indeed, one can still hear the echo of seventeenth-century writers' satirical barbs in late twentieth-century chronicles of fashion. For example, in *Hats: A History of Fashion in Headwear,* Hilda Amphlett describes a variation on the cavalier hat as follows:

> By the time Charles I came to the English throne hats had reached a perfection of grace and elegance never since surpassed ... with a wide brim cocked up at the back, allowing an ostrich feather of considerable size to be tucked between it and the crown and droop gracefully over the edge ... *"He looks for all the world, with those spangled feathers, like a nobleman's bedpost,"* wrote a contemporary.[29]

In this context, close attention to the discourse surrounding the fashionable beaver hat opens up possibilities for examining shifts in men's gendered self-expression and in their judgment of other men according to the changing norms of "respectable" masculinity. One example of these shifts can be found by critically re-engaging with chronicles of the fur trade in North America. These texts usually reproduce an illustration that portrays variations on the beaver hat from 1776 through to the mid-1800s (Figure 2.2). However, the heyday of the beaver hat was considerably prior to this period, starting in the early 1600s. The significance of this elision is that more than halfway through the two-hundred-and-fifty-year reign of beaver headgear (in the mid- to late 1700s), there was a sudden change in men's fashions, one that contemporary gender studies might well note. This shift has been variously described as the "great renunciation," "the most remarkable event in the history of dress," and, as Flugel puts it, the "great defeat" during which men "gave up their right to all the brighter, gayer, more elaborate, and more varied forms of ornamentation."[30] Prior to this period, as we have seen, men of the aristocracy, and of the merchant class who emulated them, were equally partial to "hats of rococo embellishment" and the lavish use of lace, velvet, powders, and highly ornamental dress.[31] However, by the time of the French Revolution in 1789, the European aristocracy was in decline, and the Protestant values of hard work, sobriety, and frugality were on the upswing, with the bourgeoisie beginning to reflect these values in what they wore. As Fred Davis summarizes:

> With such parallel developments as the industrial revolution and a more democratic polity ... men's dress became [a] primary visual medium for intoning the rejection of "corrupt" aristocratic claims to elegance, opulence, leisure, and amatory adventure that had been so elaborately encoded into pre-nineteenth-century dress ... [This] symbolic adherence

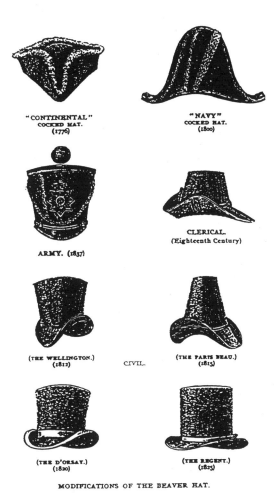

"CONTINENTAL" COCKED HAT. (1776).

"NAVY" COCKED HAT. (1800)

ARMY. (1837)

CLERICAL. (Eighteenth Century)

(THE WELLINGTON.) (1812)

CIVIL.

(THE PARIS BEAU.) (1815)

(THE D'ORSAY.) (1830)

(THE REGENT.) (1835)

MODIFICATIONS OF THE BEAVER HAT.

Figure 2.2   Modifications on the beaver hat, 1700s   From Hugh Grant, "Revenge of the Paris Hat: The European Craze for Wearing Headgear Had a Profound Effect on Canadian History," *The Beaver* 68, 6 (1988/89): 40

to the austere values of the new age [meant that] men's dress became more simple, coarse, unchangeable, and somber, sartorial tendencies that in many respects survive to the present.[32]

Yet the evolution of men's fashion worked somewhat differently in the imperial outposts taking shape in North America. Throughout the colonial period, the prescribed dress for colonial officers was characterized by what Helen Callaway calls "pomp and plumage enhancing masculinity,"[33] and the symbolism of these costumes was a crucial set-piece in the choreography of gender and empire. Nevertheless, colonial traders frequently expressed alarm about the "immoderate" fashions sported by some Indigenous men. Indeed, by the early 1800s, when the "great renunciation" chronicled above was well under way, Vibert tells us there was a perceptible shift towards a morally charged physical description of Indigenous others in travel writing. This trend anticipated the Victorian tradition of physiognomy, the assessment of character and worth from the physical features of face and body.[34] While traders on the western plateau admired the rich leather clothing of hunters, they were more ambivalent about their penchant for decorative accessorizing. Writing from the Colville region, one trader opined: "The young and especially the males ... occupy no inconsiderable portion of the morning decorating themselves; in point of time, and the degree of pains taken to ornament their hair, paint their faces &c they may compete with the more accomplished fops in the civilized world."[35] This trader's comments resonate with the early satire of extravagant European male fashions in the 1600s but even more with the bourgeois notions of a respectable and circumspect manhood, which gained greater prominence in the early 1800s.[36] For a man of enterprise, like Governor Simpson, the new head of the Hudson's Bay Company, the penchant of many Indigenous men for flamboyant dress and ritual contradicted the emerging European values of self-restraint, sobriety, and dedication to an all-encompassing work ethic. Indeed, as the nineteenth century proceeded, it was increasingly the "primitive" men in Africa and North America who were seen as having a fetishistic and feminine predilection for decorating their bodies. By the late 1800s, Thomas Carlyle noted that "the first spiritual want of a barbarous man is Decoration, as indeed we still see amongst the barbarous classes in civilized nations."[37] However, what haunts this commentary is the fact that, for well over two hundred years, the fur trade – the business upon which European exploration, colonization, and trade was reliant – was fuelled by European men's extraordinary attentiveness to displaying "all the gayer, more elaborate, and more varied forms of ornamentation" in hats.[38]

Thus, in both the anthropomorphic narratives of natural history and in the debates about masculinity, industry, and bodily decoration arising in the context of the fur trade fashion, beaver discourses served as a symbolic medium through which European explorers produced themselves as civilized, respectable, and enterprising, in contrast to Indigenous peoples. If we return to the maps and texts of early naturalists, we see that the ideal beavers were imagined as intelligent and hard-working patriarchs who ruled their lodges as their kingdom, while disabled or single beavers were condemned as lazy and cast out to become vagrants out of fear they could bring about the degeneration of the good race. Particularly in the latter stages of the fur trade, this discourse constructed an elaborate narrative through which European settlers identified with the widely celebrated traits of the beaver – industry and providence – while they relegated Indigenous peoples to the opposite end of this binary universe, castigating their subsistence strategies as lazy and indolent. Similarly, European men's attention to bodily decoration – the fashion obsession that fuelled the fur trade – was considered a mark of wealth and prestige in Europe; however, by the late eighteenth century, arguably similar preoccupations with bodily decoration among Indigenous peoples were castigated as immoderate and savage. Thus, in both the discourse about beaver society and in the notions of masculinity and bodily decorum associated with fur trade fashion, European imperial discourse characterized Indigenous peoples as an inferior race that failed to conform to civilized norms of industry, manliness, and appropriate bodily self-presentation. Yet a critical re-reading of these imperial discourses suggests that the very categories of "colonizer" and "colonized" were secured through the beaver narratives of enterprise and racial advancement. Indeed, the newcomers' symbolic investment in the beaver became one process through which European settlers identified themselves with "authentic" markers of this new land and dis-identified with that "failing race" of Indigenous peoples – the original residents of this same territory.

Commodity Beavers

The beaver was the first article of trade upon which European trade and exploration was based, and, as such, it became a crucial medium through which early settlers articulated an imagined relationship with commercial culture. Indeed, the beaver insignia was adopted for such an overwhelming number of early commercial and state purposes that it is well suited to being analyzed through the theory Anne McClintock provides in her analysis of the social history of fetishes. McClintock describes a fetish as embodying the problem of contradictory social value within the context of intercultural trade and imperial conquest. She assesses how the fetish serves to displace onto an object the "contradictions that the individual cannot resolve at a personal level ... [so that] the fetish object ... is destined to reoccur with compulsive repetition."[39] Drawing on analyses taken from early travel writing, she notes that, by the mid-nineteenth century, the fetishism of colonized

Figure 2.3   Hudson's Bay Company coat of arms From Jim Cameron, *The Canadian Beaver Book: Fact, Fiction and Fantasy* (Burnstown, ON: General Store Publishing House, 1991), 55

peoples was a well-established trope that marked them as belonging to the "earliest, primitive stages of evolutionary progress."[40] Yet, while the fetishism of colonial others was seen as a "Victorian scandal," I argue that images of the Canadian beaver suggest the fetishistic compulsions of the colonizer, not the colonized. Further, while many fetishes are marked as "impassioned objects" for their ability to materialize symbolic control over what would otherwise be a terrifying set of ambiguities, over the past four centuries images of the beaver have been drained of this complexity and are now so commonplace, so banal, that they are virtually unnoticeable.

The Hudson's Bay Company (HBC) was founded in 1670, and, as the enterprise most closely associated with the fur trade in English Canada, it was also the first to claim the beaver emblem for the Company charter and coat of arms (Figure 2.3).[41] Interestingly, while the HBC motto asserts connections with "integrity" and "progress," it also gestures towards alternate meanings that move beyond its formal declaration of moral purpose. The HBC coat of arms contains four beavers, a sitting fox for a crest, and two moose, with the motto: Pro Pelle Cutem. As beaver pelts were used to make felt for beaver hats, the traditional explanation for the Latin dictum has been "the skin, cutem, for the sake of the fleece, pro pelle."[42] However, an alternate and equally acceptable reading of the Latin refers to the risks of the business to early traders. Here, Pro Pelle Cutem means: "We risk our skins to get furs."[43] Interestingly, E.E. Rich tells us that it was not uncommon for early commercial mottos to have a "puckish" double meaning.[44] I suggest that this second reading of Pro Pelle Cutem provides a cryptic acknowledgment of another widely known yet publicly obscured aspect of the beaver legacy – European traders' ambivalence about the risks of the trade. For these men did "risk their skins" in physically dangerous work to establish fur trading posts in far-flung areas of the continent and often in hostile territory. Of course, this alternative translation of the Latin could simply be read as an assertion of bravado by the masters of the trade, and undoubtedly it was. But, at the same time, it holds a contradiction that memorializes European traders' ambivalence about the conditions of their livelihood. Not surprisingly, HBC public relations efforts have constructed narratives of the early fur trade that emphasize the heroism, bravery, and romance of the traders, not the potentially unromantic and even unmanly feelings of fear and dread implicit in the traders' show of bravado.

The transition of the beaver image from an HBC crest to a vehicle for pictorial advertisements used by a range of different commercial interests began in the mid-nineteenth century. McClintock notes that, prior to 1851, advertising was rarely used and "was generally regarded as a confession of weakness, a rather shabby last resort."[45] However, with the growing competition among several European empires it became advantageous for businesses to brand their products through corporate images, or "signatures." The impetus for this change came from a confluence of factors, including a proliferation of new products from the colonial outposts, the increased buying power of a growing middle class, the low cost of racialized colonial labour, and the savings from technological innovations associated with the Industrial Revolution. Together, these changes produced the conditions for the first real innovations in advertising.[46]

While these factors generated a need for making distinctions between different mass-produced products, historic representations of the beaver from natural history texts, explorers' travel narratives, and the ongoing commerce of the HBC already associated the animal with "enterprise" and "tradition." When the new country of Canada was inaugurated in 1867, and especially when control of Rupert's Land shifted from the HBC to the federal government in 1870, the beaver became identified as a national image, enhancing its cultural currency as a symbol aligned with stability and commerce. Towards the end of the nineteenth century, the image was taken on

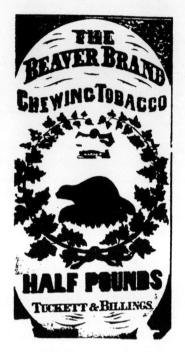

Figure 2.4 Labels for Crompton's Corsets and the Beaver Brand Chewing Tobacco From Jim Cameron, *The Canadian Beaver Book: Fact, Fiction and Fantasy* (Burnstown, ON: General Store Publishing House, 1991), 104 and 103

by a host of new enterprises, including the Canadian National Railways and widely divergent business interests, from the Canadian Illustrated News to the John B. Stetson Company. In the majority of these images the beaver signals a traditionally masculine association with industry and commerce, or the presumptively male pleasures connected to resting from one's labours, as in the labels for Sleeman's Ale, Beaver Brand Chewing Tobacco, and Crompton's Corsets (Figure 2.4).

However, in the twentieth century the image of the beaver has been used to signal both innovation and respectability in advertising, regardless of its relationship to the product being sold.[47] One obvious example of the malleability of this image comes from Roots, whose adoption of the beaver as a concept logo seems meant to signal the company's association with a benign and authenticating idea of "nature," a far cry from the dangers alluded to by early HBC traders. Recently, the company opened a new venture, Roots Lodge in Ucluelet, one of the two villages near Pacific Rim National Park on Vancouver Island, and decorated this "small, hip, family hotel" with an aesthetic borrowed from the owner's family cottage in Algonquin Park. Here, as Marnie Fleming suggests, the beaver image seems to stand in as a symbol of "solidity and permanence in the midst of an ephemeral and fragmented world."[48]

These commercial appropriations take advantage of historically laden cultural signifiers to provide a symbolic link between late capitalist consumer society and the apparently benign and authentic past of explorers and fur traders in an untrammelled wilderness. At the same time, this emblem also carries forward a series of discourses, from the early texts of natural history to the present day, whose associations have worked to eclipse other narratives. Most commercial images of the beaver have generated a set of taken-for-granted meanings associated with European order, commerce, and social discipline. However, images of order can also demarcate social boundaries, and these distinctions can signal regimes of violence and constraint.[49] As the image of the beaver became an emblem of commerce and of the country, the long and intricate history of Indigenous and Métis labour – the one essential element that made both the fur trade and early exploration possible – was eclipsed. Indeed, the beaver became an increasingly banal image representing sanitized Euro-Canadian settler traditions of economic progress and paternal entitlement. As a fetish object, then, the beaver is haunted by historical associations that are both traumatic and commonplace. Indeed, most commercial representations have come to stand in for clichéd notions of enterprise and belonging and hold only the faintest remnants of imperialist nostalgia about those whose skilful labour and intercultural connections actually enabled the beaver commerce in the first place.

Political Caricatures

National appropriations of the beaver are intimately linked to these earlier commercial uses, and the connections between the two are well illustrated in the first stamp issued by the Province of Canada in 1851 – the threepence beaver. Up until the nineteenth century, most stamps portrayed the reigning monarch. However, in 1850, the beaver was still such an important commercial symbol for the young colony that the government used its image to create one of the world's earliest pictorial stamps. Over the next fifty years, as the colony was consolidated into a country, the beaver remained one of the central images featured on a plethora of new currency, crests, and monuments.

However, one of the more populist uses of the beaver image is in political cartoons. My examination of these images is based on a review of the caricature collection of documentary art located at Library and Archives

Canada. Spanning the period from the early 1960s to the early 1990s, the collection provides access to hundreds of cartoons that use the beaver image.[50] The first, and by far the largest, group of beaver images found in this collection are cartoons that depict Canada in relation to the United States. And, in virtually all of these caricatures, the United States is presented as a strong-armed neighbour against whom Canadians must exercise constant vigilance. From the cartoons that portray the fraught and dangerous context in which Canada negotiated the Free Trade Agreement (Figures 2.5 and 2.6) to those representing the United States' sense of entitlement in negotiations on acid rain and participation in NATO (Figure 2.7), Canada, through the image of the beaver, is presented as the "little person" who must negotiate with and against an oversized neighbour. The one exception is Edd Uluschak's "Beaver Trudeau and Elephant Nixon," which appeared on 18 June 1973. This cartoon depicts Trudeau as a beaver who ties up the trunk of a Richard Nixon elephant to prevent him from drinking from a Canadian fuel barrel. Here, the depiction of Trudeau (as a beaver) shows him not as gullible, naive, and overrun but, rather, as crafty, satisfied, and successful.

Figure 2.5   **"Don't worry yourself Brian ... I have the greatest respect for Canadian culture"** Cartoon by Adrian Raeside for the *Victoria Times-Colonist*, 1985-87. Courtesy of Adrian Raeside; Library and Archives Canada, C-141006

Figure 2.6
"You're gonna LOVE this guy!" Cartoon by Denny Prichard for the *Saskatoon Star Phoenix*, 22 May 1987. Courtesy of Margaret Pritchard; Library and Archives Canada, C-140995

Figure 2.7
"Damn Chair Squeaks" Cartoon by Vance Rodevalt for the *Calgary Herald*, 30 May 1986. Courtesy of Vance Rodevalt; Library and Archives Canada, C-136647

Figure 2.8   "We've decided to skin just part of you" Cartoon by Vance Rodevalt for the *Calgary Herald*, 19 December 1984. Courtesy of Vance Rodevalt; Library and Archives Canada, C-145002

Implicit in most of these images, excepting that of the flamboyant French-Canadian prime minister Trudeau, is the discursive legacy of the beaver as an honest (if naive and somewhat hapless) representative of an unassuming country. However, when the beaver stands in for Canadian citizens in relation to various internally contested social issues, the animal tells a less benign story (Figure 2.8). In some cartoons, the beaver stands in for Canadian citizens in relation to the questionable decisions of politicians, for example when it represents a health-care system that is being subjected to

Figure 2.9 **"What do you see?"** Cartoon by Ed Franklin for the *Globe and Mail*, 1 July 1978. Courtesy of the *Globe and Mail*; Library and Archives Canada, e-010857038

ludicrous and painful government cuts ("We've Decided to Skin Just Half of You"); in others, we see the beaver in a less positive light as it represents the Canadian Union of Postal Workers engaging in strike action that garnered widespread public disapproval. Consequently, on the specifically internal terrain of national politics, as opposed to the external territory of Canada-US relations, the beaver image demonstrates considerable flexibility.

However, when the beaver stands in for "mainstream" versions of the nation in relation to its internal "others," the situation becomes even more complex. In an early cartoon entitled "What Do You See?" (Figure 2.9), we see Prime Minister Pierre Trudeau, flanked by the symbols of a beaver and a moose, staring down the telescope towards the former leader of the Parti Québécois, Premier René Lévesque. This image suggests a familiar tale of surveillance and estrangement between federalists (who are aligned with the nationalist emblems of the beaver and the moose) and the separatist French leader of Quebec. However, in the second cartoon (Figure 2.10), drawn by Réshard Gool and entitled "Jaws," the artist presents a French-Canadian critique of the inequitable power relations between the tiny "frog" (a derogatory slang term for French-Canadians) and English Canada, which is depicted as a monstrous beaver.

I argue that commercial representations of the beaver have carried forward a set of meanings associated with European order and social discipline, and my analysis of the beavers in Canadian political cartoons suggests a related story. Ross Poole suggests that national symbols mediate the "moral

JAWS

JAWS

Figure 2.10 "JAWS" Cartoon by Réshard Gool. Courtesy of Karl MacKeeman; Library and Archives Canada, C-151048

character" of a homeland.[51] The image of the beaver in political cartoons is most likely to represent Canada as a benign and moral country when it is contrasted with an external adversary, most often the United States. When the beaver is used to depict internal conflicts, it presents a more contradictory narrative. It might represent long-suffering citizens who must try to survive their government (e.g., health-care cuts) or a supposedly greedy and inefficient trade union (e.g., the Canadian Union of Postal Workers).[52] Most important, though, it usually depicts a group Eva Mackey calls "Canadian-Canadians," or those "ordinary people" who consider themselves, and are considered, to be society's mainstream.[53] In the vast majority of representations, then, the beaver image portrays mainstream white English-Canadians rather than those others who are never quite seen as part of the nation-building project.[54] Indeed, perhaps the deeply ambivalent relationship

Figure 2.11 **"Canada is a quiltwork, a mosaic, hamburger"** Cartoon by Dan Murphy for the *Vancouver Province*. Courtesy of Dan Murphy; Library and Archives Canada, C-140981

between Canadian-Canadians and those others can best be seen in the final cartoon in this series (Figure 2.11). Here the beaver (mainstream white Anglo-Canadians) must go through the meat-grinder (being ground up into a less valuable grade of meat) precisely in order to produce a multi-ethnic mosaic.

The Strange Career of the Beaver in the Sexual Imaginary

In the final section of this journey, I take what may seem like a sharp change in direction, from examining political cartoons, natural history discourses, and commercial images to examining the histories of sexuality and respectability that underpin the language of slang. In doing so, I trace the process through which contemporary references to the beaver encompass *both* nationalist associations for the mainstream of Canadian society and vernacular references that associate the word "beaver" with female genitalia.

In *Nationalism and Sexuality,* George Mosse argues that modern ideas of civility, as displayed in language and morals, are a recent phenomenon and were not generally accepted prior to the 1800s. Indeed, up until that time, customs that contemporary Westerners would view with incredulity prevailed among both the aristocracy and the "lesser" classes of society. Mosse elaborates:

> For example, at Holkham, the country seat of the earls of Leicester, ennobled in the eighteenth century, the chamber pots sit in a cupboard in the dining room. They are now merely a tourist attraction, but barely two hundred years ago they would have been used during dinner, perhaps more regularly than the knife and fork. But then, during that same dinner ... a true gentleman in some aristocratic circles would have been expected to fondle the bosom of his beautiful female partner.[55]

In this context, words that would be considered crude or even obscene by today's standards were widely employed by all levels of society.[56] The shift in language and notions of propriety came together due to the late seventeenth- and eighteenth-century rise of pietism and evangelicalism in the growing middle classes. Mosse argues that the middle classes could only partially be defined by their increasing economic activity and that "above all it was the ideal of respectability that came to characterize their style of life."[57] He goes on to say that, "through respectability the middle class sought to maintain their status and self-respect against both the lower classes and the aristocracy. They perceived their way of life, based as it was upon frugality, devotion to duty, and restraint of the passions, as superior to that of the 'lazy' lower classes and the profligate aristocracy."[58] Of course, the overwhelming growth of the middle class was also linked to imperial exploitation and the Industrial Revolution. However, the middle class's social and behavioural standards were also shaped by the Protestant religious revivals that united various Christian sects against an "unregenerate world." And, consequently, it was the dynamism of this group that changed the moral climate in both England and the "New World."

As nationalist sentiment progressed in Europe and North America from the period of the French Revolution through various wars of national liberation, increasing importance was ascribed to pietism's belief in moderation and control over the passions so as to ensure that these did not come into conflict with the demands of the family and the state. Indeed, in the eighteenth and nineteenth centuries, a lack of control over the "animal urges" was said to be characteristic of inferior classes and races and might even threaten the foundation of bourgeois society.[59] This trend included the sanitization of language, and the process was exemplified by the nineteenth-century publication of expurgated versions of Shakespeare and the King James Bible as well as in the movements for social hygiene. In Canada, these campaigns were marked by groups such as the Women's Christian Temperance Union, which pursued work against "obscene" literature through the Department of Purity in Literature, Art and Fashion.[60] In the twentieth and twenty-first centuries, however, the middle-class obsession with sexual morals has been gradually eroded not only through legal battles[61] but also through a broad trend towards permissiveness accelerated by two world wars, the feminist and sexual revolutions of the 1960s, and the popularization of sexual materials through the mass media. Perhaps what has most powerfully entrenched this change is the availability of sexually explicit material through the internet and cable television. Now, with the flick of a mouse or a channel changer, materials that many people would still be embarrassed to purchase through a retail outlet are available in the privacy of one's home. So while crude sexual expressions are still frowned upon, in many contexts there is a more widespread acceptance of explicit sexual language.

In the *Bloomsbury Dictionary of Contemporary Slang*, the listing for the word "beaver" suggests that its sexualized meanings were popularized through pornographic images and pin-up magazines in the late 1950s.[62] However, shifts in language always have a history, and a search through the *Oxford English Dictionary* and several historical dictionaries of "street literature" indicates that the term "beaver" has long been used as slang for "beard" and that the word "beard" often referenced both men's beards and women's pubic hair. Consistent with the class-based shifts in language noted above, the popular stories from Chaucer's *Canterbury Tales* (e.g., "The Miller's Tale," 1369) and *A Hundred Merry Tales* (the first English jest book, published in 1526) provide a window onto a period when the use of sexualized language was more common than it became in subsequent centuries and did not always imply a male-controlled objectification of women. In the summary below, James Henke describes an incident from *A Hundred Merry Tales* in which the reference to "beard" as pubic hair was, in fact, initiated by a witty gentlewoman:

> As the two [a gentlewoman and a male youth] are exchanging barbs, the woman comments on the youth's beard, which has not yet filled in, growing luxuriously over his upper lip but sparsely on his chin: "Sir," says she, "ye have a beard above and none beneath." He responds, "in sport": "Mistress, ye have a beard beneath and non above." "Marry," quod she, "then set the one against the t'other" which answer made the gentleman so abashed that he had not one word to answer (94). The woman is suggesting that their two half-beards, when joined together will equal a whole. The humor here is of the "beaten-at-his-own-game" school. The youth, who is losing the wit-battle to the girl, attempts to turn the tables with a smirking sexual joke only to be bested at his own tactics with an even cruder counter.[63]

This sexualized meaning of "beard" survived for several centuries, as is seen in *A Classical Dictionary of the Vulgar Tongue* (1796), which tells us that Captain Francis Grose defined "beard splitter" as "A man much given to wenching."[64]

In the 1600s, the word "beaver" was also often used as a synonym for "hat," arising from the popularity of the beaver hat. Thus, the phrases "He's sporting a handsome beaver,"[65] meaning a handsome beaver hat, or the more aggressive "cock one's beaver," meaning to "assume a swaggering air" (1642).[66] Rawson explains that "hat" is also a byword for the female genitals, with the allusion resting on the knowledge that hats were frequently made out of beaver felt.[67] Given this history, Rawson suggests that the term "beaver" may have survived as a kind of slang code among heterosexual men. One example of this can be found in *The Limerick*, first published in 1927, a section of which goes as follows:

> There was a young lady named Eva
> Who went to the ball as Godiva,
> But a change in the lights
> Showed a tear in her tights,
> And a low fellow present yelled, "Beaver!"

Thus, beaver may have been a street cry that men would use with other men, "advising them that if they looked sharp, a woman without underpants might be seen."[68]

There is no way to trace a linear trajectory from the early references to "beaver" as an alternate term for "beard," which also referenced women's sexuality (1360-1500s); to beaver as a sometimes sexualized synonym for "hat"(1600s); to the slang and street usages of "beard" and "beaver" from the late 1700s to the early 1900s; to the overtly sexual references in 1950s pin-up magazines and the "beaver shot" of pornographic movies. Nevertheless, it seems that the recent hyper-sexualization of this term probably emerged from underground usage over the past several centuries.

How, then, to understand the relationship between slang discourses that have usually worked to objectify and degrade women's sexuality, on the one hand, and the beaver narratives that reference the norms of social order associated with Canadian nation building, on the other? I argue that the link between these seemingly disparate stories can be found in the racialized and patriarchal thrust of virtually *all* beaver discourses. In the narratives from natural history, the fur trade, commerce, and politics, women were not simply underrepresented; rather, the overtly paternal nature of these discourses *worked to inferiorize their contributions to nation building.* And, when women do appear in national histories, whether as respectable wives or immoral sluts, they are always already sexualized.

To place this theme within a broader context we must remember that Canada, like other countries in the New World, first became an imagined community through constructing categories that defined some people, primarily European male immigrants, as fully entitled and deserving citizens while others – including all women – were defined as unfit to be full citizens of the "new" land. However, the specific history of Indigenous women in the beaver trade is particularly relevant here. During the first three hundred years of European trade and settlement, ongoing sexual relationships between Indigenous women and French and English traders were crucially important to the political and economic survival of the early colony. However, in the mid-1800s, as white women started to arrive in the remote outposts of Rupert's Land, a redefined colonial morality began to view cross-racial partnerships with increasing disdain. This ideology posited that the emerging British values of "civilized" manliness and "pure" motherhood might be compromised by the "degeneration" that could result from mixed-race liaisons. As Sylvia Van Kirk shows, marriages *à la façon du pays* began to be denounced as sinful and debased, and traders increasingly looked upon Indigenous women simply as objects of temporary sexual gratification, not as partners to whom they should make a long-term commitment. In this context, the stigmatization of Indigenous women as immoral sexual objects with promiscuous tendencies, which were supposedly "inherent in their Indian blood," was a crucial early development in a specifically white process of Canadian nation building.[69] Further, this same ideology has been evident in the overwhelming number of North American popular stories, songs, and pictures that have represented "Indian squaws" as depersonalized objects of sexual convenience. This legacy continues into the present, with the devastating lack of official concern about the disproportionate rates of violence against Indigenous women across the country, most obviously in Vancouver's Downtown Eastside.[70]

While publicly legitimized beaver discourses focus on narratives about Canada as an industrious and benign nation, the more secretive underground slang underscores the sexualized nature of women's – particularly Indigenous women's – absent-presence in this same national project. Thus, from the anthropomorphic maps and texts of early naturalists, in which European settlers constructed and then identified with the paternal traits of the beaver; to the racialized notions of masculinity and bodily decorum associated with changing fur trade fashion; to commercial beaver images that fetishized paternal entitlement; to the Canadian-Canadians portrayed in political cartoons – the very category of a deserving citizen was secured through these discourses of masculine enterprise and racial advancement. These beaver images articulated the investments through which Anglo-Canadian settler identity was defined.

The Beaver Bites Back

I now turn to exploring how four contemporary Canadian artists have responded to this complex beaver legacy. These artists work in spheres that range from sculpture to photography to performance, and each addresses aspects of the "secretly familiar" beaver legacy that has served to authenticate a banal symbol of national purpose. Significantly, these artists do not construct beaver stories to sketch out a utopian space separate from the confines of dominant narratives; rather, they work from the inside out, fashioning new horizons from the conflicting range of beaver narratives found in popular, historic, and official narratives.

The Spirit of Canada Suckling the French and the English Beavers (1970-71)

In 1971, the National Gallery of Canada staged a groundbreaking retrospective on the work of one of Canada's best-known artists, Joyce Wieland.[71] The exhibit, True Patriot Love, brought together a wide selection of Wieland's work, including material referencing pop culture, women's traditional crafts, classical sculpture, and experimental film, and it highlighted the artist's preoccupation with re-envisioning national narratives through a wryly feminine eye.[72] *The Spirit of Canada Suckling the French and the English Beavers* (Plate 2) is an expressively rendered miniature bronze and was first exhibited, as part of True Patriot Love, resting on a large pink sculpture called *The Arctic Passion Cake.* As Lauren Rabinovitz notes, this display, together with other items in the show, including quilts embellished with political slogans, knitted Canadian flags, embroideries depicting Canadian wildlife (while warning of its impending destruction), nationalist cartoons, and bottles of *Sweet Beaver* perfume, all evoked the atmosphere of a postmodern county fair rather than an art exhibit.[73]

In his review of the show, Hugo McPherson points out that the distinctive feature of *Spirit of Canada* and *Arctic Passion Cake* is that the two sculptures map out Wieland's own tongue-in-cheek myth of Canadian origins:

> [The] huge *Arctic Passion Cake* [was displayed] near the entrance to the exhibition in the National Gallery [and] depicted Canada as a huge landscape crowned by icebergs and snowfields ... The roughly-circular base is decorated with the crests of the provinces ... On the summit lies a murdered polar bear, slain by hunters; but the bear has made love to a beautiful woman, *The Spirit of Canada,* and further down the slope we find her giving suckle to her off-spring, the French and the English Beavers. The cake will not be eaten, but visitors are offered little *petit fours* – a taste of Arctic passion.[74]

Kass Banning argues that one of the ways in which Wieland can be distinguished from other artists of her generation is through her "constant attention to, and representation of, feminine and often domestic concerns"; and, in *Spirit of Canada*, the artist appropriates conventions from classical European carving to reimagine the nation in distinctly female form.[75] Wieland herself describes this as a commitment to "remaining loyal to myself and to my mother and my female line."[76] Thus, in *Spirit of Canada*, the artist seizes the unlikely conventions of French Renaissance sculpture for a wildly playful reimagining of nationalist narratives and uses her own body as the model for this bawdy reconfiguration.

Most critics of this work, like McPherson, conclude that the myth of national patrimony elaborated in this sculpture is optimistic and that "the beavers will grow stalwart and live in harmony with the Canadian spirit."[77]

Yet there are several aspects of this story that continue to puzzle as *Spirit of Canada* could be a hopeful rewriting of an acrimonious national history *and*, at the same time, a commentary on women's position as the caretakers of the national "family." My interest is in relating the artist's "myth of origins" to traditional narratives of "the wilderness" found in Canadian visual arts as well as to stories in which the animal and the human come together in myth and fiction.

In Wieland's *Arctic Passion Cake*, the configuration of a "huge landscape crowned by icebergs" draws on a long tradition of images of northern wilderness that are a symbol of Canadian identity, and it represents the North as an archetype of the nation. As Gerta Moray argues, the image of a national "patrimony" works to assure Canadians both of a sense of "spiritual purity" and a sense of entitlement to resources won from hard labour on the soil.[78] Jonathan Bordo suggests that two additional qualities usually mark these narratives: first, all traces of an Indigenous presence are eliminated; second, the landscape itself becomes a place of "spiritual birth, of the nativity of the modern Canadian who emerges from union with the land."[79] Indeed, he also argues that this same landscape exorcizes the "ghosts of cultural difference – difference between the Aboriginal and the invader, between the classed hierarchy of the Old World and the equal birthright of the New."[80]

Based, then, on the insights of Moray and Bordo, I argue that Wieland uses the conventions of pop art for a humorous reworking of these wilderness discourses.[81] Wieland's *Arctic Passion Cake* configures the national patrimony as a huge pink confection, an image that feminizes these traditionally sombre narratives at the same time as it suggests that this much vaulted "landscape" may indeed be a very "sweet deal." The rapacious portrayal of the hunter is consistent with an important Wieland theme: it is a humorous but direct environmental critique. Further, her formulation of a Canadian myth of origins, based on a union between the polar bear and *Spirit of Canada*, seems like a feminist reworking of the classic narrative in which the landscape itself is a place of "spiritual birth." While the story references the Roman tale of Romulus and Remus, twins who were saved from abandonment and suckled in infancy by a she-wolf and who grew up to found the city of Rome, Wieland's tale also suggests an interesting genealogy. Indeed, this narrative takes as its starting point a long tradition of bear stories that have come to inform myth and fiction.[82]

Annis Pratt, in her examination of the archetypal narratives associated with bears, suggests that these animals have traditionally been a medium for women's transformation and empowerment. In myths of old they are the "greenworld lovers," an alternative to socially acceptable partners, who fulfill "women's socially repressed sexuality and eroticism," especially when men "turn to cruelty" or attempt to control the women they love.[83] Translating these classic narratives into the contemporary period is Marion Engle's famous Canadian novel *Bear*. Winner of the Governor General's Award for best English-language novel in 1976, the book's main character, Lou, befriends a bear while working and living in the northern bush. While at first merely intrigued by the animal, by the end she has become sexually involved with it. As Christl Verduyn notes, the story "lies on the seam between fiction and reality" and uses the "fantastic" as a point of entry for defamiliarizing realist assumptions, a strategy that allows for pointed societal critique.[84]

Looking at Wieland's "Canada myth" within this context, I would suggest that, in *Spirit of Canada*, the polar bear can be seen as a vehicle through which the female protagonist gains access both to her own sexual wildness and to a sense of indigenization.[85] Indeed, the country itself is born from this cross-species relationship through which French and English beavers come to stand for the nation. Here the bear stands as the fantastic embodiment of both the wilderness and all men. Yet Wieland's work also follows the tradition of eliminating from the narrative any overt reference to Indigenous people. Indeed, the mending of the national story is reliant upon a matriarchal mythology in which it is the white woman herself, through contact with the polar bear, who becomes a "wild vessel that will make things whole."[86] The myth could be optimistic, presenting a plea for peaceful coexistence between the French and the English. At the same time, it also suggests an alternative reading: the rapacious young beavers will eventually suck the mother dry.

The Spirit of Canada Eating Beaver

In *The Spirit of Canada Eating Beaver* (1999-2000) (Plate 3), Wendy Coburn has fashioned a sculpture that responds to the complex currents that mark Wieland's work. Coburn's project began with an acknowledgment of the contemporary association between the word "beaver" and women's sexuality for, as the artist herself remarks, in the contemporary context, "no savvy person can pretend to investigate the many representations of the beaver without referring to the slang signifier ... [of] the human female genitalia."[87] Yet no other artist has taken up this challenge with quite the wry humour demonstrated in *Eating Beaver*. Coburn's sculpture was first displayed, alongside Wieland's, at the Oakville Galleries in 2000 in an exhibit entitled *Beaver Tales*. Like Wieland with *The Spirit of Canada*, Coburn uses her own body as the model for the miniature sculpture, although this time the target is a quick-witted send-up of heteronormative assumptions. While the work does reconfigure a national symbol, Coburn does not attempt to map out an alternative myth of national origins. Indeed, the objective of *Eating Beaver* was precisely to play with and against the male-authored sexual slang that so often serves as a subterranean mechanism for sexualizing women in order to keep them "in their place." Significantly, though, this intervention does not shy away from using a sexualized image in order to challenge how women have been objectified by these very representations. Instead of reiterating the maternal vision in which women single-handedly give birth to and nurture the country, Coburn's work celebrates women's entitlement to sexual pleasure through a cross-species and non-procreative form of sexual expression.

However, *Eating Beaver* does more than provide an implicitly queer perspective on nationalist discourse, just as *Spirit of Canada* attempts more than a feminist twist on the national story. By blurring the lines between "productive" and "non-productive" sexuality, and between male and female, Coburn parodies the legitimating discourses of respectability, modesty, and heteronormativity that have served to authenticate the imperial project. Indeed, the discourses that enabled *Eating Beaver* are very different from the modes of thought that have shaped modern nation making. Throughout the past two centuries, imperial discourses have been characterized by the construction of binary relationships between the human and the natural world, productive and non-productive sexuality, male and female genders, and the civilized and savage races. And, as we have seen, Canadian representations of the beaver from natural history, commerce, and politics typically reproduced these distinctions in ways that legitimated European male settlers' territorial and nationalist ambitions while delegitimizing or erasing Indigenous contributions to various beaver enterprises.

In contrast, both these art works present human sexual expression itself as unruly and unpredictable, and Wieland locates the origin of the Canadian nation not in the authentic claim of a pure northern race to its paternal entitlement but, rather, in a fantastical relationship of miscegenation that blurs the boundaries between the human and the animal. Further, while female nationalist symbols typically represent femininity through domesticated emblems of maternal womanhood,[88] Wieland and Coburn's sculptures demonstrate none of this bourgeois timidity about women's sexual appetite and power. Thus, Coburn's work appropriates the terminology that signifies women's sexuality in the service of men and inverts its meaning, presenting an image in which the beaver, as a national symbol, acts *in the service of women.* Here it is women's pleasure – not that of children, men, or the nation – that takes priority. Indeed, it is no surprise that representations of lesbianism have been thought to pose such a risk to the integrity of the nation, as Coburn's work challenges the patriarchal interpretations of women's assumed place as mothers and patron saints of both the family and the country.[89]

Souvenirs of the Self (Banff Park Museum), 1991-2000

In Jin-me Yoon's photo exhibit Souvenirs of the Self (Banff Park Museum), 1991-2000, the artist develops a series of six postcards that examine representations of national belonging through photographs in and around the town of Banff, in Banff National Park. In each of these postcards, Yoon poses her body in front of the most recognized sites in the Canadian tourist lexicon. Hyun Yi Kang describes Yoon's method as "autobiographical staging,"[90] and the juxtapositions in each image do stage an invitation to viewers to examine their own assumptions about belonging in relation to those emblems that are indexical of the Canadian nation.

The focus of my investigation is the title postcard for this series and an image that Yoon uses to frame the rest of the collection (Plate 4). In it she stands carefully posed in front of a Cabinet of Curiosities at Banff Park Museum. The cabinet holds a taxidermic recreation of a Canadian beaver peacefully chewing away at a tree stump against a painted diorama of woodland forest and stream, while perched atop the cabinet is an American beaver. The catalogue for the exhibit points out that the animals play out "the stereotypic national characteristics," showing "the 'Canadian' beaver" as "benign, docile and safely contained in the realm of the 'natural,'" while the "'American' beaver, on the other hand, is depicted as unconstrained, aggressive and active, literally on top of the 'Canadian' beaver."[91] On the back of each of the images in this series, Yoon provides a commentary that blurs the distinction between the personal signature expected on postcards and the uniform caption, juxtaposing the conventionally generic statement with a more self-reflexive one that is phrased in the third person:

> Marvel over the impressive collection of Western Canada's oldest natural history museum.
> She looks with curiosity and imagines life beyond the rigid casings.

Finally, in vertical columns on the back of the postcard are three captions, written in Japanese, Chinese, and Korean, which say "We too are the keepers of this land." However, these captions are not translated into English and so are directed primarily towards viewers from Japanese, Chinese, and Korean linguistic backgrounds. Finally, the postmark in the top right corner of the postcard reads "A 100% Canadian Product."

In a recent interview, Yoon commented that her central preoccupation in this project was to speak to issues of classification, framing, and containment.[92] In this context, the choice of the Cabinet of Curiosities as a starting place is manifestly appropriate because, as she notes, these exhibits have been driven by "a kind of humanism that classifies all living things in a hierarchy."[93] Probably the most monumental example of taxidermic display can be found in the American Museum of Natural History in New York.[94] In Donna Haraway's analysis of this institution (and of Carl Akeley, the man known for perfecting the art of taxidermy), she describes the museum dioramas as "side altars" that "tell a part of the story of salvation history ... where the animals in the habitat groups are captured in a sculptor's vision ...[as] actors in a morality play on the stage of nature."[95] Haraway maps out several key elements in a typical story: first, each grouping is modelled on the idea of perfection, and animals that are too small, irregular, or deformed never make it into the display case; second, each has to be judged to have "character"; and, third, the one essential quality for a typical animal is that it must be an adult male. In the case in which the diorama is composed of a group of animals, it inevitably represents a "perfect family."[96]

If taxidermic exhibits are "meaning machines" in the story of Man and Nature,[97] then the relations of power that frame these technologies of classification have an eerily familiar ring – and bring us back to the early natural history explorers and map makers whose writing I analyze at the beginning of this chapter. Here representations of the beaver join together qualities of industry and paternal intelligence: the ideal animal is seen as an overlord and architect, while the "defective" beavers are seen to cause the degeneration of the race. The contemporary display in the Cabinet of Curiosities at the Banff museum seems to reiterate these patriarchal narratives, with the Canadian beaver represented as a hard-working emblem of national character while the American beaver mimics the assumed national characteristics of the nation south of the forty-ninth parallel.

However, the continuing salience of these faintly comical displays concerning the moral character of a homeland take on added significance in relation to Yoon's performance. Her self-display beside the cabinet highlights how non-white Canadians, whose citizenship is so often viewed as inauthentic, are also an object of interrogation. Indeed, Yoon developed the project through a process that involved reflecting on how she was initially perceived in the town of Banff. When she first arrived at the Banff Centre for the Arts, many of the locals greeted her as a Japanese tourist. She decided to take these *mis*-recognitions as the starting place for her work:

> This prompted some thinking about my own complex history. I came as a child from Korea, and Korea has a difficult historical and colonial relationship with Japan. I wanted to examine the relationship between this history, and the way my body was taken up within the tourist space of Banff. So I decided to look at the popular representations of place, and did a loose kind of fieldwork, watching how people are trained to "see" and "frame" a desirable place for them to be photographed, and how these locations are then a metonym for something greater. For instance the *Banff Springs Hotel* is thought to harken back to some grand European past, which is basically a fiction. So the performative aspect of my work is really a response to the performance of everyday life ... I grew up feeling like a racialized object ... and kids taunted me about being a Jap or a Chink ... [M]y making art is partly a coming into subjecthood, through the possibility of actually speaking back through representation.[98]

Thus, Yoon's performance articulates a series of questions: What are the epistemological connections between the systems of thought that mark and classify animals and those that categorize human beings? How do some animals and humans take on a naturalized place at the centre of the world while others become "other"? And what forms of discursive and representational violence facilitate these everyday assumptions? In Souvenirs of the Self (Banff Park Museum), Yoon inserts her body into the photographic composition in a way that highlights the implicit hierarchy in these representations.

While travel photography, including the ubiquitous postcard, has been a significant trope through which Western explorers have constructed the "East," Yoon reimagines this format in order to take a critical look at her adopted country. Monika Kin Gagnon comments that one consistent strategy in Yoon's work is to "quote the containing structure" while disrupting the very terms by which these cultural narratives are normalized.[99] In Souvenirs of the Self (Banff Park Museum), the artist positions herself within particular narratives of Canadianness precisely in order to question their taken-for-granted status. Here, the absurd juxtaposition of the Canadian and American beavers contributes a humorous edge to querying the naturalization of particular emblems and identities. One of Yoon's objectives is to invite the viewer to cast a critical eye on the usually unspoken assumptions regarding who can be "at home" within liberal narratives of the nation and to reflect on who can take national identity for granted and who cannot.[100] Throughout, she performs "that place, where there is a slippage between humour and pain ... it's not utterly earnest, but not entirely ironic either."[101]

Speaking to the performance itself, Yoon's stance in the photograph presents a remarkable stillness. Unlike most tourist images, in which the people in the shots smile and wave to their beloved, the artist presents her body in a pose that is almost more contained than the taxidermic animals behind her. This restrained posture presents a striking counterpoint to the English text on the back of the postcard: "She looks with curiosity and imagines life beyond the rigid casings." Yoon talks about this juxtaposition by emphasizing the importance of understanding "the subject position that racism forces on people, and what it does to one's own feelings of encasement within the body."[102] And these comments point back to the "autobiographical staging" that Yi Kang notes earlier, for the artist is not only re-enacting the impact of racism on the body of the other but also using the secretly familiar discourses of anthropomorphic classification to stage the potential disjunctures between personal narratives and larger social and historical movements.

In each of these images, Yoon is shown wearing a Nordic sweater commonly sold in gift shops around Banff. According to early Canadian nationalists, the hardy and resilient northern characteristics of early white settlers were the basis of their status as a "superior race" that would eventually triumph over the "weak and effeminate" peoples of the south.[103] These assumptions about the inherent superiority of northerners remained active in statements by public officials until quite recently. For instance, the Governor General of Canada, Vincent Massey, noted in 1948 that "the vast majority [of Canada's population] springs either from the British Isles or Northern France, a good many too, from Scandinavia and Germany, and it is in northwestern Europe that one finds the elements of human stability highly developed."[104] Even more overtly racist beliefs informed Canadian immigration policy until 1967 – the first year federal legislation was changed to allow significant non-white immigration. (Yoon's family emigrated from Korea to Canada in 1968.) In this context, Yoon's costume of Nordic sweater and jeans, with its attendant associations with the pioneer spirit, highlights a potential disjuncture between her very particularly raced and gendered body and the norms of citizenship associated with northern and implicitly white visions of Canadianness.[105]

In his study of the impact of the taxidermic impulse on the writing of history in the nineteenth century, Stephen Bann comments that taxidermy's restoration of a sense of life-likeness "is postulated as a response to a sense of loss."[106] If taxidermy is a means of protecting against loss, then I suggest that, in the exhibit of Canadian and American beavers at the Banff Park Museum, we see an attempt to protect against the loss of the "benign" ideas of authenticity and Canadianness associated with this hard-working emblem. However, in *Souvenirs of the Self*, Yoon inhabits this landscape of national fantasy to posit her own set of questions – questions that inquire into the effects of this national ideology on the construction of a supposedly unmarked national identity.

But perhaps the haunting commentary in Korean, Japanese, and Chinese on the back of these postcards attempts to protect against the loss of another kind of memory. In withholding translation of the text from the predominantly English-speaking white audience, the artist is articulating a variant of what Homi Bhabha calls a "limit-text, anti-West," the point at which transcultural incompatibilities will not be negotiated any further.[107] Its assertion – "We too are the keepers of this land" – draws together another audience and, in so doing, emphasizes the long history of Asian settlement in Canada and the relations of allegiance these settlers bring to the land; at the same time, it works against official kinds of forgetting, which constitute one of the primary themes of Yoon's artistic practice.

Rising to the Occasion (1987-91)

Finally, I turn to the sculpture *Rising to the Occasion* (Plate 5), by the Ojibwe artist Rebecca Belmore, which now resides in the permanent collection of the Art Gallery of Ontario. This project first started its life in a remarkable street procession, entitled Twelve Angry Crinolines, in Thunder Bay, Ontario. Brought together by Lynne Charmaine, the parade was composed of twelve women artists who attempted to draw attention to a variety of hotly contested political issues on the occasion of a visit to Canada by the duke and duchess of York in 1987. As the artist recalled in a recent interview, while the royal visit itself was brief, it required elaborate staging:

> Prince Andrew and his new bride Fergie flew into Thunder Bay and then were whisked off to the Old Fort William, the reconstructed Hudson's Bay fort. The idea was, very specifically, to replay the fur trade history, from the point of view of the British colonialists ... [and consequently] the royals were actually taken upriver from Fort William, and put into a birch bark canoe and then they were paddled downstream to the Fort where they could be greeted by canon salutes and welcoming crowds. So

our performance was a direct response to that. And *Rising to the Occasion* was really my version of "what to wear" for the royal visit.

But *Rising to the Occasion* was not only a response to the fashion crisis engendered when the plebs attempt to crash a royal parade. The front of Belmore's costume, with its plush fabric, elaborate china plates, and trim Victorian detailing, references historic British norms of femininity. The back of her costume features an unruly "beaver dam" that mushrooms out from the baroque folds and, waving above the artist's head, two impertinent Indian braids. Embedded in the beaver-dam bustle, made of twigs and bark, are trade goods and all the bric-à-brac associated with a royal visit. Although no video cameras recorded the parade for posterity, the Canadian critic Charlotte Townsend-Gault writes about the event and pays particular attention to this artist's performance:

> Belmore was decked out in a surreal agglomeration of red velvet and beaver lodge, tin kettles and trade trinkets, worn with the hauteur and disdain proper to the artifice of a fully-fledged crinoline. Thus arrayed, Belmore was more sure of her right to be there than any Victorian grande dame in the colonies, more regal than the duchess, and, as signalled by the wired braids that waved above her head, more attuned to the cross-cultural vibes than the humiliating cliché of the Indian maiden was ever allowed to be. It has been a widely remembered performance.[108]

Interestingly, the media releases distributed prior to the Twelve Angry Crinolines performance generated considerable concern on the part of the local constabulary, and the police interrogated the organizers to ensure there would be no unseemly disruption of the royal visit. As Belmore remarks, this "added to the irony of it. Really ... what threat would we present to the royal family?"[109] Yet the law-enforcement agencies seemed steadfastly immune to the pleasures of ironic commentary. Consequently, the artists and the royals engaged in simultaneous, but very separate, performances, with Twelve Angry Crinolines parading on the streets of downtown Thunder Bay as the royals were canoed into Fort William. While there was a considerably smaller audience for the Crinolines performance, there were some striking responses. As Belmore remembers: "A few of the older women came up to me, royalists, and one of the women deliberately stomped on my dress. So there was this tension."[110] Yet this affective response was also an indicator of the performance's ability to get under the skin of local townspeople, for both the dress and Belmore's mode of performance memorialized the troubled relationship between the "cultured" norms of femininity promulgated through British imperial expansion and the "wild" and implicitly degenerate sexuality attributed to Indigenous women. As Belmore comments, "the whole idea of my wearing it [the dress], was trying to dress up for the party, but knowing that I could never 'be a lady' within the terms set by the colonialists."[111]

While the specific history of Indigenous women in the beaver trade, referred to earlier in this chapter, profoundly informs the representational choices signified in *Rising to the Occasion,* Belmore also has a more personal set of reasons for utilizing this image, for the dress materializes the contradictions in her family history. As the artist notes:

> The women in my family and in my history are still more connected to the land and the dress materializes that split. When I was growing up, my grandmother was a trapper and my mother used to skin the beaver she trapped, so I'm very familiar with the smell, the greasiness, the rancid strength of the beaver scent. If you've never seen one skinned, it's a difficult process, there is a huge amount of fat and the odour is strong.[112]

Not surprisingly, these thoughts about the beaver are of a distinctly different nature than recent commentary in the style pages of the *Globe and Mail* and the *New York Times.* Here the news is that, "in everything from high fashion, to sports, to pop culture, we're having a True North moment," with the glamorous return of fur to both the catwalks of Paris and the streets of the city.[113] Thus, while the latest hip designers are reimagining beaver pelts in a rainbow of colours and textures for everything from the classic pump to the knitted sweater, Belmore brings us back to the materiality of the beaver trade from the perspective of one who knows it only too well.[114] In her vision, the beaver is not only symptomatic of a gendered colonial legacy but also symbolizes the very material kinds of labour that have linked Indigenous women for generations. Indeed, Belmore's family has borne witness to these historical shifts from her grandmother's life hunting and trapping, to her mother's work skinning hides, to her own use of the beaver in artistic performance. Yet what stays in my consciousness is the memory of Belmore's own performance during the royal visit, at which the artist wore her surreal dress of finely tailored velvet and a wildly tangled beaver-dam bustle, evincing "the hauteur and disdain proper to the artifice of a fully-fledged crinoline." For here Belmore's very considerable performative élan breathes new life into musty fur trade narratives, reanimating "through repetition with a difference, a lost country that is relished and loved."[115]

Yet, as I note in the introduction, the forms of love articulated by each of these artists has little to do with the patriotic love of country. Indeed, their projects reject the model of *philia* whose bonds of responsibility are directed only towards fellow citizens. Rather, Wieland uses the figure of the beaver to portray fantastical relationships of miscegenation that blur the boundaries between the human and the animal, while Coburn's pleasure-seeking beaver satirizes women's role as the "mother of the nation." Similarly, Yoon and Belmore play with and against racialized narratives of classification and containment that have structured the beaver image and the nation. Indeed, these artists appropriate nationalist master-codes to trace how beaver narratives have been employed to produce gendered and racial others: strangers and foreigners. At the same time, their work also illustrates how anthropomorphic discourse is productive of who can be considered Canadian-Canadians at the centre of the nation. As Donna Haraway notes:

> The role of the one who renamed the animals was to ensure a true and faithful order of nature, to purify the eye and the word. The "balance of nature" was maintained partly by the role of a new "man" who would see clearly and name accurately, hardly a trivial identity in the face of eighteenth-century European expansion. Indeed, this is the identity of the modern authorial subject, for whom inscribing the body of nature gives assurance of his mastery.[116]

The work of these new "authorial subjects," in contrast, suggests the risky and fantastical ways in which a natural world might be reinvented in the hopes of creating a more complexly textured, and very real, material world. At the same time, it also illustrates the comic ironies and unsettling hierarchies in the beaver world we take for granted.

3

Things Not Named
Bachelors, *Dirty Laundry,* and the Canadian Pacific Railway

> From its earliest days, the train has been romanticized and even sexualized, most often as a double for male sexuality ... One of the train's great effects on modern Western culture was, in fact, its historical role in disrupting and uprooting traditional Victorian culture by literally destabilizing its social-sexual hierarchies.
>
> – Lynne Kirby, "Steamy Scenes and Dream Machines"[1]

From the late nineteenth century to the present day, the Canadian Pacific Railway (CPR) has epitomized the transcontinental bonds that unite the nation. Images of the railway in contemporary culture range from nostalgic ballads like Gordon Lightfoot's *Canadian Railroad Trilogy* to caustic political commentary heralding the railway's eclipse as a drain on the federal treasury.[2] I explore the representational legacy of the railway as a foundational image in Canadian nation building, starting with the photographs, posters, and testimonials distributed by the CPR, encouraging European settlers to undertake an epic journey to a new homeland. These images are then placed in conversation with lesser-known material from the William Van Horne collection in the Canadian Pacific Archives and a selection of photographs by the early British Columbian railway worker and photographer C.D. Hoy. My purpose is to explore the visual imaginary emerging from the rails' construction and to highlight haunting fissures in the remembrance of the railway and the nation. Then I take up Richard Fung's *Dirty Laundry* (1996, 30:30 minutes), a videotape that explores the legacy of Chinese "bachelor" workers on the CPR. Here the liminal space of train travel intersects with the contested histories associated with those who built the western sections of the CPR. Indeed, the video fleshes out a mode of reading/viewing history that is attentive to the silences that echo through narratives of the western frontier, and my own investigation follows this same method. Here I invite the reader to imagine, remember, and flesh out what Willa Cather calls "the inexplicable presence of the thing[s] not named" in the construction of the CPR and the western settlement of the nation.[3]

"Everybody Has a Train Story"[4]

The best-known Canadian train story is encapsulated in a photograph entitled *The Last Spike*, taken in Craigellachie, British Columbia (1885), and showing the CPR director Donald Smith hammering the final spike that joined the rails from east to west and, some would say, creating Canada as we now know it. While the railway has been the subject of intense debate by many of this country's eminent historians, including Harold Innis, Donald Creighton, George Grant, Hugh Dempsey, and A.A. Den Otter, one of the assumptions shared by all of these authors arose first in the work of Innis, who argues that the form of transport used in early North American economic activity was a crucial determinant of later political divisions on the continent and that forms of transportation themselves have a profound impact on national identity.[5] Den Otter builds on this idea in his exploration of the "technological nationalism" that fuelled the growth of the railway, arguing that a central feature of the new industrial imperialism and its civilizing mandate was the transportation revolution.[6] In my analysis of the semiotics of the railway, I reread the visual iconography of the CPR in order to explore how these taken-for-granted tropes articulate a white civilizing mission.

The Last Spike has been reproduced everywhere from school history texts to insurance calendars, and it signifies a crucial early moment in the iconography of nation building. This is because this photograph of the "great men" of the railway encapsulates the intersection of masculinity and technology. These themes are also evident, for example, in the celebratory notices the railway issued to mark the beginning of transcontinental travel. In the posters collection of the Canadian Pacific Archives, a newspaper advertisement regarding the first passenger train for the west reads: "CONSUMMATED! TO-DAY, AT TWO O'CLOCK P.M. First Through Passenger Train LEAVES FOR Winnipeg and the West BY THE Canadian Pacific Railway" (Figure 3.1). Thus, in the CPR's love affair with technology, the powerful speed and scheduled regularity of the railway became the emblem of masculinity's domination of nature in conquering the vast spaces of the new continent.

The gendered nature of railway discourse was evident everywhere from political debate about the effects of the tracks on the North American landscape to the advertisements issued by the CPR to encourage immigration

Figure 3.1 "Consummated!" CPR newspaper advertisement, 1886 Canadian Pacific Archives, A6355

and settlement. For example, Den Otter quotes a dramatic oration by the American senator Daniel Webster, which attempted to reconcile his support for the railway with the seemingly negative effects of the locomotives' raucous invasion of a peaceful landscape and their cut-and-slash construction techniques. The senator resolves these concerns, however, by avowing that such complaints cannot really be taken seriously. After all: "While the pastoral scene is beautiful, it is trivial and effete, and those who are disturbed by the piercing whistle of the iron horse are effeminate and squeamish."[7] Here Webster is asserting that those who object to the destructive effects of railway construction are simply allowing an implicitly feminine and therefore trivial set of worries to disrupt this important national project. These critics, he seems to say, fail to understand the inherently progressive force of the "iron horse" in overcoming a vast continent and uniting man and nation.

This "philosophy" of railways was bound up with the sense of continental entitlement characteristic of both the Canadian and American national missions. For if Canada's claim to the immense north and western territories was, on its own, an audacious act of political imperialism, then it was the railway that provided the essential technology to bring the west into this emerging Dominion. Indeed, from a Foucauldian perspective, the railway symbolizes the decentred strategies of imperial rule and is an emblem of what Cole Harris calls "the capillaries of colonial appropriation."[8] Thus, it was the railway that enabled both the United States and Canada to secure control over the western territories. And this drive for territorial mastery was portrayed in language that suggests the utter inevitability of European "progress." As Canadian explorer Allan Macdonell wrote: "The impulse of emigration to the westward cannot be arrested" and, consequently, the best one could do was to take a position in accord with this movement or be swept aside.[9] In this context, railway discourse identified technology as a key element in the nation's rise to pre-eminence, and the speed, power, size, and control symbolized by this transportation revolution were important signifiers in an implicitly masculinist national trajectory.

Doug Owram notes that one of the distinctive aspects of Canadian homesteading rhetoric, as compared to that of the United States, was the concept of "seeding" the North West with reliable men. The idea was to bring in suitable groups of farmers who would each take up a lot, build a small dwelling, and clear the land and prepare it for cultivation. When a base was established, they would send for their wives and children or find a partner through local channels. Owram tells us that: "When the captain of a militia company in Ontario proposed that he and five hundred of his men emigrate to the North West in return for a grant of land, John A. MacDonald commented enthusiastically to McDougall that 'these are the kind of men you want.'"[10] It was evident in the CPR settlement campaigns that these "ideal" men were white men, who would come either from eastern Canada, the United States, or Britain, and this is where the CPR advertised the wonders of Canadian farms. Here one group is of particular interest: the British tenant farmer. These men were thought to be used to the rigours of the land

and to have the appropriate skills. It was also thought that, arriving from the still semi-feudal confines of the "old country," they would appreciate one of the most unique things the New World had to offer them: "free" land. Thus, a significant motif in the visual iconography of the railway is the passage of immigrant groups bound with high hopes for farms in the North West. In one typical photograph, entitled "HIGHLAND CROFTERS FOR CANADA," the text the group composed to memorialize its journey records its near-utopian vision: "We're sailing west, we're sailing west, to prairie lands sun-kissed and blest – the crofters trail to happiness."

In CPR publications attempting to draw settlers to the Prairies, one of the most consistent themes was the supposed suitability of this land for farming and, in particular, for the cultivation of wheat. As Owram points out, this emphasis on wheat as opposed to other kinds of farming was no accident as wheat, along with beef, was seen to be the staple of the Anglo-Saxon peoples and, thus, as the pre-eminent food of the "civilized" world, had particular qualities attributed to it. As Thomas Spence opines, wheat "supports brain, and blood and muscle in just the proportion requisite for the highest type of manhood. Refinement, fortitude and enterprise, most distinguish those nations which most consume wheat. Beef eating and wheat-consuming races, at once dominate and elevate the rice and pork consumers with whom they come into contact."[11] Thus, wheat assumed mystical properties as a source of national and racial strength, and this was evident in the materials distributed through railway settlement campaigns. For if it was true that Canada could only expect to assume its potential as the "granary of the continent" through the CPR, then it was also true that the CPR could only begin to make money if it drew settlers to the North West.[12] Thus, in advertisements like "CANADA WEST" (Figure 3.2), the image of abundant harvests of wheat was a sign of the prosperity the railway was thought to enable. And these visuals were reinforced by extensively detailed booklets, such as the CPR-produced *Plain Facts from Farmers in the Canadian North West* (1885), distributed through the railway offices in London. Here, the CPR provided dramatic descriptions of the vast areas available for cultivation:

> Of this [western] territory 76,800,000 acres are described as pure prairie lands; 300,000,000 as part timber and part prairie, all suitable for the growth of wheat and other cereals ... [thus] the almost unparalleled fertility of the soil, the proved and healthy and agreeable nature of the climate, so peculiarly adapted to successful farming, and the facilities

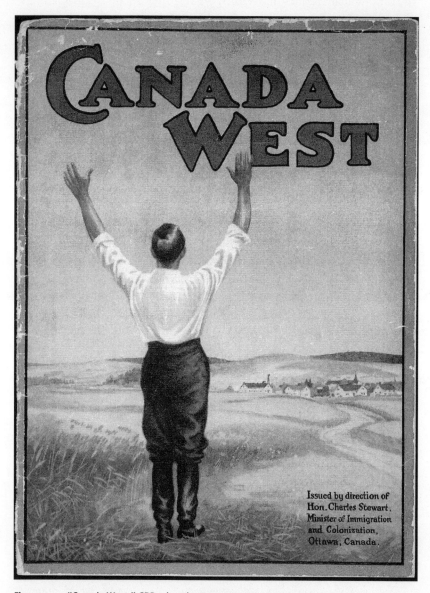

Figure 3.2 "Canada West," CPR advertisement Canadian Pacific Archives, a12987

offered by the Canadian Pacific Railway, which with its branches now runs through the most fertile parts – these are inducements that have attracted and will continue to attract the energy and capital of farmers and others in the old country.[13]

Using quotes from farmers who had already moved to the North West, the booklet maps out the profit settlers could expect from the land. Thus, *Plain Facts* concludes that, with an investment of between 100 and 150 pounds, immigrants could expect to have the value of their farm increase to 1,057 pounds within a few short years. Of course, these estimates are never restrained by the world price of grain, the cost of transport, or the uncertainty of the weather, all of which could prevent any profit. As Owram dryly concludes: "This predilection for optimism indicated a dangerous lack of understanding among officials and enthusiasts of the difficulties facing the settler" at the same time as it elided the very real difficulties involved in carving a livelihood out of a quarter section of land.[14] This, of course, resulted in inevitable disillusionment for many.

Significantly, when the CPR began construction in the North West, it discarded the original government estimates of 40 million acres of fertile land across the northern section of the Prairies and, on the advice of John Macoun, set the route of the line south instead – with the disastrous result that thousands of settlers moved into semi-arid areas of limited agricultural value. As David Jones details, the result of this policy was that the new territory opened up by the rails actually lost thousands of settlers after the original land rush. Thus, from 1915 to 1925, Canada saw a net negative migration of 413,145 people, and, during the same period, approximately 829,736 Canadian citizens migrated to the United States.[15] Further, Jones' detailed examination of the railway's apprenticeship and colonization scheme in 1929 suggests that there were repeated and bitter complaints that the CPR failed to provide the one year of work and accommodation promised by its representatives. Thus, the rosy views of homesteading in the New World promoted by the CPR's literature were often hotly debated by those who attempted to settle in the west. Indeed, many were deeply suspicious of the railway's monopolistic control of the western economy and believed it to be a symbol of eastern exploitation at western expense. Charles Mair summed up the opinion of many, early in the CPR's history, when he wrote in 1891: "the country is killed with C.P.R. extortion."[16] However, the groups who may have been most wary of the railway's expansion were not the settlers drawn to homestead in the vast North West but, rather, the Indigenous and Métis peoples over whose lands the rails were constructed. These peoples were rarely portrayed in early CPR settlement literature, and when they were mentioned in booklets like *Plain Facts* it was simply to reassure settlers of their docile status:

> No trouble whatever need be anticipated from the indigenous Indians of the North-West, for, thanks to the just and generous policy pursued towards them by the Canadian Government, they are quiet and peaceful. Reserves of land are set aside for cultivation by them, and assistance is given where necessary by the Government. This happy feature is in striking contrast with the experience of some of the more western of the United States, where disturbance and bloodshed have been of constant occurrence. The Canadian government has established Indian [residential] schools throughout the country, in which the young Indians are taught and trained, and this, together with the fact that the Red Men are in parts themselves settling down to agricultural pursuits, bodes well for their future. The establishment of the mounted police throughout the territories has taught the Indians to respect the laws of the land; and thus there is no Indian problem to solve in Canada as there is in the United States.[17]

Ironically, the booklet containing these reassurances about the government's "just and generous" policies was distributed to prospective settlers in 1885, the year of the second Riel Rebellion, which sought to bring attention to Métis and Indigenous grievances about terrible land policies and community starvation – issues that had long been ignored by Prime Minister John A. MacDonald's government.

While the CPR's paternalistic literature made every effort to construct Canada as a tolerant nation that was morally superior to the United States in its treatment of "our Indians," Indigenous and Métis communities were well aware of the dangers the railway posed to their independence and continued livelihood. For, as Hugh Dempsey documents, the CPR was, in part, responsible for the disastrous loss of game that had sustained Indigenous peoples' livelihood as well as for prairie fires that destroyed Indigenous land while damaging grazing lands and livestock. The railway was also crucial to the Canadian government's ability to mount a swift defeat of the second Riel Rebellion, and it was the railway that enabled a swarming influx of settlers, resulting in the irrevocable marginalization of Indigenous peoples to the confines of the reserves. Indeed, as Cole Harris argues, it was the railway, rather than the military, that tipped the balance of power with Indigenous peoples and made the outcome of the struggle for the western territories inevitable. Thus, for many, the CPR was a crucial symbol of the disciplines of white appropriation and control. This perspective is summed up in a bitterly eloquent speech by Chief Foremost Man (Nekaneet), who articulated the defeat of his people's hopes for constructing self-sustaining and independent communities:

> Let them [Euro-Canadians] take back the blankets and return the buffalo robes. Let them send the buffalo back, and take their own people to the reserve where they came from. Give us the prairies again and we won't ask for food. But it is too late. The iron road has frightened the game away and the talking wire stretches from sunrise to sunset. It is too late; it is too late.[18]

If the CPR materials only mentioned Indigenous peoples in order to reassure settlers of their supposedly compliant status, representations of "Indians" and "Indianness" did serve as a distinctive theme in the tourist materials that "The World's Greatest Travel System" used to promote Canada to a wider public. By the time of the railway's completion, it was clear that the CPR would have to undertake a significant program of tourist promotions to recover the cost for constructing the mountain section of the line, which had been extraordinarily labour-intensive and expensive. Thus, Van Horne devised a strategy of "capitalizing on the scenery" to entice tourists to travel the "Empire" in North America, thereby helping those sections of the rails pay for themselves.[19] E.J. Hart's extensive work on tourism and the CPR highlights how early marketing capitalized on the late nineteenth-century craze for the wilderness in order to entice travellers to make the long journey to the mountains. Thus, the CPR released its first pamphlet for distribution through its London office with the appeal:

> May I not tempt you, kind reader, to leave England for a few short weeks and journey with me across that broad land, the beauties and glories of which have only now been brought within our reach? ...You shall see mighty rivers, vast forests, boundless plains, stupendous mountains and wonders innumerable; and you shall see all in comfort, nay in luxury. If you are a sportsman, you will meet with unlimited opportunities and endless variety, and no one shall deny you your right to hunt or fish at your sweet will. If you are a mountain climber, you shall have cliffs and

peaks and glaciers worthy of your alpenstock, and if you have lived in India, and tiger hunting has lost its zest, a Rocky Mountain grizzly will renew your interest in life.[20]

Entitled *The Canadian Pacific, The New Highway to the East Across the Mountains, Prairies and Rivers of Canada* (1887), the brochure had a distinctly western emphasis, with breathless descriptions of the "grandest of all the peaks of the Selkirks – Sir Donald – an acute pyramid of naked rock shooting up nearly eight thousand feet above us, a dozen Matterhorns in one," while also marvelling at the "clearness of the air [that] brings out the minutest detail of this Titanic sculpture."[21] Here CPR advertising materials reference both Swiss landmarks and Greek mythology, illustrating the Euro-masculinist tenor of space myths used to construct the landscape and the nation. And, indeed, the echoes of Swiss and European references continued in all the CPR literature as well as in the architecture of CPR hotels from the more modest accommodations at Glacier House to the stately Banff Springs Hotel. Not surprisingly, this discourse attracted a cosmopolitan class to early Canadian railway travel, from those who came through professional connections, such as the men of the British Association for the Advancement of Science (who, in 1884, travelled as far as Kicking Horse Pass) to the journalists of the Canadian Pacific Press Bureau.

By the late 1920s, the CPR had developed a series of tourist "festivals" that were intended to pay homage to the diverse range of traditions characterizing Canada's immigrant make-up at the same time as they were to draw a wider clientele to travel the rails and to patronize CPR hotels. From the first "Folksong and Handicraft Festival" held at the Château Frontenac in Quebec City to the "New Canadian" festivals at the Royal Alexandra in Winnipeg and the Palliser in Calgary, these events constructed a romantic legacy about the diverse folk traditions of French, English, Scottish, Eastern European, and Scandinavian immigrants. While these festivals did expand who counted as Canadian beyond the original English and French settlers and were the prototype for ideas about the Canadian mosaic as opposed to the American melting pot, they also constructed a national mythology that was distinctly Euro-Canadian in orientation, as non-European peoples were never included in the railway's version of the national vision.[22] The one non-European group that *was* consistently represented in CPR promotions, however, was Indigenous people. For instance, on the fiftieth anniversary of the completion of the transcontinental line (1931), the railway published a menu for their passenger service with an illustration of "Banff Indian

Hunting Grounds," which shows two "chiefs" in the distinctive Plains head-dress hovering above a glittering image of the Banff Springs Hotel (Figure 3.3). Here the welcoming salute of the chiefs is a gesture from one group of patriarchs to the next, reassuring the visitor that no one would deny the (white) sportsman his right to hunt and fish at will.

If this rereading of the most commonplace railway images highlights the gendered and racialized tropes implicit in the technological national-ism that fuelled the building of the nation, then how might those images compare to those from less recognized sources? To investigate this question I turn to a selection of photographs by the early British Columbian settler C.D. Hoy and to material from the collection of William Van Horne held in the Canadian Pacific Archives. These alternative railway images open up some of the more contradictory stories that haunted the construction of the CPR.

In the early 1880s, the CPR recruited thousands of Chinese labourers to build the western sections of the line, and the CPR's own website notes that it was these workers who were used to construct the most dangerous and difficult parts of the railway running through the Fraser Canyon. Up until the past decade, it was thought that few images of the racially mixed, predominantly male communities that developed along the line of the rail-way's construction had survived. However, Faith Moosang's recent re-discovery of the work of C.D. Hoy has altered this representational history while also providing the largest publicly accessible visual record of Indigen-ous people in the interior of British Columbia.

Chow Dong Hoy arrived in Canada in late 1902 and originally took work as a houseboy, dishwasher, and cook to pay off the cost of the head tax and transportation for his passage.[23] Then, from approximately 1907 to 1909, he was employed by the Grand Trunk Pacific Railway as an axeman, sur-veyor, and cook. When the company laid him off, he settled in Quesnel where he founded the C.D. Hoy and Company Dry Goods Store, and from 1911 through to 1923 he also worked as the town photographer.[24] Hoy's early history of work on the railway and in other labouring occupations was char-acteristic of the limited options available to Chinese immigrants. What was unusual, as Faith Moosang notes in her study of Hoy's photographic legacy, was his decision to start his own business, including a portrait studio, in a rugged frontier town. And his approach to image making was also far re-moved from Euro-Canadian conventions. While mainstream photographic representations often fit non-European peoples into exotic or demonized stereotypes, in Hoy's images, as Moosang notes, the "frank, open look on

Figure 3.3 Cover of the CPR passenger service menu celebrating the fiftieth anniversary of the completion of the transcontinental railway, 1931. The illustration shows two "chiefs" in the distinctive Plains headdress hovering above the Banff Springs Hotel. Canadian Pacific Archives, br184

the people's faces ... and the lack of romanticism in the setting and light effects, reveal the difference between being photographed for someone else's story and being photographed for your own."[25] I examine selections from Hoy's archive in order to explore how the representational codes constituted through his work intersected with the racialized and sexualized forms of affiliation the railway engendered.

Hoy's photographs represent the polyglot worker communities typical of early Canadian settlement – but these were not the usual subjects found in early twentieth-century Canadian photography. They include Chinese, Indigenous, mixed race, and white men, women, and children who were employed in mining, salmon canning, logging, railway work, and ranching. For example, in Figure 3.4 we see an older Chinese man who, with a stoic expression, sits facing the camera. The "studio" for this portrait has been quickly constructed by placing a chair in front of a rough tarp backdrop. Given this man's age, it is likely he worked on the railway and perhaps also in the primary industries opening up throughout the BC interior. His body seems wiry and strong while his hands show the effects of labour and are placed prominently on his knees so that all his fingers are clearly in evidence. Moosang notes that this positioning of the hands, along with the clarity of their rendering, draws our eyes to them again and again. Indeed, the resolute expression of the face and the body posture confront the viewer with a remarkable sense of dignity and endurance. To this viewer, the proud portrait seems to be saying: I have worked hard, remained whole, and survived.

Most of Hoy's Chinese portraits are of individual men, and many are posed in this manner. These representations draw on the Chinese traditions that emphasize direct frontal images of the whole body presented in a static position, and they also reflect the film technology of the period, which required absolute stillness in order to avoid a blurry image. But this form of self-presentation may also speak to the context of early work on the railway and in primary forms of resource extraction, where there was considerable cause for pride in sheer survival. Indeed, as the CPR has acknowledged, Chinese men worked primarily along the steep and treacherous walls of the Fraser Canyon. To keep costs down, the crews used nitroglycerin instead of dynamite, a less expensive but less stable explosive, to do the blasting. Eyewitness and newspaper accounts of these conditions paint a horrific picture. Patricia Roy reviews this history and notes that, while neither the CPR nor the government kept track of fatal accidents occurring during railway construction, some indication of them can be gleaned from newspapers of the day, such as Yale's *Inland Sentinel*. Here, a columnist from the period penned

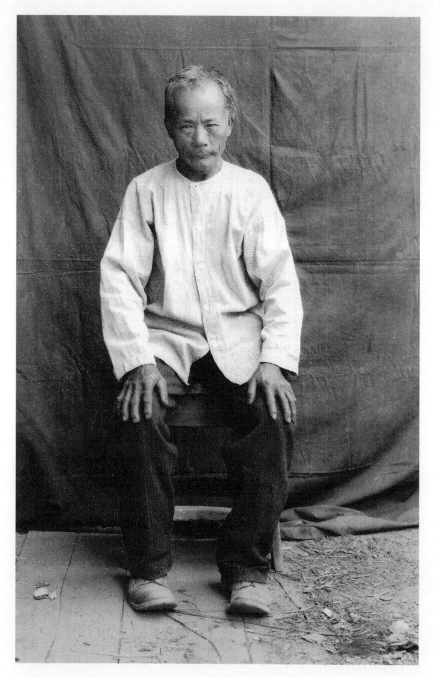

Figure 3.4   Portrait of an unidentified Chinese man, Quesnel, BC, 1911-23 Photograph by
C.D. Hoy; Barkerville Historic Town Archives, P1658

Figure 3.5   Group in front of the C.D. Hoy & Co. General Store, Quesnel, BC, 1911-23.
Left to right: Jerry (or Harry) Boyd (Kluskus); Captain Marc Mack (Nazko); John Lazzarin
(blacksmith); Chief Michel (Nazko); Unknown; Moffat Harris (Nazko); and Chief Morris
Molize (Kluskus)   Photograph by C.D. Hoy; Barkerville Historic Town Archives, P1887

a sardonic observation of an incident in which a Chinese man was blown to
pieces while setting an explosive in a tunnel. The writer remarks: "Of course
there will be no investigation – only another Chinaman gone – that's all.
Another of the same sort fills the gap and the work goes on as usual."[26] Roy
suggests that, in addition to accidents, at least fifteen hundred Chinese men
(and possibly many more) died of illness. Indeed, some contemporary commentators suggest that Chinese rail workers likely sustained one of the
worst occupational death tolls in Canadian history.[27] In contrast to the stoic
determination that often marks Hoy's images of older Chinese men, his images of Indigenous people suggest a more relaxed demeanour. Moosang
notes that Hoy's services were most in demand during Quesnel's annual
Dominion Day Stampede, and, thus, many of his photographs reflect this
carnival atmosphere. For example, Figure 3.5 suggests a coming together of
cultures that was characteristic of interior BC communities, with five
Indigenous men, one Caucasian man, and one Chinese man casually grouped
together. As Moosang notes: "The lack of stiffness or pretence in this image
is striking ...[and] it stands as a visual testament not only to the variety of

people who lived in the Cariboo, but also to the fact that not one of these men wished to avoid being remembered in this way."[28]

This photograph, as well as the numerous other images in Hoy's archive, is in striking contrast to the romanticized photographs of respectable white settlers in neat nuclear families reaping harvests of grain from prairie wheat fields. Nor do Hoy's images resemble the forms of salvage photography that were based on the idea that Indigenous cultures were dying out and needed to be preserved in their original purity. Instead, Hoy's photographs stand as a testament to the vitality of these early communities. At the same time, they also speak to the distinctly *hybrid* and disproportionately *male* conditions of western settlement produced by the railway's construction.[29]

This racially mixed and predominately male context also influenced the socio-sexual relationships that developed in the west. For example, in Figure 3.6, we see an Indigenous woman, Josephine Bobby, attired in Euro-Canadian fashion beside a man who may have been Wesley Jasper, wearing leather chaps with a decorative fringe and a leather pouch decorated with beadwork. Both figures present themselves for the camera in a direct and relaxed fashion. Nothing is known about the relationship between Bobby and Jasper. But the image should be viewed in a context that acknowledges that, in early twentieth-century British Columbia, mixed Euro-Canadian and Indigenous partnerships were still common – despite increasingly strong disapproval of these relationships. At the same time, these may not have been the only forms of coupling that characterized this territory. Figure 3.7 offers another Hoy photograph, with, on the left, a man who may be Joe Hoy and, on the right, an unidentified Chinese man. Both are impeccably dressed in starched white shirts and ties, with the man on the left sporting a vest and pocket watch, while the chiselled good looks of the man on the right are set off by the more casual attire of a cardigan and tie clip. The seated man holds the *Sai Gai* newspaper, indicating that, although the photo is set in the remote BC interior, the men are following the Chinese news of the day. There is no information available about these men: we simply observe their relaxed and confident stance. On the question of brothers, friends, cousins, or lovers, the camera does not speak.

The juxtaposition of C.D. Hoy's images with the earlier CPR images suggests that, although the railway secured a distinctly Euro-Canadian hegemony during the first decades after its construction, it also fostered a racially hybrid and predominantly male homosocial culture. For it was the railway that spurred the immigration of thousands of Chinese men to British Columbia, and it was the railway that first intensified crossracial encounters between white, Chinese, and Indigenous peoples, particularly along the line

Figure 3.6 Portrait of Josephine Bobby, possibly with Wesley Jasper, Quesnel, BC, **1911-23** Photograph by C.D. Hoy; Barkerville Historic Town Archives, P1707

Figure 3.7 Two men (possibly Joe Hoy on left) with one unidentified Chinese man holding the *Sai Gai* newspaper, Quesnel, BC, 1911-23 Photograph by C.D. Hoy; Barkerville Historic Town Archives, P1876

of its construction. From Hoy's photographic combination of Chinese and Western forms of aesthetic representation to the shifting norms of sociability and sexuality evident in his photographic archive, we can see that western Canadian culture was profoundly shaped by the racialized forms of affiliation and settlement engendered by the CPR. Thus, Hoy's photographs render more complex the narrative of white nation building and Aboriginal spectacle promoted by the settlement and tourist images discussed at the beginning of this chapter.

Indeed, these images suggest how representations of gendered and sexed masculinity were reconstituted through the crucible of the CPR and western settlement, for the hybrid worker communities first brought together to build the CPR and then to settle the surrounding territories often prompted a radical rethinking of colonial authority. Here the regulation of men's domestic lives – through laws against cross-racial relationships, the head tax that worked to limit Chinese women from immigrating to Canada, and the increasingly virulent discourse against Chinese bachelor communities – suggests how the state acted to regulate national, racial, and sexual borders.[30]

However, at least one image from *within* the Canadian Pacific Archives also troubles mainstream narratives about whiteness, masculinity, and enterprise in the building of the railway and the nation. In Figure 3.8 we see a picture from the private notes of CPR general manager William Van Horne. The sketch shows a sheet covered with figures, evidence of a mind intent on determining the costs of a complex project. In the centre is a quick rendering of a Chinese man, with stereotypical whiskers and a long moustache. Alpheus Stickney, the general superintendent of the CPR's western division, notes that Van Horne frequently made sketches on blotting pads, which he usually tore up as fast as he drew them.[31] Only three of these have survived. When I came across this image in the Canadian Pacific Archives, the staff kindly offered to copy and enlarge the sketch of the Chinese man separately from the financial doodles on the same sheet. But it was precisely this juxtaposition that rendered the image interesting and important to me. For Chinese workers were, in fact, indispensable to the CPR's early financial viability as their "cheap wages" saved Andrew Onderdonk, the contractor for the western section of the line, between $3 and $5 million and allowed him to escape bankruptcy.[32] Further, the little-known research of Frank Kunyin Moy points out that similarly cheap wages made Chinese workers crucial to the logging, salmon-canning, and coal-mining industries in British Columbia and that Chinese exports and tax revenues provided urgent monetary support to the new federal and provincial treasuries.[33]

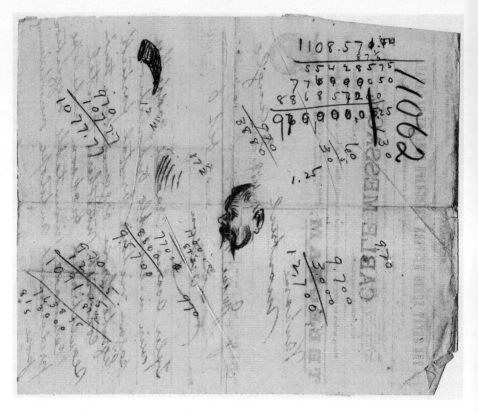

Figure 3.8   **Private notes of the CPR general manager, William Van Horne** Canadian Pacific Archives, ID11062

Like most elite accounts depicting subaltern subjects, Van Horne's sketch of a "Chinaman" awash in a sea of figures is saturated with pejorative meanings: a caricature that suggests workers who are useful, disposable, discarded. But, read against the grain, perhaps other meanings are possible. One of the late nineteenth-century terms used for Chinese workers is "living machines," an ambivalent phrase that implies no small amount of admiration. I would argue that any reading of this sketch must hold it in tension with other representations of Chinese labourers: both those men on the edges of railway construction crews and C.D. Hoy's images of labourers whose manifest sense of presence speaks to their pride in survival. Like so many of the images arising from dominant sources, Van Horne's pencil drawing suggests both a crude utilitarian stereotype and something more. Indeed, the shadow narrative arising from Van Horne's sketch indicates that the Chinese bachelor worker lodged among the financial calculations was indeed a key not only to the economic survival of the CPR but also to the financial and social viability of the early western territories.[34]

From the late nineteenth-century settlement literature to the mid-twentieth-century tourist images, whiteness and hetero-masculinity were potent markers in a powerful new transportation revolution. While images of Indianness were a frequent theme in railway iconography, most CPR advertisements reinscribed the idea that Indians are either vanishing into the wilderness or available as consumer spectacles: it was white settlers and tourists who were the legitimate inheritors of the railway and the nation. A paradox becomes evident in juxtaposing C.D. Hoy's photographs with the more populist and prosaic images of the CPR: while extolling white hetero-masculinity, the advent of the railway also fostered a racially hybrid western culture. Indeed, from the shifting norms of sociability and sexuality evident in Hoy's pictures to the combination of Chinese and Western forms of aesthetic representation evident in his photographic techniques, western Canadian culture was profoundly shaped by the very "impure" forms of affiliation and settlement the railway engendered. Similarly, Van Horne's sketch troubles the narratives that posit that only white men were sufficiently enterprising to construct the rails that connected the nation. While the photograph entitled *The Last Spike* symbolizes ideas about the "great men" of the railway, both CPR contractors and other Western industrialists knew that it was primarily Chinese workers, or the "living machines," as they were described, who were crucial to the financial viability of the railway, to the resource industries of the west, and, thus, to the early Canadian nation.

While representations of the railway inscribed the norms of whiteness, masculinity, and enterprise that are foundational to Canadianness, sexual control was also fundamental to these nationalist politics. Indeed, the early west was an arena of intensive homosocial contact between working-class men of all races, and, in this context, the question of how white men would react to this was never preordained. Would they prove a great and hardy "race," capable of civilizing themselves and this new land? Or would they degenerate into the morass of "corrupt" behaviour that was thought to characterize the "alien races"? In the second half of this chapter I explore how Richard Fung's videotape, *Dirty Laundry*, represents this history of "innocence," "vice," and "perversion." Here I ask: if the CPR has been a central icon of nation building, then how might *Dirty Laundry*'s visual text provide a different point of entry for examining "the inexplicable presence of the thing[s] not named" in the construction of the nation?

Dirty Laundry: Activist Video and the Theatre of History Making[35]

Dirty Laundry originates from the experimental documentary tradition and brings together such disparate modes as historical investigation, travelogue, and narrative drama. The video combines a montage of archival photographs, film images, and acted sequences to reconstruct the conflicting narratives associated with early Chinese work on the CPR. Overlaid on this visual material are interviews with historians, writers, and activists whose perspectives sometimes stand in uneasy relation to the archival images. As Thomas Waugh argues, the video embodies a fundamental disjuncture, where the secret compartments and corridors of a transcontinental train provide the setting for a collision of Chinese diasporas and a distinctly queer nation.[36] Further, the title references the notion that certain aspects of Chinese-Canadian history have often been considered too shameful to be re-remembered – "dirty laundry" not to be aired in public.[37] In contrast, Fung's visual work unsettles dichotomous narratives of "heroes" and "vices," and it destabilizes the very ground upon which exclusive notions of national history and racialized subjectivity are constructed.

The video begins by recording a photograph being taken of a Chinese man who is the great-grandfather of one of the central characters, Roger Kwong.[38] Then, the scene quickly shifts to archival film footage of an early railway voyage through the Rockies, with CPR workers on the margins of the tracks, their very presence a blur on the edge of our vision, indistinct and fleeting as the train hurtles forward. Here the historian Nayan Shah reflects on the nature of historical memory and the patterns of erasure and forgetting that mark the west. And then the scene shifts again to a present-day railway car in which Roger Kwong, a Toronto writer, travels through the mountains to Vancouver. The camera shows Roger's line of vision wander pleasurably over the butt of a white passenger adjusting his luggage. However, when Roger approaches a Chinese railway steward to request a seat change, the narrative shifts. Roger does not speak Chinese and cannot produce the privileged marker of linguistic belonging. "How can you be Chinese and not speak Chinese?" the railway steward asks him. The question hangs uncomfortably in the air between the two men, disrupting any easy or automatic assumption of a shared identity.[39]

The video's movement back and forth between historical analysis and fictional travelogue is based on Fung's belief that different kinds of narrative forms convey different kinds of truth. The director suggests that he didn't want viewers of the tape to feel too secure with either fiction or history.[40] Indeed, the historical and current sequences are all acted by the same cast, intimating how one generation's narratives about honour, misery, intimacy, and vice bleed into the next, and echoing the instability of the discourses of sexuality and history. Further, questions of interpretation are highlighted throughout in the video's construction as a cinematic triptych. Here the inspiration was primarily aesthetic. Fung describes most of his video work as operating in "movements," suggesting the classic forms of musical composition.[41] In *Dirty Laundry,* we see this form used to articulate the discursive tropes that have structured Chinese-Canadian history. While national histories tend to reconstruct ideas of heroes and vices, Fung deploys these notions as a narrative device, structuring the video into three sections: "A History of Heroes," "A History of Vices," and "A History of Questions." On their own, the first two sections represent a kind of controlled symmetry, re-presenting "opposite" but mutually reinforcing approaches to Chinese-Canadian history. However, their juxtaposition with "A History of Questions" ironizes these parallels while, at the same time, staging a fundamental question about the public secrets in the history of the railway and the nation.

Fung lists among his contemporary influences a variety of independent film and video makers in Britain, including John Akomfrah and Isaac Julien.[42] These artists now represent an established tradition in black British cinema, where questions of history are mapped through several different time frames simultaneously. This aesthetic is not unique to black cinema, but, as Jun Xing notes, informs much alternative Asian American film as well.[43] Indeed, Fung suggests that *Dirty Laundry* was partly influenced by Trinh T. Minh-ha's film *Naked Spaces – Living Is Round,* which articulates the fragmentary quality of knowledge through a series of unsettling visual and narrative juxtapositions.[44]

Many of these cinematic attempts to rethink historical memory employ visual and narrative strategies that are consistent with Foucault's theory of genealogy. While traditional history (and Hollywood cinema) are usually productive of links that unite events into a coherent story, Foucault suggests that "writing genealogy, on the other hand, involves the recognition of disparity, of the dispersion of origins and links, of discontinuities and contradictions."[45] Indeed, genealogical and postmodern approaches to history have pushed debates about objectivity to a critical juncture, where, as Joan Scott observes, new work has multiplied not only stories but also subjects, insisting that histories are written from fundamentally different and sometimes irreconcilable standpoints, none of which may be completely "true."[46]

Fung's visualization of a historical montage juxtaposes a series of different textures, including poems, historical dramatization, vintage newsreel, travelogue, traditional Chinese instrumental music (composed by contemporary Chinese-Canadian artist Lee Pui Ming), still archival photographs, and a variety of nationalist and honky-tonk musical tunes. These juxtapositions suggest the dialectical interplay between past and present in a way that is transhistorical. In *Dirty Laundry,* Fung draws on and reconstitutes the filaments of a Chinese-Canadian cultural imaginary to enable what Foucault calls a "history of the present." These different visual and narrative forms and historical moments allow viewers, as David Halperin observes, to re-remember a past in which "we appear different from ourselves, or from what we thought we were, and so we recover a sense of ourselves as sites of difference, hence, sites of possible transformation."[47]

Listening to "A History of Heroes"

Throughout the latter part of the nineteenth and the early twentieth centuries, the Immigration Building in Victoria, British Columbia, contained a holding area in which Chinese men were detained before they could enter Canada.[48] A dramatized representation of this holding area, along with the stone wall upon which generations of men scratched messages of despair, bitterness, and hope in rough-hewn Chinese characters, is a central image in the visual lexicon of *Dirty Laundry.* The actual wall upon which this dramatized image is based was demolished in 1977, but some photographs were preserved.[49] In *Dirty Laundry,* Fung combines these archival images with historic dramatizations to explore Chinese men's complex practices of resistance in the face of state power.

This first movement of *Dirty Laundry* starts with newsreel footage of hundreds of Chinese workers as they arrive in Victoria and are shipped to a new life in the Canadian west. The scratchy images are reminiscent of other mass shifts in population and signify both the dreams and apprehensions of diasporic populations. However, these associations are soon intercut with the haunting image of Chinese men carving on "the wall":

> Fellow countrymen, quick read this.
> Scraping together a few hundred dollars
> I left my home for a foreign land.
> Now I have been thrown into a prison cell,
> I cannot sleep because my heart is filled with hate.
> When I think of these foreign devils, my anger rises.[50]

The exercise of state power in detaining Chinese men in holding cells prior to their being released for cheap labour was a performance the meaning of which was public and clear. Here the physical act of detainment was clearly racialized. While British and European immigrants were usually screened briefly and then released for settlement (with access to land to get them started), Chinese workers were detained for unpredictable periods under conditions that articulated the following assumptions: these men are, by nature of race, incapable of citizenship and suspect of disease. They must be quarantined, controlled, and inspected.[51]

In the scene described above, Fung cites and reconstructs the Chinese detainee's performance of fury and resistance to the Canadian "foreign devils." Perhaps the power of the poems and stories render it no surprise that the wall was demolished and removed from public view. Nevertheless, this artistic reiteration suggests the dual meanings inherent in the phrase "dirty laundry." Here historical dramatization reinserts a combative "Chinese other" into the Canadian state's detached narrative of mass migration. Indeed, the wall serves as a forceful reminder of the haunting erasures that underlay tidy nationalist euphemisms of a multicultural and depoliticized history.

In a scene that follows shortly after, Fung again takes up practices of erasure and silence, but this time from a different angle. The video presents an interview with the novelist Sky Lee (with the wall in the background), in which she describes silencing as a form of self-protection. Indeed, Lee suggests that, for early Chinese settlers, some practices of forgetting were also double-edged strategies of survival:

> Chinese people clamped down on revealing who they were and we still see the effects of this today. I call it mis-placed cultural protectionism. Because we were so mis-interpreted by the racist dominant culture that we just didn't talk ... about it ... in front of them. [However] before long we found ourselves not talking about it at all. We just internalized that stigma – as shame.

Here strategies of survival produce their own lesions. Thus, Lee's analysis suggests the potentially self-destructive contradictions of Chinese settlers' resistance. Indeed, blithely ahistorical notions of "cross-cultural dialogue" pale before the effects of generations of silence. In this context, "shame" is a symptom of an imperialist history in which those traumatized by racism often carry an impossible legacy. As Cathy Caruth remarks, this trauma is a symptom of a history that cannot be possessed and yet has not been resolved.[52] These different forms of "silenc(e)(ing)" require multiple readings. Indeed, the meanings reverberate: Who has dirty laundry? Why are some

Figure 3.9   Image of Chinese detainee writing on "the wall," at the Immigration Building, **Victoria, BC** Courtesy of Richard Fung, *Dirty Laundry;* image courtesy of Vtape

ashamed and others not? For what ends are the practices of silence and era-sure? Always it is relations of power that structure these narratives, while the juxtapositions suggest the complexity of narratives through which, as Foucault says, discourse becomes "both an instrument and an effect of power, but also ... a point of resistance and a starting point for an opposing strategy."[53]

In Figure 3.9 we see a staged image of a Chinese man writing on "the wall," suggesting how the narratives of Chinese detainees form a haunting template imprinted on the stone masonry of the Immigration Building. While Chinese men were known as "bachelors," many actually had wives and children in China. *Dirty Laundry* highlights repeated instances in which archival writing on the wall suggests that these men sometimes took on the voices of their wives in order to admonish themselves for failing in their obligations to adequately support their families at home. Thus, while present-day viewers have no unmediated access to these writings, it appears Chinese men often took on women's voices in what Fung calls a kind of "authorial transvestism."[54] As Edward Said points out, the word "author" springs from the same etymological roots as does the word "authority" and is attended by potent notions of engendering, mastery, and property.[55] The term "transvestite" originates from a prefix, "trans," which means "across (transgress ... transform)," and the Latin "vestire," meaning clothe.[56] In this context, "authorial transvestism" suggests that Chinese men transgressed the (in)vestments of gender to take on the voice, manner, and concerns of women.

I suggest that the kind of authorship articulated on the wall presents the possibility that Chinese men expanded the relations of husbandry beyond property, or at least ventriloquized their wives' rebuke for their own failures in this regard. *Dirty Laundry* dramatizes this history through its re-presentation of these doubly authored narratives of bitterness and disappointment. For instance, in one dramatized sequence, we see a woman braiding her husband's hair in front of an evening fire, while a female voice speaking in the rural Toisan dialect (translated into English subtitles) angrily reproves her partner: "Not half a cup of rice can be scooped from the pot. All our things are broken. Our house is falling apart. Your gambling has driven us to poverty." Entitled "My Wife's Admonishment," this reproof articulates the words of an anonymous message from the wall. This fragment may have been written by the gambling husband himself or by a relative or friend who was sympathetic to the impoverished lives these women led. Indeed, the text suggests that some Chinese men transcribed the admonishments of their absent wives into the very architecture of confinement that awaited them in this new land – the holding cell in the Immigration Building.[57]

Here we see that *Dirty Laundry* does not simply replace one "true" narrative with another; rather, a range of doubled visual and narrative strategies work to dislodge the certainties of historical "truth" from their privileged moorings. The sequence above, for instance, acknowledges the familial loyalty and financial responsibility that tied these men to their wives, children, and homeland. At the same time, the video's central focus is an exploration of the queer possibilities implicit in Chinese men's lives as bachelors in Canada. This attention to multiple and conflicting narratives is also evident in the positioning of those interviewed for the film. As Peter Steven remarks, while most documentaries construct expert knowledge by placing interviewees in a book-lined study, here the historians, activists, and writers are all shown with fictional or archival images in the background, a visual technique that problematizes the air-tight boundaries between history and fiction. This strategy shifts conventional associations between professional status and "true" knowledge, implying "that these professionals are as tangled in messy reality as the rest of us."[58]

Indeed, the early "professionals" who testified at the Royal Commission on Chinese Immigration constitute a prime example. Earlier in this triptych, *Dirty Laundry* shows us a garrulous and self-important white miner who testified to the commission about the difficulties of making ends meet on meagre wages, ending his monologue with the rhetorical question: "How is it with the Chinaman?" A short while later, the miner answers his own query in a voice tinged with resentment and anger:

> The Chinaman can do as much work underground as I can. He has no wife or family. He performs none of these duties. Forty or fifty of his kind can live in a house no larger than mine. He craves no variety of food. He has inherited no taste for comfort or for social enjoyment. Conditions that satisfy him and make him contented would make my life not worth living ... the Chinaman comes in, taking advantage of our skill and of our toil and of our struggles, and drives us from the fields of industry which we have created and which our race alone could create.

However, in the midst of this monologue, the miner rematerializes (complete with a natty new set of clothes and more authoritative speaking voice) as Senator Jones of Nevada. Here Fung reconstructs a second performance of authorial transvestism. This time the narrative is based on a presentation by Senator Jones to the Royal Commission, in which he took it upon himself to act as a representative of "the people" and "condensed many a harangue from his white workmen" in his testimony.[59] In this instance, the senator's ventriloquism (transgressing the boundaries of class) functions in the interests of white racial dominance. Indeed, whatever the motives of Senator Jones' original performance, it is likely that its *effect* was to deepen existing cleavages between differently racialized groups of working-class men. It seems that, for Senator Jones, solidarity was rooted in whiteness. Interestingly, Jones' testimony also articulated everyday assumptions about Chinese bachelors as men who were unencumbered by heterosexual responsibilities. As we have seen, these ideas are dramatically at odds with the written texts that chronicle many Chinese men's own conflicted response to diasporic separations.

While this kind of testimony played a leading role in constituting public discourse about Chinese men, it also worked to define the racial "norm." As Nayan Shah observes in the following sequence, "whiteness" as a category was being produced during the late nineteenth century, and the classed and raced tensions informing Senator Jones' testimony illustrate precisely this process of white racial formation.[60] Indeed, as Shah is interviewed, a series

Figure 3.10 **"The Maple Leaf Forever"** Courtesy of Richard Fung, *Dirty Laundry*; image courtesy of Vtape

of visual images rearticulate his analysis with eerie familiarity. Here the video juxtaposes Shah's appraisal with those oh-so-familiar imperial tropes: soldiers on parade and eminently respectable women in all their finery on the church steps – images that imply that whiteness itself was consolidated through banal spectacles of military imperial and religious power. And, indeed, these grainy photos of masculine pageantry and feminized morality have been central in constituting white Canadian national traditions.

Further, the hackneyed cartoon that comprises the next image in *Dirty Laundry* provides an eloquent illustration of the ideas that have fuelled Canada's self-image (Figure 3.10). The drawing shows a group of European men, each representing the figure of a country (Belgians, Englishmen, Russians, Americans, Austrians, Irishmen, Frenchmen, and Scandinavians), all brought together by a Canadian Mountie who conducts them in singing "The Maple Leaf Forever." If Canada's crisis can be figured as the need to re-think colonial authority for a polyglot settler community, then images like these emphasize the transnational markers of Europeanness: all brought together to sing from the same song-sheet. Here, the words and images of the anthem illustrate the primacy of British heritage at the same time as they obscure the history of England's brutal relations with its own "internal" colonies:

> The Maple Leaf our emblem dear
> The Maple Leaf forever,
> With Lily, Thistle, Shamrock, Rose,
> The Maple leaf forever.[61]

This populist iconography illustrates different shades of imperial white: indeed, of all the "peoples" represented in this image, none stray from the "Homo Europeanus" of "superior" health and intelligence, who was assumed to constitute the national norm. With the United States as the right-hand man at the song-sheet, these symbols of nation building have been crucial to papering over the myriad racial and classed tensions that have always threatened Canada's unity. In this context, the icon of the railway is a potent, if predictable, image of white imperial progress. For it is the railway, more than any other image, that presents linear time as a forward-thrusting track through the wilderness, symbolizing an unfolding national drama of masculine vigour and racial advancement.

"A History of Vices"

The scene that sets the tone for "A History of Vices" opens with Roger Kwong nodding off to sleep as the sole occupant of a railcar – a private space that enables his writing at the same time as it facilitates a brief, and very sexual, affair with the railway steward. As Roger's head slumps to the table he inadvertently knocks off a small portrait of his great-grandfather (the same picture that opened the video), smashing the glass cover. Roger's great-grandfather worked on the railroad and his father insisted that he bring the picture along as he travelled through the mountains. However, when the portrait comes loose from its frame, a second image is revealed hidden behind the first. Here Roger's great-grandfather is joined by another Chinese man. The two men stare directly into the camera and lightly hold hands (Figure 3.11). Later, when the railway steward arrives to wake Roger, he notices the pictures. Looking at the second portrait he comments: "This is normal in China." Roger, surprised, asks what he means. The steward responds, "That men hold hands."

The question of how the "normal" is constituted in different cultural contexts and historical eras is one of the most fascinating puzzles raised in *Dirty Laundry*. In China, as in many non-Western countries, homosocial

Figure 3.11   Hidden image of Roger Kwong's great-grandfather and friend Courtesy of Richard Fung, *Dirty Laundry*; image courtesy of Vtape

norms may have produced practices of friendship that could be read as very queer in the present-day West. *Dirty Laundry* engages this arena in the third movement, after an interlude in which Roger and the steward engage in a steamy sex scene that visualizes the relatively explicit contemporary sexual identities and practices in contrast to the homosocial ambiguities of history. In this context, Roger asks:

> "You know what you were saying about men holding hands. What does it mean?"
> The steward replies: "It means that they like each other, that they're friends or brothers."
> Roger: "Not lovers?"
> Steward: "Well, it's a smart thing. If they're lovers they can hold hands and nobody asks any questions."

While the historic notions of friendship that the railway steward references problematize modern Western binaries like homosexual/heterosexual, the history of same-sex friendship in the West is also an area of considerable ambiguity. For example, for upper-middle-class men in Victorian England, life revolved around predominantly male institutions, including the public school, the university, the armed forces, the church, Parliament, the club, and the city. In this context, marriage was often deferred, ostensibly for economic and social reasons, and clergymen, schoolmasters, dons, and army officers usually remained bachelors. While the complex notions of gender and sex produced in these contexts are now receiving some attention, the disproportionate number of Chinese *and* white bachelors working on the railway and on the early western frontier (1870-1910) have attracted less notice. But many normative frontier activities were structured through homosocial pairings: cowboy bosses advised men to take a partner when exploring new trails; bachelor homesteaders often staked out their claim with a male partner to share the work and lessen the isolation; and mining claims were often worked by two men together in virtually all-male work camps.[62] Thus, the hierarchical terrain of western Canadian settlement was marked by deeply homosocial codes. But white men were rarely suspected of any improprieties – instead, it was Chinese and Sikh bachelors who were the target of charges of sexual "perversion."[63]

As Nayan Shah comments in an interview early in the second movement, the multiracial and sex-segregated societies that typified the late nineteenth-century frontier allowed for a range of sexual, racial, and gender crossings that may not have been as common in eastern Canada. Indeed, this period also witnessed a number of historic shifts in legal and sexual codes that present a telling juxtaposition of seemingly unrelated, but potentially linked, events. While Fung often uses the technique of montage to highlight these associations, the video also uses the more straightforward strategy of a printed text against a background of dramatized sequences or archival images. For instance, early in the second triptych, a text reminds us that, "in 1885, the year Canada institutes the Head Tax, Britain criminalizes all sexual activity between men as 'gross indecency.'" This simultaneous tightening of the codes that regulated men's movement across sexual and national boundaries suggests a hardening in the norms of citizenship. Here the strict enforcement of heteronormative sexual contact is only one of many forms of regulation, all of which operated to produce the ideal citizen as a respectable, white, heterosexual man. In this context, ideas about Chinese bachelors as "perverse" did the ideological work of focusing attention away from the mass of not so ideal white bachelors who thronged the bars and brothels in settlements throughout the west. Indeed, discourses regarding the "degenerate" Chinese or Sikh migrant kept the boundaries of "civililized" white society from becoming dangerously blurred.

While many different kinds of men found themselves "batching it," as the saying went, western discourse about bachelors was not a seamless whole.[64] Cecilia Danysk suggests that early journals, novels, and newspaper reports from the west represented Euro-Canadian bachelors as living in squalour, disorder, and loneliness – many of the same conditions often attributed to Chinese bachelor communities. Yet these images did not cause white bachelor settlers to be castigated as perverse. Indeed, the situation was quite the reverse: white women viewed these men with "tolerance, concern and benevolence, and often with bemused affection." Danysk continues:

> Westerners, particularly [white] women, felt a certain responsibility towards them. Part of a woman's duty in the west, claimed Mitchell, was "being kind to poor [white] bachelors round about who needed kindness badly." Bachelors were more to be pitied than scorned, and the sorrier their existence, the greater the solicitude.
>
> Bachelor homesteader S. Jickling and his partner Stan were often invited by the women in the district "for a clean bite," as they called it. Clearly, there was a special niche reserved for [white] men without [white] women. "I used to feel so sorry for those boys," recalled one pioneer: "They were so pitiful. My mother, she worried over them and she babied them and they came to her with all their troubles."[65]

Danysk argues that the major reason (white) bachelors found such acceptance was that their "condition" was temporary – it was assumed that most bachelors would eventually find wives and settle in a town or on a farm. Yet, in order for this assumption to have any meaning, these men had to be seen as marriageable in the first place, and "marriage-ability" was a quality only white men shared.[66]

Indeed, the contrast between representations of Chinese and white bachelors could not be more stark as, from the completion of the railway in 1885 through to the Exclusion Act, 1923, Chinese men were subject to a full-scale moral panic that branded them as "yellow fiends," "yellow devils," and "yellow Chinamen."[67] These designations formed condensed epithets of meaning that reproduced ideas about a jaundiced and unhealthy race that epitomized a cowardly and degraded masculinity. Gail Bederman reminds us that Western imperial cultural norms identified advanced civilizations by the degree of their gender differentiation. In civilized society, women were womanly – delicate, spiritual, and dedicated to the home – and men were the most manly ever evolved – firm of character and self-controlled.[68] In this context, racial slurs that indicated that Chinese men were "unmanly" also suggested that they lacked a masculine ability to restrain their passions. Similarly, terms like "fiends" and "devils" summoned up ideas about evil beings who were prone to any manner of perversity or licentiousness.[69]

Shah argues that, despite a widespread moral panic about the high rates of venereal infection among men, a discourse of "deviant heterosexuality" was the main explanation used to frame white men's sexual "indiscretions." In contrast, speculations of sodomy were entertained primarily when questioning the syphillic infection of Chinese men.[70] All this despite the thousands of bachelor homesteaders, like S. Jickling and his partner Stan, who settled in communities all over the west. In this context it is useful to remind ourselves that Asia and the Orient had been a site of sexualized European imaginings long before western Canada was settled.[71] I argue that the proximity of Euro-Canadian and Chinese settlers constituted a new site in which sexual paranoia about "the Far East" was utilized to constitute the boundaries of a civilized white hetero-morality. Indeed, the *Report of the Royal Commission on Chinese Immigration* contains fantastical descriptions of Chinese men's supposed affinity for a variety of perverse and outrageous sexual antics, testimony that *Dirty Laundry* appropriates for a hilarious and fleeting spoof.

"A History of Questions"

The final movement of *Dirty Laundry* opens with archival photographs of Chinese bachelors and prostitutes being submerged under a swirl of dirty water. These are the images of perversion that epitomize the supposedly shameful aspects of Chinese-Canadian history. However, *Dirty Laundry* represents these emblems of a tainted past in ways that reconfigure the discourse of shame. As Eve Sedgwick comments:

> The forms taken by shame are not distinct "toxic" parts of a group or individual identity that can be excised; they are instead integral to ... the process in which identity is formed. They are available for the work of metamorphosis, reframing, refiguration, transfiguration ... but unavailable for ... the work of purgation and ... closure.[72]

In other words, the discursive shaming of a group or individual cannot simply be purged or wilfully evacuated. But the process of disidentification can recycle this history in order to use it as raw material for a performance that reconfigures its meaning – in ways that have usually been unthinkable to those in the dominant culture.

Dirty Laundry suggests that the constructions of "shame" that emerge from a history of Chinese bachelors in building the CPR are integral to both Euro-Canadian and Chinese history. My analysis attempts to dislodge Chinese and white bachelors from the protective custody of the shadows for a much needed reassessment. I argue that *Dirty Laundry* represents the process of negotiating multiple and conflicting racial, gendered, and sexed identities as a site of constant conflict and struggle – indeed, as an integral component of the work of constructing the Canadian nation.

Fung decided to use a historiographic approach to making *Dirty Laundry* after conversations with several gay Chinese-Canadian friends prompted the realization that few had heard of the historic "bachelor societies." Indeed, the most common response to his queries was "were those the triads?"[73] Further, his own introduction to the early moral panic that branded Chinese-Canadian (and American) bachelors as "sodomites" did not come from reading the history of early Chinese settlement on the Canadian frontier. Instead, he came across a copy of *Report of the Royal Commission on Chinese Immigration* (1885) while visiting the Chinatown History Museum in New York City. It was there that he flipped through the index and unearthed the references to "sodomy" along with the attendant accusations of perversion.

However, there are multiple origin stories for this video, including that form of genealogy usually associated with family history. Fung's father travelled through Canada when he left China in 1929 for the West Indies. The route involved travelling by sea from China to British Columbia and by rail – the CPR – across the Dominion. Once on the east coast he journeyed south by sea to Trinidad. Fung Sr. travelled during the period known as the Exclusion Era (from 1923 to 1946), when no Chinese immigrants were allowed to settle in Canada, save a tiny number of merchants, diplomats, students, and their wives and servants. Thus, while prospective Chinese migrants were the target of the most racist immigration legislation in Canadian history, they were not all affected equally. A few with monied status and connections could migrate. However, for the vast majority of those who sought to escape poverty and war in China, like Fung's father, their view of Canada was shaped by the CPR. It was the railway that provided the transcontinental route for a quick passage through the country and on to other more hospitable destinations. It was only when Canada's immigration laws had been liberalized in the 1960s that non-elite immigrants from the West Indies were able to migrate to Canada and settle as citizens.

These two narratives illustrate how the question of borders – those racialized, classed, gendered, and sexed mechanisms of exclusion – continue to haunt the present. At the turn of the century, western discourse about bachelors was crucial to the forms of regulation that secured Canada's *internal* borders. Here practices of whiteness and heteronormativity were secured through a host of separations – which were anything but "natural" and not always successful. Needless to say, in the polyglot settler community of the west coast, some bachelors were assumed to be more perverse than others. My analysis examines how particular kinds of racialized and sexed masculinity were reconstituted through the banal and clichéd images of the CPR and western settlement. *Dirty Laundry* neither fashions a new coherence for this story nor provides a tidy resolution of contradictory events. But it provides a starting point for exploring the queer valence that subliminally charged the discourse about western settlement and, at the same time, it highlights the racialized codes that produced such different narratives about batching it on the frontier.

4
Banff National Park
Rangers on the Mountain Frontier

"Don't Lose the Clichés. Canada Is Nature ... That's Our Brand."[1]

In the spring of 2005, the Canadian Tourism Commission announced it was sidelining the "Mounties, mountains and moose" images as part of what *Globe and Mail* marketing reporter Keith McArthur called an "extreme makeover" for the Canadian "brand."[2] While the justification for the change was market research showing that Canada had lost much of its tourist appeal, some, like Toronto Taxi Advertising and Design chairman Paul Lavoie (quoted above), thought the new strategy dangerous. However, a glance at the new tourist slogan: "Canada. Keep Exploring" highlights that this supposed makeover operates within the same discursive landscape. For ideas about exploration have always been central to Canada's touristic identity, at the same time as they have often reinscribed a discourse of white, masculinist discovery of the wilderness terrain.

This chapter explores how wilderness parks have functioned to construct notions of gender, race, and respectability on the western frontier. My focus is on the representational legacy associated with Banff National Park, which has furnished the most recognizable images of Canada's "brand" for well over a century.[3] I combine a close reading of Robert Burns' history of the park warden service, which started at Banff National Park, with an analysis of a contemporary Banff advertising blog called *The Park Ranger*. My project is to investigate the racialized anxieties that inform white masculinities and to identify key processes through which park wardens came to be imagined as benevolent "guardians of the wild" while Indigenous men, who had formerly been the recognized experts on mountain terrain, became outlaws, mascots, or spectres. I argue that the simultaneous fetishization and erasure of Indigenous men in the new space of the wilderness has served to bolster Euro-Canadian masculinity and agency at the expense of those others, who, through the same process, were most often rendered primitive, static, and lacking.

In the second half of this chapter I turn to the work of Shawna Dempsey and Lorri Millan in their performance *Lesbian National Parks and Services* (*LNPS*). *LNPS* was created for a summer institute at the Banff Centre for the Arts in 1997, and the artists played out the piece in the day-to-day space of the town. There they handed out brochures, engaged with tourists, and staged specific events (such as setting up a recruitment table in Central Park). However, a puzzling contradiction haunted the Lesbian Rangers' performance. While Dempsey and Millan engaged in a hyperbolic display of lesbianism, they received virtually no negative response; on the contrary, they were generally treated with deference and respect. Most critics cannot fail to wonder about this. I explore the obvious question: how did they pull it off?

Overall, then, I trace the naturalization of whiteness and hetero-masculinity in representations of Banff National Park, a tourist space that is Canada's most internationally recognized emblem. The Lesbian Rangers relied on taken-for-granted ideas about this mountain wilderness to mount their performative challenges. Indeed, it is precisely because the project *works* as comedy that it so effectively stages the visible-yet-invisible effects of whiteness in the national imagination.[4] In this context I explore how whiteness and heteronormativity have operated as everything and nothing, hypervisible but never spoken. I argue that it is in the residue of such representations that the *unremarkable* and banal ties to national belonging take shape.

Rethinking the Wilderness

> I know a man whose school could never teach him patriotism,
> but who acquired that virtue when he felt in his bones the
> vastness of his land, and the greatness of those who founded it.
>
> – Pierre Elliott Trudeau, observation during a
> wilderness canoe voyage, 1944[5]

To borrow cultural historian Patricia Jasen's wonderful turn of phrase, it was the lure of "wild things" that drew thousands of tourists to Banff National Park in the early twentieth century.[6] For here the untamed heritage of cowboys, Indians, and explorers, along with the imposing mountains themselves, fostered a sense that visitors were coming to a liminal space, perched at the edge of the British Empire and perhaps even on the edge of civilization itself. These images of Banff were fundamentally shaped by the Canadian Pacific

Railway, which developed both the Banff Springs Hotel and the mineral springs associated with the park. But, at the same time as the CPR fostered images of a rough-and-ready western landscape, its publicity also assured the "class that travelled" that this wilderness kept its sensibilities in mind.[7] As one contemporary hotel puts it, "Banff answers the call of the wild in very civil tones."[8] Thus, Banff's appeal as a tourist destination has been lodged in a deeply contradictory movement, alternating between images of highly commodified pleasure and a seemingly undomesticated wilderness. And this ambivalence implies a range of other paradoxical conflicts, for constructions about "wildness" and "civility" are mediated through the cultural norms associated with gender, race, and respectability on the frontier. And, as Banff is central to Canada's touristic self-image, these intersections have come to embody ideas about the national body – in short, about Canada itself.

If we begin historically, although Banff embodies a crucial place in the Canadian imaginary, the origin of the park is linked to the first national park in the United States: Yellowstone.[9] It was the American painter George Catlin, famous for his portraits of Indigenous people during the 1830s, who has been credited with first suggesting that the United States establish national parks.[10] Working under the assumption that both Indigenous peoples and the buffalo were "under an equal doom," he imagined that the state could create:

> a *magnificent park,* where the world could see for ages to come, the native Indian in his classic attire, galloping his wild horse, with sinewy bow, and shield and lance, amid the fleeting herds of elk and buffaloes. What a beautiful and thrilling specimen for America to preserve and hold up to the view of her refined citizens and the world, in future ages![11]

While Catlin's vision of national parks was crucially reliant on forms of racialized spectacle in which Indigenous people's own interests in the politics of land were nowhere to be seen, the idea of a park in which human and animal "specimens" were preserved for public view suggests illuminating connections between parks and other national institutions, namely museums. The first commissioner of national parks in Canada, appointed in 1911, suggested a similar connection. In his writing about the origin and meaning of wilderness reserves, J.B. Harkin argues that parks belong to Canadian citizens "in the same way as our National Galleries and National Museums do."[12] And, as both the public servant Harkin and scholars like Benedict Anderson note, museums have been an important foundational tool for developing the idea of a nation.[13]

There is, however, a longer history for "emparked areas,"[14] one that can be traced to the Anglo-Canadian "mother country" of England. As E.P. Thompson has powerfully illustrated, seventeenth-and eighteenth-century English parliamentary acts of enclosure also worked to create private emparkments, thereby dispossessing thousands of rural inhabitants of their land. Here the abolition of common pastures and the use of game laws to restrict hunting to landholding gentry were part of a larger project: destroying the means of subsistence for a poor rural peasantry. In the tumult that followed, the peasants protesting the enclosures were often characterized as a "wild" and "undisciplined" race. The most notorious law passed in the enclosure movement was called the Black Act (1723). It created fifty new capital offences for those who blackened their faces to raid private emparked areas, royal chases, and forests. Thompson vividly describes the malicious extent to which customary usages of the land by common people were withdrawn and rural inhabitants persecuted, and how the "blacks," often highly organized and mounted, ran a running battle of "agrarian warfare" with forest officers.

While there are many differences between the history of legal and social attitudes towards land tenure in England and in Canada, I suggest that there are clear parallels between English and North American emparkment projects. The people most affected by these projects differed – "barbarian" peasants in England and "Indian savages" in North America – but each group was marked as uncivilized and subjected to a rupture of traditional assumptions of common land use through custom. Each endured the encroaching and, in the end, drastic imposition of capitalist property relations. Also noteworthy is the role of English forest officers, whose policing of peasants' agrarian warfare calls to mind the running battles that, from the outset of emparkment projects throughout North America and elsewhere, park wardens have engaged against "poaching" by Indigenous people.[15]

While the English emparkment movement naturalized a class order, in North America, as the American scholar William Cronon famously notes, the creation of ideas about wilderness and national parks were "in a very real sense to protect the nation's most sacred myth of origin."[16] More specifically, in Canada and the United States, national, provincial, and state parks naturalized the idea of the wilderness as "virgin" territory through the erasure of Indigenous peoples' prior claim on the land.[17] As Kent McNeil argues, notions of scientific racism were crucial in judging Indigenous peoples as unfit to claim territory (in and around Banff and elsewhere) upon which they had lived for generations. Here an imperial romance with the wilderness frontier(s), and social Darwinist notions about Indigenous peoples as morally infantile and unfit for citizenship, enabled European settlers to characterize these spaces as "free land" and to represent Indigenous peoples as having no legally recognizable land tenure.[18] A century later, continuing battles over land claims remind us that the preservation of the wilderness in and around Banff has been crucially reliant on the takeover of Indigenous territory. For example, it has taken almost one hundred years for the Siksika Nation land claim for areas of Banff National Park to be settled, while many aspects of Treaty Seven, negotiated with the Stoney Nakoda people of that region, remain troubling and controversial.[19]

These processes are historical, but they have also had a profound impact on the contemporary space of Banff. As architectural critic Trevor Boody notes, the town's development of an increasingly generic Rocky Mountain resort aesthetic threatens to obliterate its own "rough history," while at the same time ensuring that planners now "enjoy the freedom to concoct a smoother, freeze-dried substitute."[20] Thus, throughout Banff, a very particular vision of nation building has settled into every nook and cranny. As Jody Berland elaborates:

> [Banff National Park] has been maintained for nearly a century as a kind of *natural* museum, in which mountains and trees function as testimony to the past ... as display objects in a museum without walls whose vistas commemorate the territorial triumphs of the land's founding fathers.[21]

This imperial respatialization required that Banff be stripped of a whole range of earlier and/or alternative cultural meanings. While a few Indigenous people continue to work in the park as wilderness guides and as cultural producers, they have been primarily visible in decorative mascots or through ritualized events like the Banff Indian Days.[22] As Tolly Bradford highlights, the policy of the parks department has been deeply implicated in this marginalization, for, in creating the park, the Canadian state was responsible for preventing local bands from continuing Indigenous patterns of land use. Yet, clearly, the parks department, along with numerous entrepreneurs in Banff, still had an interest in employing the *image* of Indianness to attract tourist dollars. Thus, some Indigenous activities, such as beadwork and horsemanship, were deemed worth preserving, while others, including subsistence hunting and traditional religious and cultural events at the base of Cascade Mountain, were seen as a threat to the government's exploitation of the park resources.[23] Consequently, the vision of Indianness promoted at Banff National Park has often used a discourse of Indian exoticism and difference while reproducing the idea that it was white tourists who were the legitimate heirs to the wilderness.

As Jensen points out, the idea of national parks as a place of rejuvenation arose at a time of widespread anxiety about the moral character of urban life. At the turn of the twentieth century, popular Canadian magazines expressed increasing fears that men in white-collar work were suffering the effects of "overcivilization" and effeminacy – problems that could weaken citizens' personal and racial health. The best cure for this "brain-fag,"[24] they opined, was a wilderness holiday, a form of recreation that was acquiring increased popularity among the middle and upper classes.[25] Canadian historian Mark Moss argues that the back-to-nature and physical culture movements were thought to "help arrest the deterioration of Canadian manhood." Indeed, "Nature ... was the antidote required to reinvigorate a 'rapidly deteriorating race.'"[26] Thus, ideas about wilderness and, by extension, wilderness parks such as Banff, were particularly important for men and boys who needed to release their pent-up frustrations with "urban confinement" and to encourage those "manly qualities" that urbanization put under threat.[27] Consequently, the wilderness ideal was envisioned as a male homosocial space beyond the feminized, mundane, and domestic details of daily living.

If these were the anxieties that characterized the early twentieth century, then is it possible to see them reflected in early debates about the founding of Banff National Park? Certainly discussions within the national Parliament highlighted the class conflicts implicit in this masculinist discourse. Here, members of Parliament charged that Rocky Mountains Park (later Banff National Park) would simply serve the wealthy and "citified" elite, not the majority of Canadian taxpayers. As John Kirk, the opposition member for Guysborough, commented:

> Why should [the government] go into the business of preparing public parks as a resort – for whom? Not for the people of Canada, not for the people who pay the taxes, but for the wealthy people of the cities of the Dominion and the cities of other countries.[28]

But perhaps this debate is not surprising, given that the majority of the population knew far too much about strenuous labour on farms and in factories, in mines and logging camps, to regard hiking in "wild" backcountry land as a relaxing ideal. In contrast, it was those characterized as "fagged-out cits," or city dwellers, seemingly emasculated by the comforts of civilized life, who were eager to preserve some remnants of the wild landscape and the regeneration it promised.[29] In the wider public media, periodicals such as *Canadian Magazine* dispensed a steady stream of articles and poetry that made connections between northernness, nationality, and racial health. "For all those wishing 'to get closer to the primeval conditions of nature,' promised one writer, 'Canada, the future country of the world, peopled with a vigorous northern race, offers herself disdainful of competition.'"[30]

Thus, for those with the ability to travel, Banff was the ideal mountain getaway. Tourist writing from the 1890s notes its "exhilarating atmosphere, full of ozone, purified by frost and forest," which is said to be of particular benefit for "overworked business men" who "absorb its quiet peace gratefully, and declare it to be the most invigorating spot on the continent."[31] Not only did it offer a luxurious hotel, Swiss guides for a vigorous mountain trek, and abundant hunting in season (during the early years), but it also had mineral hot springs, an asset that "promise[d] to be of great sanitary advantage."[32] Thus designed, the early Rocky Mountains Park provided all the "tonic[s] of the wilderness" one could need to ward off physical degeneration and mental distress.[33]

Wardens of the Wilderness

The men responsible for maintaining order in the wilderness of national parks were park wardens. While Mounties and wardens have often performed similar cultural roles, in the early years of Rocky Mountains Park the North-West Mounted Police also did much of the actual work of "blazing trails to the far ranges" – work usually associated with park wardens.[34] Robert J. Burns argues that early park wardens at Rocky Mountains Park needed to know how to survive in regions far from settlement while also having sufficient education to report to the federal civil service. As Burns notes, the "delicate task here was to pick individuals who had not been too blatant in their violation of existing poaching and weapons violations."[35] This ruled out the local Indigenous Stoney peoples who were *the* experts on mountain terrain and survival; however, as Catriona Sandilands notes, "it would have been both legally impossible and culturally unthinkable for them to represent the state of which they were, following Treaty Seven, effectively wards."[36] Yet the first chief game guardian, Howard E. Sibbald (Figure 4.1), was well aware that his recruits would only be effective if they knew the terrain from a poacher's perspective, and, consequently, he required men who

Figure 4.1 First Chief Game Guardian Howard E. Sibbald Whyte Museum of the Canadian Rockies, V 408 NA-63

brought together an interesting masculine confluence: straddling the boundary between the warden and the "outlaw."[37]

I want to reflect on the racialized masculinities produced through this union by exploring how white men were legitimized as park wardens, while Indigenous men were made into outlaws when the first superintendent of

Rocky Mountain Park, George Stewart, recommended that Indigenous peoples be permanently excluded from hunting in the region.[38] I trace this development through the narrative supplied by Robert Burns in *Guardians of the Wild: A History of the Warden Service of Canada's National Parks* (2000). Burns was a historian for Parks Canada from 1976 to 1995, and he provides a systematic review of park wardens' early game protection strategies in Rocky Mountains Park and, later, Banff National Park. A consistent theme in his narrative concerns repeated tales about former or future wardens and prominent Banff citizens caught poaching within park boundaries. In the first of these stories, Burns tells us that "the most celebrated early poaching incident occurred in 1912, when Sibbald and deputy guardians J. Warren and Bill Peyto prosecuted former Chief Game and Fire Guardian Moore ... [and] the prominent local figure J.I. Brewster for killing two mountain sheep in the park."[39] Burns goes on to highlight the "popular attitude(s) towards game protection" by recounting a story covered in the *Banff Crag and Canyon* in 1913. Though the tale depicts an incident from Yoho Park in the United States, Burns uses it to illustrate the attitudes that seemed to be common among park warden staff on both sides of the border.

> A small group of tourists including a British army officer, at Field early this week expressed a burning desire to see "a live b'ar" in his native haunts. So Jack Giddy hooked up a team and toted the party out towards Emerald Lake. Meeting a slide in the road they left the rig and ran plumb into a grizzly. The bear arose on his haunches when Jack pumped a bullet into him and then charged the party. A couple more well aimed shots put bruin out of commission. The tourists expressed their perfect satisfaction.[40]

Burns ends the story by noting that the "free-wheeling, gun-toting teamster, Jack Giddy is the same John M. Giddie who would be Chief Warden of Yoho National Park in 1920."[41]

Burns argues that the chief threats faced by wildlife were from local residents, especially the guides and outfitters who led hunting parties through the parks' (then) legitimate hunting areas. The wardens were well-equipped to counter their efforts as they were "often former trappers and guides themselves, [and] knew their adversaries and their methods from personal experience."[42] However, during early debates over park boundaries in 1911, it was the rhetorical threat of "indians [sic] and others ... [who would] go in there during open season and slaughter and kill what it has taken years to protect and shelter"[43] that fuelled the arguments made by Superintendent

Howard Douglas to his superiors in Ottawa. Indeed, while park regulations required guides and packers to be licensed to work in the park, and licences were supposed to be routinely denied to anyone convicted of poaching violations in 1914, a new "informal" process evolved whereby men could re-apply for licensing after signing a bond for their future good behaviour. However, Burns notes, as evidence of the "background of continuous infractions," that in 1916 a "prominent Banff outfitter James Simpson was convicted of killing two mountain sheep in the park and his license was 'permanently' cancelled. In 1918, Simpson reapplied for a guide's license and was soon back in business."[44]

While it was indeed the case that "Indians" continued to maintain their traditional patterns of land use, which, after 1890, included activities then categorized as "poaching," it seems clear from Burns' narrative about "continuous infractions" that Euro-Canadian settlers, including park wardens, also hunted in and around the park boundaries and that these practices were viewed with considerable tolerance. Indeed, as Sandilands notes, Burns employs these stories about white men's antics to highlight idealized norms of a rugged, white masculinity and the "glory years" of the park warden service.[45] Their behaviour might have skirted close to the outlaw, but they were, after all, the Queen's representatives, in charge of preserving the wilderness of Banff for the enjoyment of citizens and tourists. Indeed, these tales serve to create some humorous narrative interest in his description of the early years of the parks, and Burns rehabilitates the warden image through arguing that, by the early 1920s, wardens were beginning to exercise a more consistent policy, prosecuting poachers across all the Rocky Mountain parks.

While the wardens laboured to preserve this wilderness for tourists, the Indigenous Stoney community, who had traditionally hunted within the area now defined by Banff National Park, faced a different set of challenges. Initially, most members of the band simply used the reserve as a base camp while continuing to trap and occupy their traditional hunting grounds in the mountains. However, in 1903, the boundaries of Rocky Mountains Park were extended, and, in 1909, the Rocky Mountains Forests Reserve was created, moves that dramatically limited Stoney hunting in the region. In this context, early park wardens spent considerable time policing Indigenous hunters who were now seen to be trespassing when inside park boundaries. Further, between 1914 and 1929, Stoney access to land *on* the reserve was eroded through the Seebe Dam (1914) and the Ghost Dam (late 1920s) – the latter of which flooded part of the reserve territory – and by mineral exploration as a result of the interest generated by finds in Turner Valley. At the same time, the "pass system," which regulated the movement of

Figure 4.2   Harold Fuller and cougar he shot at government stables, Banff, 1925. Game guardians (later wardens) trapped wolves and other predators so more "beneficial" animals would flourish. They were permitted to retain the pelts for their own profit. Whyte Museum of the Canadian Rockies, V628-242

Indigenous people off the reserve, also restricted the Stoney people's ability to find work in nearby towns.[46] Consequently, by the mid- to late 1920s, Stoney options for remaining economically self-sufficient, particularly through their traditional occupations of hunting and trapping, had been significantly curtailed. The poor soil of the reserve made agriculture, which was encouraged by both the government and the churches, very difficult. All these factors together ensured that the Stoney people were more economically impoverished relative to other bands in Alberta, and they became increasingly dependent on government assistance. [47]

A fascinating example of how national park policies regarding hunting and game preservation were influential in producing differently racialized masculinities can be seen through an exploration of park practices concerning "predator control." Burns tells us that, from the early years of Banff's development, it was generally accepted that game guardians should trap wolves, coyotes, mountain lions, and lynx under the assumption that, if the "harmful" animals could be eliminated, then the "beneficial" animals would flourish (Figure 4.2).[48] In 1918, the first commissioner of national parks,

James B. Harkin, made official what had already become policy in practice: "wardens were to be permitted to retain for their own profit the pelts of 'noxious' animals they might kill in the line of duty ... This was a strong incentive, as a warden could supplement his salary substantially by trapping predator fur-bearers in the park."[49] Indeed, as many wardens had been trappers before joining His Majesty's Service, these skills allowed them to top up their salary from 10 percent to well over 50 percent.[50]

By the early 1930s, people at headquarters were starting to shift their views on predator control so that the parks were no longer simply considered as "nurseries or 'reservoirs' for game animals."[51] However, park wardens were strongly invested in the earlier system, and, consequently, it took several decades for the new thinking on wildlife protection to take hold. This continued involvement of wardens in trapping predators was particularly striking, given the increasing evidence that populations of elk and other large game in Banff and other western parks were growing too fast, resulting in damage to their natural habitat and the townsites – precisely because of the lack of predators![52] Thus, starting in the 1920s in Buffalo National Park and by the 1940s in Banff and Jasper, the parks service initiated an annual slaughtering program. As Burns describes it, "park officials had stepped onto a long and slippery slope which ... would see 'guardians of the wild' shooting big game animals in the scenic parks in a desperate attempt to control their numbers."[53] While many of the townspeople in and around Banff approved of the cull as it addressed the problem of "nuisance" animals, park officials were anxious to avoid the leaking of unauthorized reports about the slaughtering program to the media. In 1944, when Banff chief warden Mitchell did give an interview to the local paper, he stressed that the cull was necessary to avoid overuse of the range resources, which could put the large game species at risk of starvation.[54] The wardens' own role in promoting the overpopulation of elk and other large game by destroying their natural predators was never mentioned. Also interesting is Burns' description of where the meat from this cull was distributed: it went to relief camps in the parks, to Indigenous and Inuit groups – with the Stoney reserve mentioned specifically – and was also sold to commercial packers.[55]

How, then, might we understand the connections between hunting and game preservation in the wilderness of Banff National Park and the racialized masculinities associated with park wardens? First, it seems clear that state policies, from the Indian Act to the prohibition on Indigenous hunting in Banff National Park, legally constructed Indigenous men as outlaws and poachers, while park wardens (many of whom had been trappers before being hired) became legitimate "guardians of the wild," to borrow the title of Burns' book. Thus, the early (white) mountain men, who were now park wardens, were established as emblems of manliness and racial fortitude, while Indigenous men, who had formerly been the recognized experts on mountain terrain, became outlaws, or, given the high death rate in Indigenous communities during this period, spectres.[56] In the parks program of predator control we find a particularly ironic example of this binary. Burns makes clear that park wardens' continued trapping of predators actually upset the balance in the park habitat and promoted the growth of large game to the point of starvation. Nevertheless, they continued these practices until well after the Second World War and viewed them as essential to nature conservation. As the wardens in Banff and in other western parks took charge of the problem of excessive numbers of large game through an annual slaughter, this practice came to be seen as a job that required excellent marksmanship, clear organizational skills, and careful public relations. Further, the distribution of the meat from the cull facilitated a performance of white benevolence as wardens organized donations to Indigenous reserves. Thus, the forms of masculinity reinscribed through the Park Warden Service highlighted white men as rugged, enterprising, and even benevolent in their efforts to protect both wild game and the natural wonder represented by the parks – while also feeding impoverished Indigenous communities. As several scholars have now argued, it is clear that it was the actions of the state, including those of national parks, that obstructed economic self-sufficiency in Indigenous communities. Nevertheless, the marginalization of Indigenous men from most forms of paid employment, in parks and elsewhere, allowed them to be depicted as lazy freeloaders who lacked ambition and had to rely on charity from the state – such as the elk meat sent from wardens at Banff National Park.

BanffNationalPark.com

While this analysis might complicate popular understandings of park wardens as respected icons of conservation, how do contemporary images of the warden service connect to this legacy? I explore this question by examining a blog called *The Park Ranger*, available at the website BanffNationalPark. com. Written by John McKiernan, *The Park Ranger* is designed as a subset of the CanadianRockies.net advertising site. While CanadianRockies.net provides travellers with a series of links to accommodations, leisure activities, and dining options, the two blogs on the site, *The Park Ranger* and *Mountain Man,* highlight two distinct personae evidently deemed fitting for the Banff National Park locale. Given that the majority of visitors to Banff rarely stray far from the highway and rely as much or more on commercial materials than on Park Services information to guide their visit, I explore how this commercial appropriation of the park warden image rearticulates earlier gendered, racialized, and sexed ideals associated with Banff National Park itself.

From April 2008 to May 2010, *The Park Ranger* posted fifty-seven blogs. The blogger used a variety of discursive strategies to establish his legitimacy as a Banff "insider" whom tourists could trust to get value for their money. Most obvious was the writer's use of locally grounded storytelling, personal anecdotes, and a self-deprecating sense of humour to establish *The Park Ranger* as a "guy's guy" who could help others navigate the wilderness of the tourist experience. *The Park Ranger* persona, however, does more than simply establish the writer's pedigree as a "real guy," with all the predictable (hetero-sexist) trappings. Close attention to the ways in which these posts portray the natural world, along with material and food cultures, also illuminates how *The Park Ranger* reinsribes the ghostly absent-presence of Indigenous people through a distinctly white Canadian masculinity.

Just as early architectural and CPR advertising for Banff worked to establish the town as a European outpost at the edge of empire, so the "facts" provided on *The Park Ranger* blog highlight the town's European heritage. Thus, we are told that Banff is "derived from Banffshire, Scotland, the birthplace of two of the original directors of the Canadian Pacific Railway" (2009). Additional facts use the quantitative language of science to inform us about the largest lakes, the oldest mountain ranges, the longest cave system, and the millions of visitors who visit every year. The tenor of the relationship between humans and the natural world takes shape more fully, though, through *The Park Ranger*'s recommendations for outdoor activities. Here disproportionate space is given to pursuits that require high levels of skill or the services of a guide, including whitewater rafting, bobsledding, caving, dogsledding, mountain biking, helicopter tours, rock/ice climbing and mountaineering. Similarly, when *The Park Ranger* discusses skiing, it is only the most challenging runs that garner attention. Although the blog is framed in a contemporary idiom, these posts suggest forms of recognizable hetero-masculinist bravado: "These rivers are not for the faint of heart ... The Kicking Horse is not one of your wimpy streams from back home" (2008). Indeed, even when describing activities such as fishing, the blog strives to emphasize masculinist forms of competition. Thus, in a posting dated March 2010, *The Park Ranger* highlights the game fish native to Banff, including the cutthroat trout, bull trout, and Rocky Mountain whitefish.

Having started with this virile description, however, *The Park Ranger* is then forced to admit that the much less fearsome-sounding brown trout is probably the most pursued fish of all the mountain trout varieties. No matter, fishing on Minnewanka Lake still provides a "fisherman's paradise" where you can "catch the fish that will earn you bragging rights over all your friends" (May 2010).

In discussions of the great outdoors, however, *The Park Ranger* cannot completely avoid those activities that have Indigenous origins, in particular canoeing and dogsledding. Yet, even within this context, the writer manages to employ the discourses of history and tradition to claim the heritage of these activities as distinctly *Canadian*. Thus, in May 2010, he opines that "canoeing and Canada go together like McDonald's and obesity. Long before the white man landed, canoes have been the preferred form of transport, and there are few better places to do it than right in the center of Banff on the Bow River." Similarly, in a post from February 2009 he notes that dog-sledding has "a pedigree that goes back well before European settlement ... [and] is probably the oldest winter recreation in Canada." Thus, in each post he acknowledges, without naming, other peoples and land uses while simultaneously occluding them: in this case by describing dogsledding through a eugenics-inflected language about the "pedigree" of the sport, not the people, before European settlement. A similar absent-presence is evident in the last post in this series, dated May 2010, regarding "Cave Tours in Banff and the Rockies." Featuring a link to Canmore Cave Tours, the blog tells readers they will "find out how both humans and animals have used these caves." Yet it provides no information about the pictographs (similar to those at the Grotto Canyon) that are seen on this tour and that have great spiritual significance for Indigenous peoples in this region.[57]

Among *The Park Ranger*'s blogs related to the natural world, posts about bears and bison are of particular interest. Here *The Park Ranger* cannot resist including a series of telling asides that construct bears as a central attraction of the wilderness experience. Thus, in a post on "Jogging in Banff" (April 2010), the blogger recommends a path "surrounded by overhanging trees" on the outskirts of the town, and concludes with the following comment: "there might be a just-woken Grizzly Bear watching you from the trees [but this just] makes you run faster. Fear is a beautiful motivator." Under the heading "The Park Ranger's Three Fav Restaurants in Banff," the one that tops the list is "off the beaten track" and appealing because he "often sees bears on the road linking the restaurant to the highway." Some might think this would be an indication of the restaurant's improper garbage storage, but, for *The Park Ranger*, these sightings are just another opportunity to establish a he-man persona capable of handling whatever the wilderness has to offer.

There is quite a different tenor, however, in the one post on the bison. Here the haunting legacy of earlier generations of imperial trade and settlement and their impact on the natural world constitutes a sober undertone. Entitled "Bringing Back Bison to Banff" (March 2009), the post chronicles the efforts of the Eleanor Luxton Historical Foundation, in partnership with Parks Canada, to gain support for the reintroduction of the "last big mammal that's missing from our ecosystem." While *The Park Ranger* starts with an effusive commentary, the tone quickly changes: "this Park Ranger thinks it would be great to see bison back roaming the ranges. It was our ancestors' fault that they were driven close to extinction, [so] a quiete [sic] prairie that they can call home is the least we can do." Thus, it is in the near-extinction of the bison,[58] the animal most closely associated with the Indigenous Plains cultures, that the blogger is finally able to articulate a sense of Euro-Canadian responsibility for dispossession; however, in his discourse, the *people* who were also devastated by mercantile capitalism, imperial settlement, and national parks, still remain lost in the wilderness.

The gendered and racialized tenor of *The Park Ranger* persona is also evident in posts relating to material and food cultures in and around Banff. Most obvious are the ways *The Park Ranger* blogger establishes his heteromasculinity in posts about real estate. Here he is careful to describe the restrictions on purchasing property within Banff National Park, but he quickly finds a solution in the nearby town of Canmore. He describes the situation as follows: "Canmore is equally beautiful, less touristy and it has a café that is seemingly staffed with Miss Universe contestants. Prices are cheaper; it is outside the National Park boundaries ... and they have a café with gorgeous staff ... did I already say that?" (March 2010). When talking about rental lodging, however, his tone is more domesticated. In July 2008 he describes two rental options, one hotel with kitchenette and a bed and breakfast in Canmore: "The smarter and prettier side of my family had us bunk up at ... a nice little bed and breakfast ... [T]he folks who run it are the best." Here the gendered language gives a nod to his presumably female partner while reinforcing the idea that women are delicate and demanding creatures that require a "nicer" quality of accommodation than a more utilitarian hotel might offer.

In his many restaurant reviews, *The Park Ranger* blogger depicts himself as a guy whose ideal meal is one of "meat and more meat." In this context, St. James Irish Gate Pub is number three on his list of three favourite restaurants, but he cautions that it's "not really the type of place that you take a girl on a first date (although I learned this the hard way) but great considering it's ... tasty, warm and just an all round cool bar" (February 2009). Again, "girls" require the finer things in life, including a better place to eat than this Irish Pub. But the pub is perfect for an implicitly Euro-Canadian masculinity that requires warmth, comfort, beer, and big portions. Among the fifty-plus restaurant reviews, there are a few in which the blogger breaks from this persona – but it is clear he does so with reluctance. For example, in March 2010 he reviewed Miki Japanese Restaurant, starting with this line: "I am only recently a fish man." While this opening implies that anything other than meat needs to be approached with extreme caution, the Miki's "all you can eat" special won him over, along with servers who were "extremely attentive." Overall, however, restaurants that veer from purportedly Euro-Canadian food cultures are almost inevitably described as places he is compelled to go to because of special events. One exception is the Stoney Nakoda Casino (April 2010). After reassuring his readers that the casino is not "a seedy place ... [with] sweaty men (I describe myself) pushing over each other trying to get the last of their chips onto the roulette table," *The Park Ranger* blogger goes on to say that it would be a great location for a stag. Interestingly, after well over a dozen reviews of bars and pubs, it is only the Stoney Nakoda Casino that is judged appropriate for this sexually charged homosocial gathering. Given the lack of any other details that would explain this anomaly, his representation seems to repeat the racialized assumption that Indigenous spaces provide an unspoken permission for Euro-Canadian men to let out their "wild side."

Overall, then, I argue that *The Park Ranger* blog manifests aspects of the national, racial, and gendered anxieties that continue to be implicit in contemporary Canadianness. Returning first to the blogger's commercial endorsements for outfitters and guides, we see that disproportionate attention is given to extreme risk-taking activities: conjuring up imperial histories in which men conquer the wilderness and their own gendered anxiety through masculine bravado. Indeed, the tone recalls the mountain men (later park wardens) of the early national parks, when the blogger describes competent outfitters and guides who "get the job done," while "girls" are mentioned when they look good, make a terrific cup of coffee, or demand the finer things in life, such as better accommodation. In the blogger's commentary on restaurants, he suggests how touristic discourse can produce an imagined sense of place by reinventing the "home-places" signified by particular foods.[59] These culinary homes in the wilderness are premised on

reinscribing the idea that men are distinguished by their hearty male appetites and that a particular connection exists between men and meat so that
animal flesh is a consummate male food and eating meat an exemplar of
maleness.[60] Indeed, the blog's devotion to meat repeats the racial discourse
employed in the settlement of the west, where wheat and beef were assumed
to be the pre-eminent food of the civilized world, providing just the right
nutrients to support national and racial strength.[61] It is clear in *The Park
Ranger*'s reviews of Japanese and Indian restaurants that these foods do not
fit within the blogger's culinary home-place and are "add-ons" of food cultures that seemingly lie outside the norms of Banff. Yet Japanese and Indian
communities have more than a century of settlement history in the Rocky
Mountain region. Consequently, I suggest that *The Park Ranger*'s construction of food cultures could be likened to what Thomas K. Nakayama and
Robert L. Krizek describe as a "white rhetorical strategy,"[62] one that clearly
implies certain kinds of belonging for the blog's assumed readership – and
certain kinds of exclusions for others.

In sum, this review of the early warden service's "golden years" in Banff
National Park and of the contemporary commercial appropriations in *The
Park Ranger* blog suggests that images of the wilderness, and the men who
make it safe for tourists, are deeply performative. In the early representations, where the wilderness is a seemingly empty space available for national consumption, and in more recent commercial adaptations, wilderness
discourse is a disciplinary practice that has often worked to reproduce a
host of exclusions while normalizing particular representations of bodies
and place.[63] R.B.J. Walker writes that "claims about history are also usually
indispensable to claims about nation."[64] However, historical claims are not
written in texts alone: they are sedimented in the Canadian imaginary
through the iconography that shapes the banal and everyday associations
with being Canadian. If the norms of national identity have been hailed
into being through the associations sketched above, then how are visual
artists attempting to disrupt these connections? The rest of this chapter
examines the *Lesbian National Parks and Services* reconfiguration of the
wilderness and the surprising, troubling, and sometimes hilarious results of
this performance.

Reading *Lesbian National Parks and Services*

> [Performance art] is visual art that happens to move in real time.
>
> – Martha Wilson[65]

Art may lay bare the contradictory dimensions of ... memory
as it vacillates between the imaginable and the unimaginable.
Recognizing [this] ... we reevaluate our approaches and criteria
for looking.

– Kyo Maclear[66]

I suggest that historic and contemporary images of national parks have a conflicted legacy that is deeply implicated in the national project of whitening the wilderness and the nation. In *Lesbian National Parks and Services (LNPS)*, Dempsey and Millan's fulcrum is an examination of gender, sex, and authority in the space of the great outdoors. In *LNPS*, the artists rely on taken-for-granted ideas about the innocent character of the landscape they inhabit to serve as the backdrop for a performative challenge to masculinist and heteronormative assumptions. My interest in *LNPS* is to examine how this performance and its reception rely on rearticulating whiteness in the wilderness ideal. This discussion examines how the project's queer subversions reconfigure an icon – the Park Ranger – whose historical traits are manliness, white racial fortitude, and (hetero)sexual restraint.[67] At the beginning of this chapter I suggest that the Lesbian Rangers had no overtly negative reactions to their performance. The artists themselves have suggested that many observers of the *LNPS* performance seemed to refuse the blatantly lesbian aspects of their work. What can we learn from this resistance? And how might it intersect with the norms of innocence, masculinity, and respectability that national parks, and thus Park Rangers, have embodied throughout the past century?

Performing Art: Performing Deconstruction

Shawna Dempsey and Lorri Millan arrived in Banff in their
turquoise 1963 Pontiac Laurentian automobile, dressed from
head to toe in khaki gear. From their boots to their caps, they
inhabited the uniform of the Park Ranger, complete with
accessories. With the jingle of their key chains, you could
hear them coming.

– Kathryn Walter[68]

Performance work draws from the conceptual art movement of the 1970s, which shifted the focus from art objects to ideas and process.[69] Like much "disturbatory art," performance often collapses boundaries between the sacred and the profane, the public and the private, with marked irreverence for established discourses and institutions.[70] Most important, performance follows a distinctly different set of conventions than acting in theatre and film. Canadian filmmaker Lynne Fernie suggests that performance artists "don't try to make you believe in this character ... [T]hey're more deconstructive than [film actors]."[71] Or, as Martha Wilson puts it, "the goal of theater is the suspension of disbelief and the goal of performance art is to bring you up short."[72] *LNPS* was a site-specific piece created for a summer institute at the Banff Centre for the Arts in 1997. It was performed as part of a larger program in which artists explored the concept of masquerade by creating new work that critiqued cultures of consumption and spectacle.[73] This concept originated with the Situationist International (SI), a group of European intellectuals who analyzed commodity culture in their own political and artistic practice. The SI explored how commercial images overdetermine social codes and channel desire into spectacle and consumption. Working primarily in the 1960s, its purpose was to destabilize these signs by constructing events or happenings that used the street as an arena for art and politics.[74] These ideas are consistent with the broader goals of performance art, which often attempts to reach a wider audience by taking art out of the museum or gallery.

The role of performance art viewers is also different from that of other art viewers: indeed, the startling contradictions of performance art often challenge passive modes of visual consumption by interrupting normalized flows in time and space. The concept of going "undercover in public space" highlights the necessity of infiltrating taken-for-granted images and spaces in order to transform the cultural logic from within. In this context, I suggest that the Lesbian Rangers' masquerade can be read as asking witnesses to *dis-identify* with simple sight and to consider how unexpected and invented images might shift common-sense assumptions.

As interlopers inhabiting the bodies of Park Rangers, Dempsey and Millan used their role as private investigators in public space to *queery* the mythic figure of the Park Ranger – always straight, upstanding, and courteous – at the same time as they satirized the commodification of Banff National Park. Locating themselves on the main streets of the town (Figure 4.3), the Lesbian Rangers handed out brochures, engaged with and assisted tourists, and staged specific events. Their pamphlet highlighted the *LNPS* insignia with a picture of the intrepid Lesbian Rangers surveying the mountain landscape. Inside the brochure was a handy map of Banff, pointing to actual tourist sites *and* imaginary institutions such as the "Invisible Lesbian

Figure 4.3 Shawna Dempsey *(left)* and Lorri Millan *(right)* as the Lesbian Rangers in Banff. The two women talked with tourists about the mission of the Lesbian National Parks and Services. Courtesy of Shawna Dempsey and Lorri Millan, LNPS (1997 and ongoing)

Heritage House and Gardens" and the "Invisible Plaque Dedicated to our Founding Foremothers." These performances, as Kyo Maclear remarks, suggest an ongoing "site gag" highlighting "the artifice of sight-seeing, [and] homing in on endemic preconceptions that shape the scripts for travel."[75]

My examination of Dempsey and Millan's performance begins with a question: if the image of the Park Rangers served as a respectable foil for a degenerate yet peculiarly natural sexuality to infiltrate public space, then how did the specifically *lesbian* subversions operate in this performance? Despite, or perhaps because, of the seeming incongruity of it all, Dempsey and Millan constructed the *LNPS* uniform and insignia, as well as their own personal demeanour, to appropriate exactly the authoritative persona of the park warden. As Millan comments, lesbians "are in a culture where we have no authority, so ... since no one will give it to us [we constructed the *LNPS*] to just take it, and see what we could do from this position as artists."[76] As their performance unfolded on the streets of Banff, the khaki uniform, military-style caps, and the large "RANGER" lettering on their shoulder badges all had an impact (Figure 4.4). Dempsey and Millan *inhabited* the Park Ranger and utilized their professional charm to be serious but friendly and helpful.

Figure 4.4 **Lesbian National Parks and Services insignia** Courtesy of Shawna Dempsey and Lorri Millan, LNPS (1997 and ongoing)

Simultaneously, the *LNPS* also ruptured traditional ideas of plausibility with the hyperbolic display of LESBIAN (on their chest/cap badges and brochures) and, thus, challenged the heteronormative assumptions from which the Park Ranger draws his authority.

Responses to the *LNPS* suggest that the historic resonance of the Park Ranger icon – embodying manliness, whiteness, and (hetero)sexual restraint – usually overdetermined the artists' queer subversions. The actual performance was received with relative equanimity: the predominant response from tourists and residents alike was characterized as "respectful" and distinguished more by "awe than suspicion."[77] Further, most passersby appeared not to recognize, or resisted recognizing, the queer nature of the performance. Indeed, Millan believes that many actually believed the Lesbian Rangers were men. This last response suggests that authority itself is overdetermined and that, in the eyes of many tourists at Banff, the colour and gender of authority are white and male.

So how did the tourist-friendly artists manage their actual engagements on the streets of Banff? In short, they assisted with photographs or directions, engaging passersby in conversation about the mandate of the *LNPS* when possible, being sure to get a brochure into their hands before they left. This process produced several memorable encounters. Perhaps the most striking involved a middle-aged white Canadian man who spied the RANGER label on Dempsey and Millan's shoulder badge and approached them to engage in conversation. As Dempsey describes it:

> When he got up to us he read the label of my shirt insignia out loud: *L E S B I A N* National Parks and Services. Realizing that he didn't know (or couldn't acknowledge) what he was dealing with, he suddenly had to improvise. His conclusion – "Now that must be *Federal,* isn't it!"[78]

Here that oh-so-Canadian method of distancing oneself from "the problem," the federal/provincial wrangle, is employed for the most unexpected of ends. When Dempsey responded (herself improvising), "Well no, actually we're international," the man remained steadfastly puzzled. Millan continues: "By the time we parted I still don't think the penny had dropped for him. Perhaps then he thought 'lesbian' was one of those supposedly obscure central European countries."[79] Others caught on to the odd nature of the performance more quickly, although they also decided it was something with which they did not want to be associated. As Millan relates:

> Your average [white] guys would come up in baseball caps and plaid shirts and say, "So where's the good fishing around here?" And as we would launch into our response, which we would usually have to improvise, you could see them reading our caps (*L E S B I A N* National Parks and Services) and the wheels turning in their heads ... and something would come over them and they'd say, "Oh thanks ... " and excuse themselves very quickly ... So it was during the course of answering these questions that the fact that the frame was hanging a bit crooked on the wall would dawn on them. I used to think it would be nice if we had a little video camera on those pamphlets to see what happened when they opened them and read it.[80]

However, these resistant readings were not the only response. Indeed, the artists' appropriation of a national icon for "other" purposes blurred the boundaries of the real for even the most knowing observers. Coincidentally, the savvy cultural critic Kyo Maclear was also at Banff in the summer of 1997 for an arts journalism residency and was asked to provide an "eyewitness account" of the Lesbian Rangers.

It is amazing, but I have yet to see them out of uniform or off duty ... Gradually the surrogate rangers are becoming ever more real, ever more familiar ... [T]he conceptual satire seems to have titillated visitors (myself included) to the point that we have become willing participants in the masquerade. Are we falling prey to parody? Or is the fiction unravelling the real, its centre and margins ... The *LNPS* make it clear that the social scripts, determining who will be loved, hated and revered, can be easily scrambled. Identities can be cross-wired and reprogrammed because they are based on unstable attributes.[81]

Some attributes, however, are more "unstable" than others. For example, whiteness remains a necessary and stable background, while the "Lesbian" on the Lesbian Ranger badge reminds us that Park Rangers, and other national icons, are only imaginable as straight. These queer significations highlight the continued force of heteronormativity in the imaginative construction of wilderness space at the same time as some observers' "titillation" signals the instability of (hetero)sexual assumptions.

While Maclear's analysis points out the instabilities in a supposedly fixed and normative sexuality, the issue of gender requires further analysis. Judith Butler argues that queer performance can be subversive to the extent that it reflects on the imitative structure by which hegemonic gender is produced, so that resistance is never pure but comes into being through the frame, and at the fissures, of existing discourse.[82] In this context, I ask: when the Lesbian Rangers rearticulated the masquerade of identity, did they "do gender" in ways that repeated and displaced through hyperbole the very constructs that they mobilized?[83] In addition, how does the *LNPS* vision of gender and sex as a mix of unstable attributes compare with the gendered and sexed performances of other Park Rangers and workers in related hotels and leisure parks?

According to white women involved with the US Park Services until the 1960s, the masculinized system of parks had quite fixed consequences for them. In their words, "the best way to get into the Park Service [was] to marry a ranger."[84] In the year 2000 in Canada, women and racialized groups still faced startling systemic inequalities. In Canada, only 14.8 percent of wardens were women, and just 1.3 percent were people of colour. Clearly, women, and racialized women and men in particular, still battle systemic discrimination.[85] However, the requirements for those who *have* managed to gain employment as Park Rangers are equally worthy of note. Specifically, women tend to be clustered in "soft" employment as park interpreters or "communicators." In Canada and the United States, the Park Service textbook suggests that the ideal qualifications for these jobs are "sparkle," "a sense of humour and perspective," "articulateness," "self-confidence," "warmth," "poise," and the ability to "greet everyone with a smile."[86] As Carolyn Dornsife comments, it is hard not to come to the conclusion that the Park Service considers women – and, I would add, a particular kind of woman – as ideal for these positions.[87] Needless to say, these "qualifications" exist within a representational economy that anticipates their opposite: namely, that a particular kind of man (racially fit and chivalrous?) is ideally suited for ranger positions in wildlife management, law enforcement, and visitor protection.

Research on women's employment in private leisure parks and hotels provides an interesting addendum to these observations. Here employers require women to be "fresh," "attractive," and "caring," and to wear uniforms designed for the tourist gaze. Some informants suggest that, if applicants are considered "too ugly" and/or "too manly," they are simply not offered a job.[88] In addition, women are required to maintain these "correct" forms of appearance in order to stay employed or management will have, in their words, "no choice" but to dismiss them.[89]

Thus, despite the expansion of opportunities for women to work in the wilderness, it seems that the appearance of hetero-femininity – just as *The Park Ranger* blog suggests – remains a key "skill-set" in eligibility for paid employment.[90] Gender, therefore, is inextricably tied up with sex – with distinctly monetary results. What makes the *LNPS* insertion of *lesbian* so incongruous is that the performance makes obvious what can rarely be said: that the "taming of the wilderness" is crucially reliant on the taming of women through techniques that work to fix and stabilize a heteronormative femininity.

I argue that the Lesbian Rangers used their ambiguously "feminine" qualifications to stage and rework gendered norms. Using their "self-confidence" and "sparkle," the Lesbian Rangers inverted the process of "interpreting the wildlife" for very different ends than those intended by the Park Service. For instance, in the section of the *LNPS* brochure entitled: "Answers to Frequently Asked Questions," one reads: *Are some animals particularly dangerous?* The answer:

> Four-legged lesbian herbivores are apt to rut frequently, throughout all four seasons. Be they elk, moose, mountain sheep or goats, lesbians are powerful beasts who are unhappy to be interrupted.

Similarly, under the heading of *FLORA AND FAUNA*, the brochure reads:

> We at Lesbian National Parks and Services like to think of Flora and
> Fauna as two women in a long-term relationship. They've had their ups
> and downs, but really they are most vulnerable to damage by outside
> forces ... So, while you are at the park today take the time to look around,
> and question the heterosexual model. Ask yourself what is "nature." Ask
> yourself what is "natural." And please, be careful not to step on any
> lesbians.

In the first quote, the artists mimic the language of "Wild Kingdom" nature
shows to re-sexualize the supposedly natural, not-sexual lesbian. Appro-
priating the landscape of Banff, the *LNPS* questions the basis upon which
some sexualities are constituted as natural while others are constituted as
deviant. Indeed, from the perspective of the Lesbian Rangers, lesbians do
not simply have a right to exist, they are an important resource. As the artists suggest in their tongue-in-cheek conclusion to the final report:

> Despite the challenges encountered by our first field team, the Rangers
> succeeded in establishing a beachhead in the heterosexual wilderness.
> We feel that the team's approach (exploiting rampant consumerism as a
> model by which to achieve explosive homo growth) will be studied for
> years to come ... [I]t seems possible that within this framework, the
> introduction of homosexual species indigenous to the area might lead to
> expediential multiplication, transforming the gay-wasteland-that-is-
> Banff into a virtual Galapagos of homosexual wildlife.

Here Dempsey and Millan employ a multitude of places and images as the
foil for their puns. Configuring themselves as undercover naturalists they
reverse normative preoccupations with "degeneracy" in order to direct their
critical gaze at *hetero*sexual space. Then they appropriate the military image
of "establishing a beachhead in the wilderness" to reconfigure the very process of shifting sexual subjectivity. Vowing that they will not be outdone by
the "hets" consumer model, the Lesbian Rangers propose fostering "explosive homo growth" while, in the same moment, satirizing the commodification of Banff itself. Indeed, it seems the Lesbian Ranger performance "did
gender" in ways that made use of their "humour" and "sparkle" for purposes
that the Parks Services could never have anticipated.

Throughout all the *LNPS* brochures and reports, Dempsey and Millan
inhabit the booming voice of the ranger as "expert" and use him for their

own ends. Never before, however, have we heard an expert talk about the desirability of achieving "explosive homo growth." The norm is still quite the reverse. Discourses that work to prevent the development of lesbians are still unimaginably common, including not only those related to their invisibility in wilderness parks but also in public schooling, the church, medicine, the military, and most aspects of mass culture. Indeed, unlike many other activists who challenge sexual regulation, Dempsey and Millan do not simply rely on the tactics of assimilation or apologetics regarding the "gay lifestyle." Instead, their provocative and only partly tongue-in-cheek timeline suggests a much more incendiary approach:

Week 1 – needs assessment and general survey of the area
Week 2 – implementation of homosexual agenda
Week 3 – recruitment

Here the artists' use of the phrase "homosexual agenda" references an expression commonly used by fundamentalist Christian organizations like the Eagle Scout Rally for Family Foundation. This group supplies the video *Suffer the Children,* which is specifically aimed at combating the "homosexual agenda."[91] The movie has been widely distributed to conservative educational and religious groups in both the United States and Canada and features lurid accounts of the "deadly" sexual practices said to be endemic to gay male culture. It also includes testimonials from ex-homosexual men claiming they have been "cured." Lesbians, however, seem miraculously not to exist. A key argument in this video, and, indeed, in the Canada-wide lobby against anti-homophobia education in public schooling, is that *information* about lesbian and gay lives constitutes "proselytization."[92] This markedly successful strategy positions homosexuality itself as a contagion.[93] Consequently, Dempsey and Millan use this reference, along with their clearly stated objective of "recruitment," to situate and identify the stakes involved in queer visibility. And this is particularly notable in Banff National Park, in the Province of Alberta, one of the most conservative jurisdictions in the country.[94] Here *LNPS* presents a flagrant challenge to the guardians of "family values." Indeed, the Lesbian Rangers' methods materialize Millan's rhetorical challenge: "Well, why not recruit? The Rangers are the perfect citizen. So why wouldn't you want your child to grow up like us?"[95] This appropriation engages the scare tactics of the family values lobby directly – but with ironic humour. At the same time, the humour is uncompromising: from the brochure's references to the "Invisible Museum of Homosexual Mountain History" to the current directives to "go forth and multiply,"

Dempsey and Millan's performance presents an explicit argument that lesbian lives are not simply tolerable but *desirable.*

The connections between queerness and whiteness come most clearly into view through a closer analysis of the Lesbian National Parks and Services Recruitment Drive, detailed in Field Report No. 56 of the project. Here Dempsey and Millan describe the performance in Central Park, Banff, where they calmly recruited all manner of people, including children, into the Ranger Program (Figure 4.5). The pair provided a wry description:

> Today's recruitment drive was very successful. The colourful "Lesbian National Parks and Services WANTS YOU!" banner and the pink lemonade attracted countless passersby, who were most interested in the Service and how they might become involved. Among our more animated guests was a day camp of thirty thirsty children who were very excited by our Junior Ranger programmes. (On a personal note I must say it is extremely satisfying to have eager young faces look up at our crisply uniformed selves with naked awe and respect.)

Anyone who has ever been involved in anti-heterosexism work in schools, or kept track of provincial responses to human rights work on lesbian, gay, or bisexual issues, particularly in Alberta, cannot fail to be astonished by this. So how *did* they pull it off?

I have argued that Banff is one of the primary sites of Canadian tourism's objectifying gaze. While most tourists remark that they want to "see something a little different," the success of any tourism enterprise rests on ensuring that differences "do not disturb" or, at least, that the spectacle is manageable and predictable for the consumer.[96] Given the relative scarcity of lesbians in popular culture, particularly in 1997, perhaps the simplest explanation for the response to the recruitment table is that many passersby could refuse it as unrecognizable. In other words, in a context in which they would not expect to see any reference to (homo)sexuality, perhaps tourists simply did not – *would not* – process what the term meant.

Alternatively, perhaps tourists *consumed* the spectacle of the Lesbian National Parks and Services Recruitment Table as an incidence of manageable, almost absurd, difference. Certainly, one of the key reasons for this was the *space* in which the recruitment table was located: the wide-open arena of a park. The discursive rules of engagement are far different in parks than, for example, in schools. In a park, one can imagine tourists taking in the spectacle of a recruiting table and banner as just one more, albeit odd, difference. Tourists are, after all, on holiday and differently positioned in

Figure 4.5   Recruitment drive in Central Park, Banff Courtesy of Shawna Dempsey and Lorri Millan, LNPS (1997 and ongoing)

relation to the everyday practices of respectability. While most could just veer in the other direction with no "harm" to the children, others could avail themselves of some lemonade, even chat with the "girls," and then move on. Indeed, if we do not assume an exclusively heteronormative audience, it is possible that some passersby, including the day camp coordinators, may have been "undercover" themselves.

In a park, the Lesbian National Parks and Services Recruitment Table conjures up images of Girl Guides (indeed, senior Girl Guides are actually called "Rangers"). It is exactly this contrast between the way these visual references hail wholesome images of innocence and the project's stated intent – to *recruit* for the Lesbian National Parks and Services – that makes it funny.[97] Importantly, this image of innocence only works for a majority white audience when it is materialized through whiteness, specifically

Dempsey and Millan's white female bodies.[98] Girl Guides, Boy Scouts, Park Rangers, and similar wholesome figures can only be seen as benign, normative symbols if they are racialized as "just people" – something representations of people of colour have never been.

Kobena Mercer argues that white people "colonize the definition of normal" and, in so doing, mask whiteness itself as a category.[99] Similarly, Richard Dyer suggests that white dominance often marks itself in contrast to what it is not and that it is seen as everything and nothing – everywhere but never spoken.[100] In this context, nationalist figures – like Mounties or Park Rangers – are usually imagined as both white and innately benign. Indeed, as Maclear argues, many of us have been semiologically trained – in summer camp, Girl Guides, Boy Scouts, or grade-school trips to parks – to see Park Rangers as "our friends."[101] I argue that this is precisely the contradictory axis upon which the *LNPS* project turns: queer subversions actually *stage* an opportunity to observe the supposedly 'benign' and banal whiteness associated with the image of Park Rangers. For, as I note earlier, there are very specific kinds of displacement that mark the histories of racialized groups in and around the Rockies, and it is only our forgetfulness of these legacies that makes the commodification of Banff thinkable. As Maclear comments:

> Without leaping into the archives, how are Banff initiates to know that the land they walk on [was] part of a Siksika Nation land claim ... that the Rockies served as a physical and symbolic border for Japanese Canadians who [after their internment during the Second World War] were not allowed west of the mountains until the late 1940s ... that the peaks are unmarked graves for Chinese railroad labourers who *died in the thousands?* We turistas are encouraged to be flat broke on thought, dizzy on scenery ... stone[d] on beauty and apathy.[102]

It is precisely our elision of these histories that haunts the visual repertoire informing the present. Indeed, the one visual memorial near Banff that references the Chinese men who worked on the railway was called, for most of the twentieth century, "Chinamen's Peak." Recent protests have forced the Alberta Historical Board to concede that the name is racist and disparages the memory of workers who built the most dangerous sections of the railway.[103] Nevertheless, the decision to rename this one peak among the hundreds of mountains in Banff National Park (most with colonial settler monikers) seems half-hearted at best. Here the story of how this landmark gained its name is telling. Apparently it was "christened" by local residents because a miner of Chinese origin, inspired by a wager, was the first person to ascend it. Rumour has it, however, that this miner was disbelieved upon his return and so had to make a second ascent, this time constructing a cairn that was more visible from Canmore.[104] This local narrative re-remembers a wilderness in which the not-quite-virile-enough non-white Canadian *does not belong* and *cannot be believed.* At the same time, the "real men" (we know these are white men) who first told this story would, if they scaled a nearby peak, have been believed the first time.[105]

I argue that, if the artists associated with the *LNPS* project had not been white women, their performance would have been received with less equanimity – perhaps as threatening, perverse, or inscrutable, it's hard to say. But whatever the effect, racialized artists would not have been able to draw on a "benign" visual repertoire of Park Rangers in anything like the same manner. Thus, I suggest that the Lesbian Rangers' whiteness and gender were both crucial to the project. Indeed, it was precisely the juxtaposition of references that hailed banal and wholesome images of innocence with the project's intent to recruit for the Lesbian National Parks and Services that, for many audiences, made the *LNPS* both surprising and funny.

Re-Envisioning Resistance

> I keep waiting for the artists to get out there to help decode the things that I don't see.
>
> – Joel Garreau[106]

I argue that the Lesbian Rangers' performance enacted an examination of gender, sex, and authority in the space of the great outdoors. But their performance also relied on earlier incarnations, starting a hundred years prior to Dempsey and Millan's visit. For it was the early Euro-Canadian mountain men who first established the Park Ranger as an emblem of manliness and racial fortitude. Yet, in their role as guardians of the wild, they were also preceded by the English forest officers who imposed private emparked areas and royal chases, protecting them against rural peasants characterized as a wild and undisciplined race. This chapter attempts to unpack these complicated legacies and to explore how ideas about whiteness, masculinity, and benevolence are rearticulated in Burns' history of the warden service, in *The Park Ranger* blogs, and in lesbian performance art. In each of these historical and contemporary examples, wilderness discourse relies on seemingly benign forms of gender performance to reproduce a host of exclusions while normalizing particular representations of place.[107] All of this analysis suggests new possibilities that emerge when observers tour the wilderness while being more attentive to the necessary tensions that fuel its contradictory meanings. For it is in places like Banff National Park that whiteness works "best" as everything and nothing, hypervisible but never spoken, and so reinscribes a Canadian ideal.

5

Playing Indian
Indigenous Responses to "Indianness"

I have traced how three foundational images – the beaver, the Canadian Pacific Railway, and Banff National Park – have materialized the "regime of the open secret" in ways that both reflect and produce discourses of white national belonging. A central thread in this analysis is Canadians' parasitic relationship to Indigenous peoples. Indeed, I have explored how our benign national imaginary is centrally reliant on a flight from history, so that nationalist images serve as a nostalgic return to the past where a denied history of Indigenous erasure and spectacularization reasserts itself. In this chapter, I suggest how these ghostly "Indians," who are both acknowledged and refused, also impinge on the present, or move from one "present" to another, and, in so doing, are paradigmatic of the forms of banal possession that make white Canadian identity itself ghostly. How then to engage with these forms of haunting – which continue to possess the living – in ways that enlarge our cultural memory and lead to a different kind of remembering?

I take up this task by exploring three Indigenous responses to the phantoms of Indianness. I start with a Canadian Anishinaabek community's engagement with a classic narrative of the noble Indian: Henry Wadsworth Longfellow's poem *Song of Hiawatha* (1855). Longfellow's epic is generally viewed as an assimilationist narrative that justifies white conquest, yet, from 1900 to 1968, Garden River First Nation, adjacent to Sault Ste. Marie in northern Ontario, worked with local entrepreneurs to stage a hugely successful theatrical run of the play. This Indian *Hiawatha* became an international sensation and was performed for thousands of people in tours to major cities in Canada, the United States, Europe, and England. Based on interviews with surviving members of the cast and with Garden River First Nation elders, I examine how this community appropriated Longfellow's epic for its own purposes, and I explore the contradictory meanings the play had for performers, community members, and those who witnessed the performance.

Next I focus on the work of two contemporary urban Indigenous artists who use a hybrid set of strategies to play with and against legacies of Indianness. I begin with Iroquois photographer Jeffrey Thomas, whose humorous juxtapositions of subjects, ranging from contemporary Harlequin romance novels to iconic Indian monuments, suggest the ways that Indianness is both integral to and estranged from popular and historical memory. The Cree/Irish/English painter Kent Monkman provides another perspective on "Indian play," with a sometimes lyrical and at other times bawdy investigation into the relationship between Eros, religion, and European conquest. Both Monkman and Thomas depict Indians who play against type, often in humorous vignettes that reinterpret the dramatic thrust of narratives of nation making. Employing mimicry, irony, and visual spectacle, these artists *intensify* the specifically erotic representations of Indianness in ways that ask viewers to consider how Euro-Canadian nostalgia and desire in relation to Indian play continue into the present moment.

Reimagining the Noble Indian

Henry Longfellow's *Song of Hiawatha* was the most popular poem of the nineteenth century and was required reading in North American public schools throughout most of the twentieth.[1] Published in 1855, it tells the story of the miraculous birth of an Anishinaabe prophet, his childhood adventures and marriage to Minnehaha, his loyal friendships and great acts of endurance, and the devastation caused by disease and famine. By the end of the narrative, Hiawatha foretells the arrival of the strangers "with white faces," offers protection to the "Black robes," and symbolically dies by withdrawing from his community into the west. Imposing a Christian framework on the Anishinaabe oral legends, the poem presents an account of gentle heroism and doomed retreat from a world on the verge of the cataclysmic changes of colonial rule.

When it was first published in 1855, *Hiawatha* was popular both on the page and in theatrical performance. Then, in the early twentieth century, a host of Indigenous pageants revitalized the epic as a "pan-Indian fusion event" for a new century.[2] Perhaps the most well known Canadian group to stage *Hiawatha* was the Garden River First Nation in northern Ontario. Its pageant ran intermittently from 1900 until 1968 and enjoyed hugely successful world tours, visiting Chicago, Buffalo, Cleveland, New York, Boston, France, Holland, Belgium, and London.[3] In the early 1900s, the performance was staged east of the Garden River Reserve at Kensington Point, and, in 1937, the *Sault Daily Star* boasted that the troupe had been invited to per-

Figure 5.1   Cast of *Hiawatha* at Toronto Exhibition, 1937 Photographer unknown; image courtesy of Clarence Boyer, Batchewana First Nation (2006)

form *Hiawatha* for a two-week run at the Toronto Exhibition, which had grandstand seating for twenty-thousand (Figure 5.1).[4] While Garden River First Nation is now rather removed from what are thought to be the centres of metropolitan culture, in the mid-1800s some members of this community were well acquainted with the rigours of international travel and inter-cultural performance. As early as 1843, Chief Shingwaukonse and several other members of Garden River First Nation travelled to England with local entrepreneur Colonel Arthur Rankin, who formed a brief partnership with the American artist George Catlin. There the Anishinaabe met with Queen Victoria, and later the group performed for several months in Catlin's "Indian Gallery" at Egyptian Hall.[5] Further, in 1872, Chief Buhkwujjenene undertook a series of lectures and speeches in England to raise funds for a school.[6] But these leaps into the international spotlight were not without their own history. For the location of the Garden River First Nation, at the junction of Lake Huron and Lake Superior, was a site of considerable strategic importance both prior to and during the fur trade, with the North West Company establishing a post there in 1783. Consequently, the people in this region had long acted as intercultural brokers in the economic, social, and religious trade between different Indigenous groups and, later, with Euro-Canadian settlers. But before we can examine the Garden River First Nation's appropriation of *Hiawatha*, more needs to be known about the origins of the poem itself.

Longfellow drew from two major sources in his development of *Hiawatha:* (1) the Finnish epic *Kalevala* for the poem's aesthetic form and (2) the writing of ethnologist Henry Rowe Schoolcraft for a record of Anishinaabek mythology.[7] As Michael McNally notes, Schoolcraft's ethnography must be viewed in the context of his work as an American Indian agent as, in Odawa and Ojibwe circles, he "is notorious for having orchestrated the dispossession of their Michigan lands."[8] Schoolcraft believed that the removal of Indians from Michigan was "best for Indigenous people and settlers alike," and thus persuaded the Anishinaabe leaders that they had no alterative but to sign the Treaty of Washington, which, when ratified by the Senate, limited the protection of reservations to five years.[9] Schoolcraft married Jane Johnston, an accomplished Anishinaabek woman, and from her and her family learned the Ojibwe language and oral histories.[10] Longfellow's central protagonist, "Hiawatha," is actually an amalgam of the Anishinaabe trickster figure Nanabozho and the famous Iroquoian leader Hiawatha. The historical Hiawatha was a widely recognized figure in the nineteenth century and was credited with negotiating peace between the disparate groups in the Iroquoian confederacy.[11] In contrast, the Anishinaabe oral legends are mythological accounts of Nanabozho (variously Manabozho or Nanabush), which show him as a sensual and lewd trickster.

The original poem that Longfellow submitted to his publishers was entitled *Manabozho,* but the publishers decided to rename it *Song of Hiawatha* after the better-known Iroquois prophet. Thus, in Longfellow's epic poem the central character Nanabozho, now known as Hiawatha, was transformed from a trickster into a tragic hero. The poet worked with both the Iroquoian and Anishinaabek sources in ways that significantly shifted the meaning of the original narratives. In his version of the story, peace between the disparate Indigenous communities arrives not through the highly skilful diplomacy of a historic leader but, rather, through a benevolent act of Gitche Manito, the Great Spirit. In addition, the fictional character of Nanabozho is cleansed of his sensual and disreputable characteristics, which are transferred to the characters of Hiawatha's loyal friends. Longfellow made two other major additions for the sake of the non-Indigenous audience: (1) a romantic storyline between Hiawatha and Minnehaha and (2) Hiawatha's welcome of the Jesuit priests and departure into the west. These examples illustrate a general trend. Longfellow consistently altered his material in ways that Christianized the original stories, dehistoricized the narrative, and, through excessive idealization, tended to dehumanize the Indigenous characters.[12] Thus, the *Cambridge History of American Literature* sums up what has been the dominant interpretation of *Hiawatha* in the past two decades of scholarship:

> By ... yoking Native American mysticism to the principles of Christianity, Longfellow creates a god-hero whose exploits belong to legend but whose purpose is to sanctify the rise of a Western, Christian, agricultural empire ... The sensual, earthy elements of the legendary materials are made genteel for Longfellow's audience; and Hiawatha appears not as the devious trickster figure of the Nanabozho legend, but as a classical hero who bestows order upon his nation and prepares the way for the Euro-American arrival ... Hiawatha's message ameliorates white conquest, and in his death and disappearance he, like the Indians of America, is symbolically absorbed by the West – the Christian eternity, the temporary home of removed Indians, and the ultimate goal of Euro-American manifest destiny.[13]

Quite unlike this narrative, the Anishinaabe legends found in Schoolcraft's work often point symbolically to the disastrous results of white conquest. In one, Nanabozho is described as a trickster/warrior who is living in the ice of the Arctic Ocean. The Anishinaabe narrator tells us: "We fear the white race will someday discover his retreat and drive him off. Then the end of the world is at hand, for as soon as he puts his foot on the earth again, it will take fire, and every living creature will perish in the flames." Similar to other stories of this period, this narrative appears to displace onto white settlers the annihilation suffered by First Nations peoples as a result of European settlement.[14]

If we return, then, to the Garden River First Nation's performance of *Hiawatha*, an obvious paradox presents itself. Given the conflict between the Anishinaabe mythology and Longfellow's poem, how did this community reappropriate a narrative that, in substantive ways, conflicted with its traditions? Certainly, critics like Dean MacCannel view the kind of "ethnic tourism" that these performances exemplified as largely exploitative of those who participated.[15] And within the field of art history many scholars view commodified forms of performance as illustrative of a problematic *in*-authenticity.[16] Informed by my interviews with elders and surviving cast members of the Hiawatha play in Garden River, along with the recent work of American scholars such as Philip Deloria and Michael D. McNally as well as Canadian historian Karl Hele, I argue that the Anishinaabe appropriation of Longfellow's text to validate their cultural difference was both clever and accommodating. For the Anishinaabe actors in *Hiawatha* had their own objectives in engaging with the popular epic, and contemporary analysis must contextualize this performance within a historical milieu in which "resistance" was often misread.

Appropriating an Epic

In the late 1890s, when members of Garden River First Nation first began to consider performing Longfellow's poem *Hiawatha*, at least some people in the community were already well aware of the epic. One of the Anishinaabek leaders during this period, George Kabaosa, noted that he had been taught the poem in Sunday School during his youth.[17] Further, contemporary interviews with Garden River First Nation elders indicate that their ancestors were informants for Henry Schoolcraft and that some community leaders were aware that Longfellow drew his stories from Anishinaabek oral traditions.[18] The initiative for starting the pageant emerged through collaboration between the colonization agent for the Canadian Pacific Railway, Louis Oliver Armstrong, and the people of Garden River, who each had compelling, though different, interests in promoting tourism along the new line running to the Sault. In 1899, Kabaosa and his nephew Wahbunosa visited the Sportsman's Show in Boston, both to perform in the exhibition and to visit Alice Longfellow, the poet's daughter.[19] Their mission was to invite her to visit the region and the peoples from which Longfellow had drawn his inspiration in writing the epic poem. The *Sault Daily Star* highlighted the story, noting that Kabaosa was a "fine figure of a man with a great gift for oratory" and that Alice Longfellow accepted the invitation. In 1900, she, and two of her sisters, came to Kensington Point, where members of the Garden River First Nation presented *Hiawatha* in a spectacular location along the river.[20]

No doubt Alice Longfellow's admiring review of this performance, along with the promotional efforts by Armstrong and, later, the *Sault Daily Star*, was crucial in ensuring the pageant moved from the relatively limited exposure available in northern Ontario to national and international venues. However, this publicity would have had no foundation without the skills of Garden River First Nation members and their ongoing commitment to international performance. And, while the motivations for local entrepreneurs may be relatively obvious, the incentives for members of the Garden River First Nation are more complex. Certainly, economic stimulus was one powerful factor, for the Robinson-Huron Treaty of 1850 had ensured the Garden River First Nation had few rights in the development of the mineral and timber reserves on their land, and the conditions for farming were not ideal.[21] Consequently, many community members needed to supplement their income through other means. In this context, one of the options for participation in the cash economy was the sale of souvenir items to the local tourist market as well as in Sault Michigan and other venues. Indeed, for many Indigenous groups, this trade offered a welcome opportunity for travel as well as the chance to resist official pressure to adopt an exclusive and settled agricultural lifestyle.[22] Thus, the Hiawatha pageant presented an opportunity to participate in a potentially lucrative tourist economy.[23]

The rationale for the Hiawatha play, however, went well beyond the revenue that would accrue to the community. Both members of the contemporary Garden River First Nation and articles published in the early 1900s suggest that the pageant was seen as a vehicle for preserving and presenting Anishinaabek cultural heritage. Language would have been an important aspect of this project of cultural preservation. The actors performed *Hiawatha* in Ojibwe, while a narrator read appropriate sections from Longfellow's poem in English. The significance of Ojibwe as the language of performance is particularly important when one realizes that the local idiom was discouraged by the Canadian state and usually forbidden in the local residential school.[24] Thus, the play both preserved a space for the public use of an Indigenous vernacular and legitimated its currency in the circuits of international performance. Equally important, the Anishinaabek actors were not passive participants in performing Longfellow's epic but actually controlled aspects of the performance.[25] Thus, the Garden River pageant included Anishinaabek legends, songs, and dances that were presented in a tableau, along with sections of Longfellow's narrative that were read in English by Armstrong. This structure of a "play within a play" separated the Anishinaabek actors' performance from the English narration and was further emphasized by the physical production, which was staged on a floating platform in Lake Huron set a small distance from the shore.[26] Thus, the audience would sit on the shore to watch the actors perform various tableaux on their island stage, and speak their lines in Ojibwe, while the narrator, located on the shore, would read sections of Longfellow's narrative in English.

Given this design, it is not surprising that it is the more performative elements of the play, rather than the English narration of Longfellow's epic, that stand out in the memory of Garden River First Nation elders when they recall the pageant. For example, Betty Grawbarger, whose uncle, John Erskine Pine, performed as Hiawatha in the 1930s, spoke of the importance of ritual dance in the pageant.[27] One of her central recollections involved the use of revered objects like Chief Shingwaukonse's war club. She notes: "My uncle John, he used Shingwaukonse's war club in the dance ... That was really quite meaningful to the people ... they all waited for that scene."[28] Observers of the 1901 performance also note that Rebecca Kabaosa, who played the part of Minnehaha, wore many richly worked garments, including a two-hundred-year-old wampum, a valuable heirloom of the community.[29] Given the prohibitions against the use of ceremonial dance in the Canadian Indian Act, and its rules against wearing traditional clothing and engaging in ritual performance, it is not surprising that the Hiawatha pageant became one of the few public arenas in which people could memorialize these practices. Thus, when performers used sacred objects, like the war club or the wampum, they brought the legacy of an honoured community leader and respected community objects into the context of intercultural performance. Similarly, the role of the drum was also crucial. Indeed, Grawbarger suggests that the subtle shifts in tone characteristic of drumming in the Hiawatha pageant may have been closer to Anishinaabek traditions than drum performance in contemporary Powwows. She notes: "That drum talks to people, the people that really know it. I would never understand that. But people back then, the old people, they knew that. So if there was a change in the drum beat, they just knew what they should be doing."[30] Jean Pine, who performed as Minnehaha in the 1937 Hiawatha pageant, noted that, in addition to drumming, the production also emphasized the traditions of communal participation in performance. Indeed, as McNally's analysis of similar performances in Michigan indicates, it seems that, in Garden River, the pageants became a vehicle for sustaining and preserving a repertoire of song and dance that was deeply connected to Ojibwe identity. Pine also described the preparations for the pageant in the 1930s, highlighting how community elder Albert Williams taught them the proper techniques for dancing on land cleared especially for this purpose.[31] This collective effort was strongly aligned with Anishinaabek tradition, in contrast to what she described as the contemporary Powwows' emphasis on more individualized "money and competition."[32] Thus, these interviews suggest that, for the elders and actors

Figure 5.2   Portrait of Jean Pine
as Minnehaha, 1937 Photographer
unknown; image courtesy of Clarence
Boyer, Batchewana First Nation (2006)

who participated in *Hiawatha* in the late 1930s, the pageant provided a performative space for rituals in music, storytelling, and dance – activities that were officially discouraged or forbidden in most other public contexts.

The elders' memories of *Hiawatha*, however, did not simply relate to its importance in memorializing aspects of their culture. For many in the casts that toured internationally, these expeditions were also a rare and exhilarating opportunity for travel. Jean Pine's mother performed as Minnehaha in the early 1900s, and she (Jean) took up the same role in 1937 (Figure 5.2). Pine noted that her mother enjoyed going "to England and touring all over the States," while her own performance before thousands in Toronto was "very exciting," providing, as it did, an opportunity for train trips, restaurant food, and meeting a host of new people.[33] While performers had an opportunity to make brief excursions into the city and sample the rides at the exhibition, they were also required to be "on display" for more than the evening show. Indeed, Pine's recollections include a demanding regimen of posing for pictures and talking with tourists in a kind of informal "Indian gallery" during the day, while *Hiawatha* performances were held in the evening. In one interview with Jean Pine, along with relatives Alice Corbiere and Joe Corbiere, the memory of this daytime display generated an ambivalent response. While Pine remembered how draining it was to "smile all the time," especially as "people wanted pictures even at lunch!" – the memory was also a source of considerable amusement. Indeed, Joe Corbiere joked that, given Pine's beauty, she could well be remembered as a kind of "Paris Hilton of an earlier age, as her picture might be all over the world ... in family albums and on postcards, people would have asked themselves 'who was that beauty from Garden River?'"

While Pine's image might conjure up ideas of a rather delicate "Indian princess," her stories from behind the scenes suggest quite the opposite. Over the course of three interviews, Pine frequently remarked that, when she and her friends toured the exhibition grounds after their nightly pageant, they sometimes had to endure degrading comments from local youth. But it was only in my last interview with her, conducted in August 2008, just a month before she died, that her response to that harassment became clearer. When asked if she sometimes had to deal with "propositions" from local youth, Jean Pine, Joe Corbiere, and I had the following exchange:

Pine: Just in the evenings, we took turns, Rose Nolan and I,
           beating kids up.
Corbiere: What!
Pine: Beating kids up!
Corbiere: Now you're blaming it on Rose!
Pine: Those kids would see us walking to the Hiawatha play and
           make war whoops. So Rose would say "Be quiet!" and then, if
           they didn't, she'd turn around and grab those kids and nail
           them to the ground.
Francis: She didn't put up with anything.
Pine: No!

While no shrinking violet in confronting these catcalls, Pine also provided what seemed to be a shared critique of the exhibition managers, who offered the Hiawatha troupe accommodation in tents on the exhibition grounds with no access to hot water. This, she noted, was in stark contrast to the lodgings offered other stage performers. Pine recounted that one of the actors on her tour was so infuriated at the lack of appropriate facilities that he said he should be introduced as "Chief DirtyNeck from TheNeverWashTribe."

Pine's commentary about the conditions that shaped the public tour of the Hiawatha pageant demonstrates a no-nonsense pragmatism and an ironic sense of humour. These performers knew that the Hiawatha play could never be an "authentic" demonstration of Anishinaabek culture. Indeed, in my interviews, surviving cast members and elders showed no interest in the play serving as a vehicle for supposedly "pure" stories. While some postcolonial critics point out that, despite input from the performers, the pageant retained its Christian influences, Garden River First Nation elders did not interpret this hybridity negatively. Early in my interview with Betty Grawbarger, she noted that Chief Shingwaukonse (her great-grandfather) had converted to Christianity in 1830 but had nevertheless kept his medicine bag and continued to participate in the Midewiwin Society.[34] Thus, she argued that the revered chief had set an example of being affiliated with a church while *at the same time* continuing to practise older spiritual traditions. It seems likely that many of the performers in *Hiawatha* also held dual affiliations. In this context, one might speculate that one advantage of staging *Hiawatha* in Ojibwe is that it facilitated a performative double-coding, whereby the Anishinaabe actors could reference spiritual and cultural traditions embedded in the Ojibwe language and style of the show. Thus, the staging of *Hiawatha* would have allowed the predominantly white and English-speaking audience to listen to narrations of Longfellow's poem while watching an "authentic" performance. At the same time, the actors – performing in Ojibwe and at a distance – were able to gain an audience for the aspects of their culture they were willing to present in public while also keeping any underlying meanings associated with their own cultural and spiritual knowledge to themselves.[35]

Observed from another angle, then, the Euro-Christian influence on the legends retold in the Hiawatha pageant may have had consequences that can only be understood if *Hiawatha* is viewed in the context of the performance options available to Indigenous peoples in the early twentieth century. As the contemporary Anishinaabek curator Clarence Boyer comments, "Many people in that period didn't believe Indigenous people had any culture to share, other than performing in the rodeo or with Buffalo Bill Cody."[36] One advantage of presenting the Anishinaabe cultural heritage in Longfellow's poetic garb was that it allowed the performers to appropriate an "empowered" author whose text positively affirmed the Anishinaabe's cultural difference, while the actual style and language of performance facilitated layers of meaning other than those included in Longfellow's original text. And these meanings would *only* have been available to other Ojibwe speakers in the audience.

Boyer's comments also highlight the gendered subtext shaping *Hiawatha*. In a context where Wild West and rodeo shows were the chief venue for the public performance of Indianness, they often reproduced Indians with a distinctly "savage" flare. In Longfellow's play, however, the figure of Hiawatha suggests quite a different kind of manliness – one that has significantly more cultural capital than can be found in the Indians featured on the Wild West circuit. Indeed, Hiawatha personifies a gentle and compassionate leader – an Indian Messiah. While the narrative suggests that this Messiah figure still took it for granted that he controlled women and the natural world (quite unlike the gender roles in precolonial Anishinaabe society),[37] in a Euro-North American context, his character enlarged the borders of a performative Indian masculinity in ways that were, for the time, rare. For women, *Hiawatha* includes only the most conventional roles: the "Indian princess" figure of Hiawatha's bride, Minnehaha, and the Grandmother who raises Hiawatha as a child, Nokimas. But these parts did ensure that there were significant roles for women in the cast, and, judging by archival photographs of early performances, a considerable number of female actors were able to travel with the pageant.[38]

While many of the Indigenous performances of *Hiawatha* in the United States were mounted by teachers and students in "Indian schools" as part of an attempt to raise money for those institutions, the production organized by the Garden River First Nation was a distinctly different phenomenon.[39] Here Anishinaabek people, working closely with local entrepreneurs, initiated a performance that quickly became an international sensation. I have highlighted the ways that the people of the Garden River First Nation intervened in the production through negotiating which parts of Longfellow's poem they would and would not perform while also establishing the choreography of ritual dance and song. Further, the language and staging of the performance allowed for a double coding of the cultural traditions presented onstage in ways that allowed *Hiawatha* to serve as a vehicle for preserving and presenting Anishinaabek cultural heritage. At the same time, the Garden River First Nation's appropriation of the poem also ensured that the community gained some benefit from an empowered author who had employed its cultural traditions to craft his narrative. While all of these elements underpin the Anishinaabe participation in *Hiawatha*, one other rationale emerged from the interviews with Garden River First Nation elders. This motive had less to do with the pageant itself, and it directed my attention instead to the everyday life of those on the reserve and those who had attended Shingwauk Residential School during the early decades of the twentieth century. While my questions did not raise the issue, interviewees interrupted my queries to speak of the ways in which the Hiawatha pageant operated within a broader context, one in which they had been denied a myriad of other opportunities through the betrayals in the treaty-making process. In particular, they spoke about Chief Shingwaukonse, whose savvy political leadership was, and is, well remembered in that community. If we return to that chief's own words about relations with Euro-Canadian settlers – which can be found, for example, in an 1849 letter to the governor of Montreal – we find an eloquent and bitter critic of imperial expansion. He noted how the white settlers had "swept away all our pleasant land ... [and told us] 'willing or unwilling, you must now go ... I want this land to make rich my white children.'" His reply to these actions was succinct: "We are men like you, we have the limbs of men, we have the hearts of men, and we feel and know that all this country is ours, even the weakest ... animals of the forest when hunted to extremity, though they feel destruction sure, will turn upon the hunter."[40] These interviewees also made a point of describing how their grandparents and cousins had suffered in the Shingwauk Residential School, where children faced compulsory attendance enforced by the RCMP, severe corporal punishment if they attempted to run away, the frequent death from tuberculosis, and, for some, physical and sexual abuse.[41] When these conditions are put together with the efforts of the school and the Indian Act to purge the Anishinaabek language and culture, then the Hiawatha pageant would have to be seen, by contrast, as a remarkable respite from the brutal rigours of colonial exclusion. Indeed, as Lana Grawbarger remarked, the Hiawatha pageant "would have been idyllic" compared to the other options available to community members for sustaining their cultural and economic survival.[42]

Despite the Anishinaabeks' intentions, however, scholars like Alan Trachtenberg – who reviewed press responses to *Hiawatha* – suggest that audiences simply saw the play as providing a comfortably bloodless version of imperial memory.[43] Trachtenberg reviews newspaper accounts that suggest a familiar typology: the characters portrayed in *Hiawatha* are the "good Indians," who are not to be confused with "poor degenerate Indians" or the "hapless creatures as creep about the stations and reserves in the west."[44] In these readings, the proof of Hiawatha's nobility can be found in his "knowing and foretelling the fading out of his race."[45] But not all reviews follow this simple trajectory. Indeed, my reading of William Edgar's article "Hiawatha as the Anishinaabes Interpret It" (1904), and Frank Yeigh's "The Drama of Hiawatha, or Mana-Bozho" in the *Canadian Magazine* (1901), suggests a more contradictory story. Edgar's article makes a point of emphasizing the influence members of the Garden River First Nation had in shaping the script and production, noting: "The Indians give their own interpretation of the Hiawatha legend, and they certainly go about it in a serious and conscientious way."[46] But most interesting is each author's description of the ending of the play, as this is the section of Longfellow's narrative that has most disturbed postcolonial critics. While most commentators view Hiawatha's death and disappearance into the west as a symbolic amelioration of Euro-North-American manifest destiny, these two early reporters register a more complicated response. In the *Canadian Magazine* (1901), Frank Yeigh describes the ending of the play as follows:

> Every auditor was breathless as, with long strides, Hiawatha passed down the sloping bank to the water's edge where floated his wonderful canoe ... Standing erect in the graceful craft ... the stalwart form faded away, in a literal sunset glow, his comrades on the shore responded in weird chants that strangely affected every listener. Fainter and fainter grew the song from the solitary occupant of the receding boat, wider and wider grew the gulf between. Even the waves upon the margin sobbed, "Farewell, O Hiawatha!"[47]

Edgar is equally effusive in his narration of the 1904 performance:

> The play closes with a most effective and beautiful scene – the passing of the Anishinaabey messiah – a picture that will remain long in the memory of the spectator and haunt him with its fascinating melancholy. When Hiawatha steps into his birch bark canoe and begins his death chant, the sun has declined until its rays make a glittering pathway leading to the islands of the west. As he moves from the shore ... the wailing voices of the warriors and squaws take up the refrain. The departing chief stands erect, with his face towards the setting sun ... His boat moves rapidly westward, the tribe and the chief chanting antiphonally. The scene is inexpressibly sad and beautiful beyond words.[48]

How, then, to understand these responses to the epic? Early sections of the reviews suggest these critics were comforted by the manifest *rightness* of Hiawatha's passing – after all, this portion of the play signalled the legitimacy of their very presence. But their narration also implies that the ending was unsettling. Clearly, the actors brought remarkable resonance to their performance. So what might this ending have meant for them? Perhaps Hiawatha's symbolic death and departure into the west allowed the performers to memorialize losses that continued to cut deep into that community and landscape,[49] for the play did memorialize a precolonial period that both the actors and audience knew would not come again. Indeed, the final scene allowed actors to materialize their links with those absent by giving them symbolic voice and name. But, if the passing of Hiawatha memorialized, at least in part, the ending of a way of life overtaken by the brutal realities of colonization, then I suggest that these actors also used the narrative for another purpose: to symbolically enter the culture of modernity, at least partially, on their own terms. For the play allowed them to engage a project of cultural translation through which they made use of Longfellow's poem for their own ends. Thus, I argue that the Garden River First Nation's cultural reinvention of the Hiawatha pageant did, in part, destabilize Indigenous stereotypes through the expressive and disturbing force of the actors' performance, for, through this play, the audience was a witness to the consequences of a colonial legacy. The question was: how would they respond? Most probably romanticized the ending, with a classic expression of what Renato Rosaldo calls "imperialist nostalgia": absorbing the pathos and cathartic release of the final scenes while avoiding the idea that they might be implicated in its catastrophic meaning.[50] But others may have sensed that this performance also implied a necessary haunting. For at least some must have known that those who "departed to the west" would surely return.

Primitivization and Performance

Despite the acclaim that accrued to the Garden River First Nation for its staging of the Hiawatha pageant, the legacy of this theatrical tradition seems to have produced an ambivalent response among some early members of the cast. For example, one of the contemporary elders whom I interviewed about the Hiawatha legacy, Angela Neveau, noted that her grandfather performed in *Hiawatha* in the 1930s but never spoke of it to members of his family. In fact, she discovered his affiliation with the play only recently, when she saw his picture in a photograph of the cast members at the museum in Sault Ste. Marie. In our interview she reflected on the context for Indigenous performance when she was growing up: "Being Indigenous wasn't 'in' at the time. In the 1950s, '60s and '70s, Indigenousness wasn't the thing to be. I think it only started to become 'cool' in the 1980s. It is more open now. Although there still is prejudice; in our city here it is really alive."[51]

While the contemporary context for Indigenous performance is, indeed, different from that faced by early actors in the Hiawatha pageant, the two artists whose work I discuss in the second section of this chapter also use tactics of appropriation as a central tool to reconfigure stereotypical images of Indianness. And, as more direct narrators of their own story, their forms of artistic poaching represent a different set of visual and discursive strategies than those found in earlier appropriations. I begin with Iroquoian artist Jeff Thomas, whose photographic work has been shown in England, Europe, and North America and whose practice also includes major projects of archival research and curation for Library and Archives Canada and the Museum of Civilization.

Much of Thomas's work focuses on what he calls the "monumental landscape" documenting his response to representations of Indianness found in national statuary and commercial buildings throughout North America. However, in a 2004 show at Gallery 44 in Toronto, Thomas also set aside a separate alcove in the gallery to highlight a more personal set of images: his ongoing chronicle of photographs of his son Bear. He began this section with a photograph of Hayter Reed, the Canadian deputy superintendent-general of Indian affairs from 1893 to 1897 (Figure 5.3). Reed had a crucial role in the history of Indian residential schools and, thus, in the legacy of state intervention in relation to Indigenous children. The photograph Thomas has chosen shows him at the Governor General's Historical Fancy Dress Ball in Ottawa in 1896, dressed as the Iroquoian chief Donnacona. It was Donnacona who first greeted Jacques Cartier on his voyage down the St. Lawrence River in 1534 and whose village, Kanata, became Canada's namesake. Reed made his mark by lobbying for at least two crucial amendments to the Indian Act. In 1894, the act was changed to ensure that all Indigenous children were compelled to attend school, usually residential school, and those parents who refused to give up their children were fined or imprisoned. And, in 1895, another amendment enshrined the active suppression of ceremony and religious practices.[52] By the late 1800s, it was already common for white people to "play Indian," so Reed's own performance of Indianness at the Governor General's Ball in Ottawa in 1896 should not surprise us. But what is striking is the *juxtaposition* of Reed's Indian performance with his determined attempt to separate Indigenous peoples from their own cultures. For it was Reed's intervention to ensure compulsory

Figure 5.3   Haytor Reed dressed as the Iroquoian Chief Donnacona with his stepson Jack Lowery at Governor General's Historical Fancy Dress Ball in Ottawa in 1896   Photograph by W.J. Topley, Library and Archives Canada, PA-139841

residential schools and to criminalize religious and ceremonial practices that made it illegal for Indigenous peoples to maintain their cultural heritage themselves. Indeed, these were the regulations against which the Garden River First Nation's performance of *Hiawatha* must be viewed.

Thomas's response to Reed's legacy comes with a series of images of his son Bear with a host of contemporary and historical artefacts: T-shirts of the five-hundredth anniversary of Christopher Columbus's arrival, urban graffiti about "cultural revolution," and one-way signs in front of the Parliament Buildings. Each constitutes a visual invitation to consider how certain markings of racialized identity cannot be separated from the historical images that ghost them. In the photo entitled *Bear with Indian Scout* (Figure 5.4), we see Bear with a "full-blooded Indian" T-shirt defiantly posed at the Champlain Monument in Ottawa, his arm casually flung across the scout's knee, signifying his identification with the Huron Wendat statue. At the same time, his stance as an Indigenous rapper reconfigures stereotypic imaginings about the stoic and silent Indian. While Bear embodies the impulse to herald identity as performative, the photograph suggests that the urbane rapper is still inextricably bound up with these earlier representations. At the same time, Bear's in-your-face stance presents a hybrid culture that is defiantly and irreverently reinscribing itself.[53]

In an installation entitled *What's the Point?* Thomas works with the next incarnation of the Indian Scout statue originally located at the foot of the Champlain Monument in Ottawa. In 1996, the Scout was the focus of a protest by the Assembly of First Nations (AFN), which objected to the statue's subservient position in relation to Champlain. After extended public debate, the Indian monument was moved to a garden of indigenous flowers in Major's Hill Park across from Parliament Hill. However, despite the AFN's hopes that the Scout's new location could rehabilitate the statue, this new site represents equally problematic views of the "Indian." For, in this new site, not only are Indigenous people equated with the "natural" flora and fauna of the landscape, but the National Capital Commission also declined to include any marker that might trace the Scout's historical relation to the Champlain monument. This elision effects an erasure of its own: a *vanishment* of the imperial history that was the origin of the problem in the first place.

While Thomas's exhibit responded to the visual problematics signified by the Indian Scout, it also suggested a mode of viewing public art that did not require, as did the AFN, that the Scout be censored or relocated. I examine Thomas's photographic work precisely because his images attempt to

Figure 5.4   *FBI, Bear with Indian Scout.* Bear Thomas, son of photographer Jeff Thomas, wearing a "Full-Blooded Indian" (FBI) t-shirt, with arm around Indian Scout statue when it was originally located at the base of the Champlain monument   Photograph by Jeff Thomas

reconfigure, rather than to censor or relocate, monuments that echo historical inequities. In *What's the Point?* Thomas re-presents the Scout through five photographs that provide a 360-degree view of his chiselled shoulders, bulging biceps, rippling chest muscles, and revealing loincloth. The sculpture's well-muscled form is consistent with historic images of the noble savage, an impression that is reinforced through Thomas's juxtaposition of these images with pictures and text from Harlequin romance novels. In Plate 6, we see a composite image of one of the photographs juxtaposed with a Harlequin book cover.[54] Between the photo and the book, Thomas inserted a line of text taken from the Harlequin novel that accentuates the erotics in both the story and the photographic images.

This threefold composition highlights how both historic statues and popular culture images of the Indian present a *primitivized* masculinity. And in both Thomas's photographs and the novel's pictures and text, it is the eroticized elements of Indianness that are particularly available for the viewer's attention. For instance, under an image of the Scout's magnificent chest we read: "Her eyes focused on each portion of his copper body that shone back at her in the moonlight. His bare bronze chest swollen with pride." In another excerpt the text informs us that "his breechcloth lifted from his long muscled legs in the gentle breeze." And the series continues: "He was a man of thick muscle, broad shoulders, and a chiselled face of nobility and intelligence," but "it was his eyes that mesmerized her most. They were dark and deep like midnight, inviting yet dangerous. Seeing how enchanted she was by his difference made Bold Wolf's chest swell with pride."

The visual semiotics suggested by Harlequin novels implies that, for the imagined white female reader, the well-muscled Indigenous male signifies a twin set of dangers and desires: namely, the fear of a raw and potentially violent sexual primitivism together with the lure of erotic pleasure. No doubt the narrative tension generated by these images generates precisely the kind of unstable excitement that fuels the popularity of these novels in the first place. Thus, the Indigenous protagonist stands in for a naturalness that seems to come before the artifice of civilization. Like the garden of indigenous flowers, these novels present Indians that are valorized as being closer to a "free" existence in nature. However, in this most popular of incarnations, the Harlequin novels accentuate the Indians' primitive power precisely in order to constitute the visual field through which white female protagonists can attain a sense of unfettered sexual fulfilment and psychic escape.

But what of the method Thomas uses to draw viewers into exploring this contemporary and historic legacy? For while *What's the Point?* critiques the primitivization of Indigenous men, it also intensifies the specifically erotic aspects of this representation in ways that ask us to consider how our obsession with the body of the Indigenous other continues into the present moment. Indeed, Thomas's juxtaposition of the statue's well-muscled physique with contemporary Harlequin novels plays white imaginings of Indianness back against themselves at the same time as it pokes fun at the earnest sobriety and anxious guilt that has often characterized Canadian responses to this colonial legacy.[55] Thus, in Thomas's photographs, public statuary is not simply an embarrassing relic of an imperial past; rather, it invites us to see once again, and to see differently, how ideas about race, the body, and the nation are reproduced in a myriad of everyday places from pulp novels to public art. Consequently, the intent of *What's the Point?* seems to be the formal staging of a joke, where the incongruity of these images begs viewers to engage in that old childhood game "which of these things don't belong together?" while, at the same time, being jolted into realizing the uncanny similarities between the different elements.

National statuary has often fashioned homage to the original inhabitants so as to highlight their manly physique. The continuities, however, between these historical representations and images from popular culture suggest that, in portraits of the Indigenous man, the racial balance of power usually remains the same. Indeed, most representations of "noble Indians" present bodies that seem perpetually tamed, whether they are subdued at the feet of Champlain, domesticated in a garden of flowers, or acting as a spectacularized fantasy for the sexual pleasure of white women. Thomas's juxtaposition of these images invites viewers to consider how the sexualized Indian has rarely been represented in ways that assume his own autonomy. Of course, some might observe that, in Hollywood movies, Indians are seen to operate through an erotics of violence that results in constant threats to white women. But I suggest that these seemingly contradictory images (of tame and savage Indians) are mutually reinforcing poles of the same binary. Whether Indians were portrayed as bloodthirsty or noble, they were always primitivized, and they have rarely been depicted in ways that portray their exercising a sense of legitimized agency for their own ends – whether this be national or sexual.

In Thomas's installation, the witty threefold juxtapositions of the Indian Scout, Harlequin romance novels, and text invite viewers to consider the continuing salience of Indian play. Indeed, the exhibit reappropriates these images not in order to censor them but, rather, in order to make them available for comment. Thomas's photographs are intended to provoke dialogue. From Haytor Reed's Indian performance, to the chameleon-like Indians in popular culture, to the tame yet still eroticized statues in official representations, to the assertively performative Bear portraits, all of Thomas's work is a deeply engaging meditation on the notions of Indianness that are hidden in plain view.

"The Correlation of Eros and Conquest"

Kent Monkman is a multidisciplinary artist whose work ranges from figurative painting to film and performance. A member of the Fisher River Band of northern Manitoba, he now lives in Toronto. Over the past decade, Monkman's work has gained national and international attention. His work is included in public collections at the National Gallery of Canada, the Art Gallery of Ontario, and the Montreal Museum of Fine Arts and has been displayed in England, the United States, and Europe.

In the series of paintings known as The Prayer Language, the artist takes up the gendered legacy of colonial relations through the iconography of the Cree language, which also has a specific connection to his own family history. Monkman is the son of a Cree evangelical minister and a white artistically gifted mother. In The Prayer Language, Monkman draws from this background to produce a remarkable group of paintings that engage with some of the most troubling narratives in Canadian/Indigenous history – narratives that the Anishinaabek elders from the Garden River First Nation also drew to my attention. In a painting that is emblematic of the whole series, *Safe in the Arms of Jesus* (Plate 7), the viewer's first impression is of a shimmering canvas of translucent script. These are the syllabics that Monkman transcribes from his father's Anglican hymnbook. Each painting reproduces the words for a particular hymn, but suspended behind this text are visceral forms that resemble entwined bodies. While the artist draws inspiration for these human forms from erotic photographs of men wrestling, the figures are ambiguous and provoke a host of questions: "Are these bodies conjoining in ecstasy or struggle? Power and subordination? Pleasure or pain?"[56] Indeed, the juxtaposition of Christian verses, which allude to the comforting possibilities of spiritual touch, with the sensual and/or violent movements of the entwined figures, illuminates how representations of the body inevitably bring up questions of power. As Monkman elaborates:

> In this series of work I am exploring the significance of power in relation to touch and sexuality. Foucault described sexuality as "an especially dense transfer point for relations of power ..." I am interested in how the discourse about, and practice of, sexuality and touch relate to hierarchy,

domination and subordination ... [particularly in] the correlation of Eros and conquest to European and Native American contact.[57]

The traditional teachings of the church have played a prominent role in regulating and disavowing the diverse forms of sexual expression that were characteristic of many Indigenous groups. And the figures wrestling in the background of these paintings can also reference the disturbing forms of struggle associated with religious involvement in Indigenous education. Here the linking together of language and sexuality results from the church's central influence in the development of the Cree language. The invention of the Cree syllabics has been credited to the Methodist missionary James Evans, who was stationed in Norway House in northern Manitoba from 1840 to 1846. While Evans was a skilled linguist and constructed the first printing press to popularize these Cree symbols, his actual role in the creation of the syllabics is now disputed. In the most complete biography of Evans to date, Roger Burford Mason argues that Evans did invent the syllabics but notes that a number of sources suggest that his knowledge of Cree was limited.[58] Evans' collaborators, including Benjamin Sinclair, a Cree man from Norway House; Henry Steinbauer, an Indigenous missionary; and Sophia Mason, a mixed-race missionary, all had greater familiarity with the structure and feel of the Cree language. As translation requires fluency in the relation between Cree and English, Mason concludes that the work of these Indigenous collaborators has "perhaps not been given the prominence it deserves."[59] Monkman suggests an even more radical possibility: that the Cree syllabics, written as sacred writings on bark scrolls, predated Evans by at least a century and that Evans was taught the symbols by a Cree informant.

These competing narratives suggest the difficulties in reconstructing colonial history. But the story of the syllabics is even more complex for, while written Cree is intimately connected to the racialized history through which the church evangelized Indigenous people, the commercial interests of the Hudson's Bay Company also had a determining influence on this legacy. During James Evans' period in the north, the HBC still had legal title to all of northern Manitoba and the Northwest Territories. Thus, the missionary's efforts to set up a school for Indigenous children and his vocal support for HBC workers who were lobbying for shorter work hours brought him into prolonged conflict with the Company. Further, during the final year of Evans' ministry in Norway House, he was accused of sexual impropriety with several First Nations women. Religious trials in both Norway House and England cleared him of these charges, and, based on a review of the current literature, it seems likely that another white missionary may have been guilty of these accusations.[60] Yet the very ambiguity of the historical record is itself a testament to the deeply troubled history that has marked Canada's colonial legacy. For Evans' work in education and the evangelization of Indigenous people was allowed by the HBC only in deference to the inevitable influx of white settlers and the consequent need to prepare Indigenous people for assimilation into Canadian nation building. The racialized assumptions guiding this process are clear and highlight the difficult history of both commercial and religious involvement in colonization.

Monkman tells us that Christianity took root in his family through the artist's great-grandmother, Caroline Everet, who was born in 1875, over a generation after James Evans left northern Manitoba. Everet lived in the Cree and Saulteaux community of St. Peter's, where Cree was used for all religious gatherings regardless of which language the people actually spoke. Consequently, the Saulteaux referred to Cree as "The Prayer Language." While the Christian beliefs of Monkman's grandmother were passed down through his family, the Cree language was not. In a story that highlights the ironies of this linguistic legacy, Monkman notes:

> My father learned some Cree as a child, but had to study Cree with white teachers, in a missionary language school, to prepare him for a Christian ministry to his own people. When I was a young child, my family lived on various remote northern reserves while my father ministered in his newly honed Cree tongue ... As I cannot actually read syllabics or speak Cree [the process of inscribing the syllabics in each painting] both reinforces my distance from the language and brings me closer to it.[61]

Thus, the very process of making these syllabics engages the artist's alienation in relation to his own linguistic history. And, while most Canadian viewers may see the syllabics as "exotic," they are one of the earliest written languages in Canadian history. And the alternating obliteration and retrieval of the Cree language depicted in Monkman's story is itself a metaphor for the broader project of assimilation that the Canadian state has pursued with such vigour.

Monkman also talked about the very physical process of making the syllabics: the paint is poured down letter by letter, then allowed to dry so that edges form and can be squeegeed off, building up shapes layer by layer. Based on years of experimentation, the artist describes the process as a careful balance "of accident, control and manipulation" in working with paint. This practice seems to echo the experience of learning a language, with children learning basic sounds and then building up, layer by layer, to a larger vocabulary. While the syllabics have become a very personal way for Monkman to make his mark with paint, they also speak to both the weight and the transience of language and human experience. Indeed, both the haunting tenderness *and* the threatening violence of the human forms behind the syllabics assume additional layers of meaning through Cree linguistic history. There is a sexual playfulness and excitement in these bodies as they reach for each other in the shadow of the script, but there is also the possibility of menace. I suggest that The Prayer Language draws on the legacy of Cree anti-colonial memory and a queer aesthetic sensibility to speak to the dangers and the possibilities implicit in physical and communicative touch. But if these paintings bring together painterly expressionism with flesh, they also invite us to consider how the history of specific languages and communities serves as a prism through which to reconsider the secrets of national memory. For these shimmering images speak to the fragility of both language and the body, reminding us, as Matthew Teitelbaum suggests, that "art is made as a homage, and rooted in connectedness to others ... [I]t is made to open up and, finally, to extend the space of memory."[62]

In his series The Moral Landscape, Monkman undertakes a very different kind of exploration of the relationship between Eros and the conquest of Indigenous peoples, this time through a cheeky appropriation of the genre of landscape painting. The romantic landscape began to figure prominently in North American consciousness around 1825, and it remained influential in Canada until the early years of the twentieth century.[63] These artists were devoted to an optimistic interpretation of the New World, where spectacular representations of nature assumed both a religious and nationalist mantle as a metaphor for European settlers' triumphant claim to the land.[64] In a recent interview, Monkman talks about his childhood fascination with Bible study books, noting that landscape paintings remind him of those early images, in which the quality of light and the element of romance underscore a connection to a Christian ideology.[65]

Monkman notes that these early masters were known as painters of a "moral landscape" because many saw their world through a profoundly religious lens, and they conveyed this sensibility in pastoral canvases on which light shines from the heavens, conveying God's omnipotent presence. In a deliberate counterpoint, Monkman appropriates the term used to describe this earlier work for his own series, The Moral Landscape, at the same time as he articulates a sly and pointed appraisal of the assumptions implicit in that genre. The paintings explore homoerotic connections between Indians and cowboys in risky vignettes that reverse the dramatic thrust of traditional narratives. The contemporary feel of these cowboy and Indian figures also alludes to influences from the genre of gay pornography, where artists like Tom of Findland have defined a gay aesthetics whose influence has also affected popular culture. Thus, The Moral Landscape highlights the sexual subtext of representations that range from the nineteenth-century landscape painting to the Hollywood western, while simultaneously conveying a wry critique of the inequitable power relations between Indigenous peoples and European colonizers.

In Plate 8, we see a postcard that Monkman produced for the twenty-fifth anniversary issue of the magazine *FUSE*, located in Toronto. The painting is of a benign landscape with an expanse of puffy white clouds and invitingly blue sky, while the text across the top declares CANADA with a red maple leaf beside it. Yet our eye is drawn from the bold text to the foreground of the painting, where a cowboy is bending over a fallen tree trunk, and an Indian dressed only in a loincloth is grasping him firmly from behind. Initially the meaning is unclear: is this rape or an erotic fantasy? Several elements of the painting suggest that the cowboy may welcome the brave's advances. First, the cowboy's gun seems to have been carefully set aside just to the right of the kneeling man, well within his reach if he wanted to put an end to the encounter. And, second, his posture, as he swivels around to look at the brave, indicates considerable fascination, as well as alarm, as he offers his (attractive) butt to the dashing brave behind him.

While Monkman's postcard satirizes the ideas of national entitlement and heterosexual bravado that permeate representations of the frontier, it also opens up a series of questions. For popular representations of the west have usually failed to comment on the homosocial context of men's relationships on the open plains, which represented both a society of boundless opportunities and a space in which the restrictions of "civilized" society were conspicuously absent. If the early North American west was an arena of intensive contact between men of all races – as it was – then the question of how white men would react to the more diverse sexual practices common among many Indigenous peoples was not preordained. Indeed, many commentators in the nineteenth and early twentieth centuries openly questioned whether white settlers would prove a great and hardy race, capable of "civilizing" themselves and this new land, or whether they would degenerate into the morass of corrupt behaviour that was thought to characterize the more "savage" races.[66]

Yet Monkman's painting is attempting more than a critique of the colonial and heterosexist assumptions that usually characterize representations of the frontier: it is also taking up the nature of representation itself. The artist has borrowed the title for the work, *Ceci n'est pas une pipe*, from a famous modernist painting by the Belgian Surrealist René Magritte. The original painting was of a literal pipe, inscribed with the words *Ceci n'est pas une pipe* (This is not a pipe), while the painting itself was entitled *The Treachery of Images.* The painting was part of a series that highlighted the difference between representation and the objects being represented, often by the incongruous combining of images and text. Here the title's reference to the "treachery" of the visual suggests the disturbing ways images can mislead viewers. If Magritte's work was concerned with the ways meanings are both conveyed and betrayed through symbols, then how does this relate to Monkman's *Ceci n'est pas une pipe?* As Monkman is playing with and against the norms of landscape painting, one concern is to highlight the deeply ideological uses of this genre, where representations of a fecund and light-filled country were usually seen to reflect European settlers' divine entitlement to the land.[67] However, Monkman also plays with the norms of the surrealist tradition, which bring ordinary objects together in surprising combinations to create visual puns. His reconfiguration of the usual dynamics between cowboys and Indians builds on this legacy, inducing a visual double-take for viewers. Indeed, this pun brings to mind a play on Monkman's title, which could have read "This Is Not a Peace Pipe," to counter common nationalist histories suggesting Indigenous peoples' peaceful acquiescence to European settlement as well as to refer to the Indian's forceful "taking" of the cowboy with an object that is, after all, anything but a pipe.

The second of Monkman's images, entitled *Portrait of the Artist as Hunter* (Plate 9), portrays the rolling landscape of the Great Plains and the excitement of a buffalo hunt, with cowboys and Indians seeming to be united in a common front to fell the majestic beasts. As we examine the painting more closely, however, we realize that the Indian in the foreground seems a little unusual. Indeed, this figure is the artist's alternative persona, Miss Share Eagle Testicle, a figure he describes as "a glamorous half-breed drag queen," in full make-up, her long black hair flowing behind her as she gallops through the fray.[68] An even closer look, however, reveals that the comely young rider is not focused on the proud animals that surround her; rather, she is hunting men.

In this work Monkman is, once again, playing off a famous historical painting entitled simply *Buffalo Hunt* by the landscape artist John Mix

Stanley. Monkman notes that many landscape artists painted themselves into the adventurous scenes they depicted on canvas, a sleight of hand that allowed them to construct *themselves* as the ultimate manly men. Artists who travelled to the western frontier often required patrons to fund their expensive journeys, and, if their final works were evidence of the wealth and status of those who funded them, they also conveyed a certain cachet about the virile artist-as-explorer. In keeping with this tradition, Mix Stanley's painting included a dashing portrait of himself and fostered a self-aggrandizing mythology, one that is now impossible either to prove or to disprove. In Monkman's *Portrait of the Artist as Hunter,* he has fashioned an alter ego so grandiose that she tops the self-promotion displayed by Mix Stanley. However, if Miss Share Eagle Testicle's flamboyance matches the level of bravado portrayed in Mix Stanley's work, this flare for drama does not come through an uber masculine persona; rather, Monkman's deliberately over-the-top figure plays off the performer Cher, whose own "half-breed" persona is a glamorous bi-racial (Armenian and Cherokee) interpretation of a Hollywood stereotype. Indeed, Share allows the artist to reclaim the romanticism of the original canvases while inserting a very contemporary drag queen aesthetic. Monkman notes that, just as early landscape artists presented their paintings as ethnological documentation of Indigenous life, so he uses The Moral Landscape as a pictorial journal of Share's, and other Indigenous men's, "sexual exploits among the white men of North America."[69]

But, once again, Monkman's performance is not a simple reversal of colonial caricatures; rather, he uses a queerly expressive form of self-presentation that combines the masculine elements of his physique with the hyper-feminine mode of the drag queen in ways that unsettle the forms of masculinity and respectability so valorized by most early Canadian figurative painting. As Jose Muñoz notes, masculinity is a "cultural imperative to enact a mode of power that ... invalidates, excludes, and [works to] extinguish faggots, effeminacy, and queerly coated butchness."[70] In contrast, Miss Share Eagle Testicle refutes the masculinized image of the noble savage *and* the heroic explorer – and substitutes her own, far more glamorous, alternative.

In this chapter I have explored how a variety of engagements with Indian play challenge the project of national regeneration. As Philip Deloria comments, many "Indian performance options" have been notable for the ways they contributed to the profoundly creative process through which American, and, I argue, white Canadian, settlers imagined themselves and their country anew. Yet the shifting terrain of meanings associated with these images suggests that it is never possible to assume that they are received in the ways they are intended. Freud suggests that the ability to mimic is tied to power and that people use this form of play to deal with powerful and overwhelming situations. Thus, mimicry allows them to "abrogate the strength of the impression and ... make themselves master of the situation."[71] In the context of Canadians' largely unacknowledged imperial history, the continuing draw to mimetic forms of Indian play has most often worked to assure white citizens of their own sense of authentic belonging while, in the same moment, providing an uncanny reminder of the colonial legacy. Yet the workings of mimicry are still more complex than this. Indeed, I have explored three examples of the ways in which Indigenous people have also engaged this legacy, though from the perspective of very different histories and for their own distinct purposes. In the Anishinaabek performance of *Hiawatha,* and in the work of Jeff Thomas and Kent Monkman, we see how artists have reappropriated the legacies of Indianness and created new hybrids in places we would least expect.[72] Yet perhaps we should not be surprised. For if decolonization theory suggests that imperialism is a virus that is always finding new ways to recreate itself, then Indigenous resistance to this legacy is equally pervasive, persistent, and creative.[73]

6

Conclusion
Living in "Haunted Places"

Haunted places are the only ones people can live in.[1]

– Michel de Certeau

If, as Michel de Certeau suggests, all spaces of human habitation are *necessarily* haunted, then the question I want to pursue in this conclusion is less about the presence or absence of ghosts and more about the ways we might engage them. For, as Derrida notes, ghosts are "always there ... and they give us to rethink the 'there' as soon as we open our mouths."[2] My study of the banal images of Canadianness highlights not only the ways in which the ghosts of the past continue to inform, sometimes even to possess, the living but also the possibilities for spectral themes to provide a necessary and even positive introjection. For, while the images highlighted in the previous chapters articulate a kind of cultural haunting, they can also be reimagined in ways that produce sufficient distance from the past to recast those stories. As Avery Gordon argues, an engagement with ghosts can provide an opportunity to reflect on "the political status and function of systemic hauntings" and the ways in which collective ghosts "conjure up social life."[3]

To draw together the themes mapped out in the earlier chapters, I start by proposing a method that invites us to think *through* enchantment. Here I employ the work of Martha Kaplan, who, in her research on the colonial encounter, uses the term "state familiars" to encapsulate the seemingly magical power of the flag and the printed word to transform the "flotsam and jetsam of empire" into beings entitled to imperial protection.[4] Though distinctions must be made between colonization in Fiji, where Kaplan originally developed this idea, and a Canadian settler context, I believe Kaplan's term is also useful in my project. In Canada, however, the term "state familiars," while extremely suggestive, does not imply that the banal objects explored in earlier chapters obtained their authority only through their imposition by an imperial power bent on conquest; rather, Canadian state familiars emerged from a process more closely described through the notions of power explored by Foucault, whereby influence accrues not simply through the extrinsic activities of the state but also through multidirectional and productive forms of power that have worked to produce freedom *and* constraint.[5] Thus, state familiars emerged, as often as not, from the interaction between state power and settler identifications, and as liminal objects occupying a position on both sides of the threshold between the territory that was and a new country in the making.

When national images are reconceptualized as state familiars, a "state of activity"[6] can be set up between the taken-for-granted and the new in ways that excavate four uncanny links between the emblems surveyed in earlier chapters. To start, however, I must provide a short reprise about the nature and characteristics of familiars. According to Emma Wilby, the familiar was used in early modern England and Scotland to denote a witch's demonic spirit *and* personal helping spirits, often defined as fairies.[7] Both familiars and fairies were considered to have supernatural powers, and they were seen as valuable since they offered various kinds of material assistance. Although the familiar is most notoriously associated with the provision, to their master or mistress, of powers to harm or take revenge on their enemies, witch trial confessions suggest that the familiar usually promised "freedom from want."[8] Of course, the familiar/fairy also wanted something in return, and the most common bargain was the soul.[9]

How, then, might the idea of the state familiar allow us to highlight significant connections between these banal images of national belonging? First, the term challenges the conceptual separation, still common, between magic and the nation. For, despite Benedict Anderson's early analysis of the nation as the work of the imagination, much scholarship still assumes that nation-states are constituted primarily through law, rational discipline, and commodification. Yet, ever since the Enlightenment, there has been widespread acknowledgment of a distinctly communal set of phantoms as "enlightened" people began to speak more about the ghosts that haunted national rather than familial communities. As I note earlier, in Europe this was the ghost of communism, and in North America it was the spectral return of slaves and Indigenous peoples.[10] Modernity, however, as Peter Pels argues, has generated additional enchantments, and "modern technologies of conduct – both ritual and rational, symbolic and substantial – determine the content and form of modern magic."[11] Thus, the effort to distance the magical from the "real" produces its own uncanny reminders. To reiterate using just one example from the images explored in earlier chapters, we saw how the beaver usually mediates a series of narratives about industry, masculinity, and respectability, which established it as a benign and authentic image of the Canadian nation. And yet this same term has an equally long history in the subterranean language of sexual slang, suggesting surprising undersides to these legitimating narratives. In this context, state familiars (like early familiars/fairies) can be seen not simply as providing an obfuscating cover but also as being profoundly creative. This is because the image of the beaver, among others, has provided an astonishingly supple vessel for a host of conflicting meanings. And, indeed, it is precisely this enchanting malleability that has ensured its continuing longevity.

Second, while the popularity of national images is sustained through their captivating elasticity, all of these symbols also signify a common dream, one to which virtually all migrants to this territory have held fast – the dream of a materially better life. If we look to the early lore about witches' familiars, we find once again a compelling parallel as those accused of consorting with the supernatural usually justified their turn to magic on the basis that these beings made a crucial promise: *freedom from want.* While there has been a complex range of reasons why beavers, railways, and Banff National Park came to signify national purpose, all of these images also encapsulated this dream. The railway is the best exemplar for, when it advertised abundant harvests of wheat under the title CANADA THE NEW HOMELAND, these images were meant to be a sign of the prosperity it would enable. Further, while the rails' speed, size, regularity, and control were a source of great wonder, it was this technology's ability to enable the preservation of Euro-Canadian control over the west, to facilitate the movement of troops to defeat the second Riel Rebellion, and to enable millions of settlers to reach the western territories that ensured its place in the Canadian imagination. For, then as now, the dream of a materially better life was intimately tied up with access to land. And it was the CPR that enabled the defeat of Indigenous resistance and secured the west for settlement, in the process providing Euro-Canadian settlers with freedom from want and ensuring its centrality as a crucial symbol in the imagination of the nation.

Third, the bargain struck by those who harboured familiars was not one-sided, nor has it been for nations. The price, for the person who gained the help of a familiar, was the soul, or, to put it in more secular terms, the capacity to become self-aware. I suggest that the project of gaining freedom from want has been facilitated by a flight from self-reflexive awareness regarding how the past impinges on the present – and state familiars have, most often, articulated that flight. The irony is that, insofar as Canadians consume versions of a past *that do not nourish,* the living can themselves become ghostly. Indeed, I suggest that Canadian state familiars have memorialized the past as a form of banal possession, so that the present continues as a failure of memory to render history useable. Thus, banal forms of commemoration also function as a haunting – for they are the affective process through which we remember how Euro-Canadian settlers became free from want, while the deeply racialized process through which this was, and continues to be, accomplished is forgotten.

Finally, the idea of state familiars may be useful in helping us reflect on national emblems as images that both conceal and reveal a public secret. At the beginning of this book I asked the following question: when emblems of national belonging convey a knowledge that is both articulated *and* refused, what might this teach us? In the following chapters I explored how the "regime of the open secret" operated through discourses of national belonging. But not everyone "belongs." Historically, Indigenous peoples have been *most central* to the visual iconography of Canadianness and *most disenfranchised* from the benefits of national belonging. Thus, images of Indianness have been used to draw strength, power, and a benign sense of dignity into, in particular, the Euro-Canadian identity at the same time as Indigenous people have been profoundly disenfranchised through a legalistic set of discourses and practices that continue to destroy individuals and communities. Indeed, when we return to images of Indians in the visual iconography of the beaver, the CPR, and Banff National Park, we find that their simultaneous fetishization and erasure has served to bolster Euro-Canadian agency and has most often rendered "the Indian" as primitive, static, and/or lacking in agency.

Yet nationalism is not an unchanging construct. As many authors have remarked, one of the most important emblems of Canadianness to emerge in the past forty years has been the idea of this country as a uniquely *multicultural* nation. This symbolic reorientation, from images that epitomized a distinctly white process of nation building to emblems that herald a distinctly multiracial citizenry, has gained prominence with several important shifts in policy, including the Immigration Act, 1967; the inclusion of multiculturalism in the Canadian Charter of Rights and Freedoms (1982); and the passage of Bill C-93, the Canadian Multiculturalism Act, 1988.[12] These shifts are much heralded, particularly on Canada Day when the media feature prominent stories proclaiming this country to be – to quote a 1 July 2004 article from the *Globe and Mail* – "a happy land of tolerance."[13] But while these representations construct a national face fit for a new millennium, perhaps it is not surprising that they also reinscribe Canada's historic self-image as a particularly benign, enterprising, and tolerant nation.

However, when we assess these widely publicized images of Canada as a successful multicultural country in connection with the critical literature on this topic, we are confronted with a very different picture. A wide range of authors, including Himani Bannerji, Eva Mackey, Sherene Razack, and Richard Day, among others, argue that discourses of multiculturalism function as an important site of racialized governmentality.[14] Carrianne Leung's work provides a recent elaboration on these themes, assessing how multiculturalism has been articulated as the heritage of national identity. Referencing former prime minister Jean Chrétien's farewell speech at the Liberal convention in November 2003, she notes how multiculturalism is portrayed as a utopian social experiment:

> The rest of the world looks to us as a model, as a beacon. Look at the people in this great hall. You see in this one location all the faces, all the races, and the colours, and religions that make up this planet. This is the Canada of today.
>
> And this is our mission to the world. To show how it is possible to live together in diversity and in harmony. But to fulfill this mission, we have a solemn responsibility to speak to the world in our own voice – an independent voice.[15]

Leung points out that this articulation of multicultural heritage portrays difference not as something residing in particular groups but as *"owned by the nation itself"* (emphasis in original). Thus, contemporary multiculturalism "overcomes the history of Canada" and works as "a central legitimating myth ... providing the discursive shift to universalism, liberalism and transcendence ... [so that Canada can] distinguish itself as unique from amongst other nations, especially carving out a distinct identity against the foil of US hegemony."[16] Most often, though, this celebratory narrative fails to reckon with the treatment of the many racialized communities who are *not* new to the nation: from the Chinese and South Asian workers on the railway to the black Loyalists and former slaves who entered Cananda from the sixteenth to the nineteenth centuries. As Rinaldo Walcott argues, black communities in particular have faced a history of deliberate and ongoing erasure that has been accomplished through the demolition or renaming of black historical settlements, coupled with linking contemporary blackness with newcomer urban communities, illegal immigration, and crime, resulting in a process of racialization that runs from invisibility to contemporary forms of stigmatized racial hypervisibility.[17]

However, given that the public discourse of multiculturalism emphasizes the period after the Canadian Multiculturalism Act, 1988, I want to
briefly highlight research on the economic differences between Canadian-
born citizens and racialized newcomers to explore how the populist image
of Canada as a uniquely multicultural society compares with new immigrants' experience of the nation. Here there is a striking consensus regarding *increases* in economic inequalities. Analyses from Statistics Canada
provide a historical tracing of the prospects facing newcomers and point
out that, in 1980, on average, male immigrants earned 17 percent less than
their Canadian-born counterparts and that, by 2000, this gap had more
than doubled, with newcomers making 40 percent less than Canadian-born
workers of similar age and education.[18] Predictably, the picture is even worse
for women: in 1980, recent female newcomers were paid 23 percent less than
Canadian-born women, and, by 2000, this gap had almost doubled to 45
percent.[19] Overall, these analyses suggest a weak link between education
and employment, which is particularly striking as newcomers are better
educated than are their Canadian-born counterparts. As a recent *Globe and
Mail* article reports, these problems have only been exacerbated by the 2008
recession. Based on the labour force survey from November 2010, research-
ers found that, in Toronto, Canada's traditional immigration capital, the
overall jobless rate dropped to 6.7 percent, while the level of unemploy-
ment for those who had arrived in Canada in the past five years was three
times that number, at 19.7 percent, the highest since Statistics Canada started collecting data in 2006.[20] Thus, for racialized newcomers – who are
emblematic of the "new face" of Canada – it seems that the public discourse
of multiculturalism stands in harsh contrast to their actual struggles for
equitable participation within the Canadian nation. In this context, it is
striking that Indigenous people are the only group in Canada who endure
worse levels of economic disenfranchisement. Indeed, the Canadian
Department of Indian and Northern Affairs reports that "First Nations ...
quality of life ranks 63rd, or amongst Third World conditions,"[21] and
Statistics Canada reports that, in 2000, 42 percent of Indigenous people in
urban centres lived on a low income compared to 17 percent among other
Canadians.[22]

A recent report of the UNESCO World Commission on Culture and
Development cited Canada's approach to multiculturalism as "a model for
other countries."[23] Yet, Yasmeen Abu-Laban and Chris Gabriel conclude
that Canada's current policies seem to suggest our attachment to multiculturalism is increasingly articulated through what racialized newcomers

have to offer the country in terms of cheap labour and access to global markets. This version, as they note, "provides a very narrow rationale for the existence of multiculturalism ... because the emphasis is not on national inclusion and belonging, but rather on national and global competitiveness. This appears to be contrary to a multiculturalism based on respect and recognition."[24] These conclusions are reinforced by Nandita Sharma's work on migrant workers, which argues that nationalist formulations of "home" continue to be informed by racialized and gendered practices that exclude non-elite workers from the Global South while contributing to the neoliberal restructuring of the labour market in Canada.[25] Thus, the new image of Canadian identity as a tolerant and multicultural nation seems to fit the deeply racialized pattern of the old image, so that what Sharma calls "homey forms of racism" continue to pervade our material and symbolic national identity.

The previous chapters traced the ways in which the cultural imaginary of Canadianness has traditionally drawn strength from a host of nostalgic ideas about "Indians" while, at the same time, doing everything possible to disinherit actual Indigenous people from their land, identity, and culture. In the current context, images of a uniquely multicultural nation are being used to construct a more up to date version of a benign national collectivity. Yet racialized groups are experiencing a re-entrenchment of the current "global apartheid" *within* Canada in ways that undermine possibilities for an equitable, multiracial nation.[26] Indeed, it seems that those most likely to serve as the face of the nation – Indigenous people as token Indians and racialized groups as emblems of multiculturalism – are also the most disenfranchised from equitable forms of economic and cultural participation within the Canadian nation. Indeed, this dual process of spectacularization and marginalization of "others" is a key mechanism through which whiteness continues to colonize the definition of "normal" in Canadian social life.

This is a very different conclusion from that drawn by John Ralston Saul, whose recent book, *A Fair Country*, also argues that Canada has yet to acknowledge the unconscious current of indigeneity that informs national identity. However, while Saul suggests that the Métis origins of Canada are what inform our national commitment to diversity, he fails to reckon with how those racialized as diverse – Indigenous people and people of colour – are systematically excluded from Canada's commitment to fairness. Thus, while he argues that the concept of "métissage" (understood as the tradition of the "expanding circle," or the accommodation and acceptance of diversity that characterized many Indigenous groups) has pervaded Canadian society, I argue, in contrast, that the symbolic and material legacy associated with Canadianness points more towards a denied racist history that continues to reassert itself in the present day.

How, then, to engage with this troubling historic and contemporary legacy? The analysis contained in the preceding pages suggests that we might start through forms of memory work that acknowledge the national imaginary as a palimpsest, or "a parchment that has been inscribed two or three times, the previous text having been imperfectly erased and remaining therefore still partly visible."[27] This imperfect erasure, or the ways that the past continues to impinge on the present, has material and symbolic consequences. Bonita Lawrence and Ena Dua conceptualize one aspect of this palimpsest in their analysis of the present-day colonial state and the contested nature of the land, arguing that "we all share the same land base and yet [must] question the differential terms on which it is occupied [in order to] become aware of the colonial project that is taking place around us."[28] In this context, the ongoing challenge, as Cynthia Wright and Nandita Sharma argue, is to create strategies for decolonization that work through the current divides between Indigenous people and migrants and that challenge the colonial state and its inevitably hierarchical relations, opening up, instead, spaces for radical resistance.[29]

The artists whose work I explore start this process by suggesting how memory work on the palimpsest of the national imaginary can move towards new forms of resistance through alternative symbolic visions. Massumi describes these artistic challenges as experiments in "walking as controlled falling."[30] This proverb suggests that, though there are always constraints – gravity, balance, and the need for equilibrium – it is still possible to move forward by playing with and against those limits. Jean Ziegler uses a similar metaphor to describe activist work at the 2003 World Social Forum in Porto Alegre, Brazil. "We know what we don't want, but ... there is no [predetermined] way; you make the way as you walk. History doesn't fall from heaven; we make history."[31] I argue that the work of memory, art, analysis, and activism can be combined in the risky and unpredictable process of "making the way as we walk." My hope is that this method might constitute an antidote to the alienation and amnesia that domination produces – in short, an antidote to the continuing lure of ghostliness.

Fountain

I conclude with the work of Rebecca Belmore, whose recent video *Fountain* suggests how blood, water, and fire might breathe new life into an old story. Like her earlier work, *Rising to the Occasion,* discussed in Chapter 2,

Belmore's recent and widely celebrated video finds its roots in performance, a medium she describes as both Indigenous and international. *Fountain* was made for the Canadian Pavilion at the Venice Biennale (2005). In an interview with Scott Watson, Belmore locates her drive to inhabit a performative persona in childhood.

> It has a lot to do with becoming aware of my identity and my own specific Ojibwe body at a very young age. I recall a very specific moment. In fact, March 22, 1965. I climbed aboard my first school bus with my mother. We were simply hitching a ride to the grocery store. I remember my shock at seeing a sea of mostly white faces staring back at me. I mark this as the beginning of confronting the idea of "persona," of the need to project an energy or whatever you want to call it ... [I]t has to do with having a particular history, a particular political history, of being born into a political situation ... I had no choice. It was a way for me to have control and create an autonomous space for myself.[32]

Belmore belongs to a generation of Indigenous people who were discouraged from learning their language and culture so that they could step more fully into being "modern." Nevertheless, in her youth she was also a witness to the lived reality of a trapping economy and knew of her grandmother's participation in religious and cultural rituals that are now rarely practised. Thus, despite the fact that Belmore cannot speak the Ojibwe language, she believes she was given "just enough information" to reinvent this legacy through her own creative reflexes.[33]

The inspiration for *Fountain* came through a series of road trips to personally meaningful sites in northwestern Ontario and to a friend on the Prairies. With water as a recurring theme in that travel, and knowing that the piece would be set in Venice, a city threaded with canals and the port of many colonial maritime journeys, Belmore decided to focus on the element of water. *Fountain* is a two-and-a-half-minute video loop, and in Venice the video is projected from behind onto a screen of water. Indeed, Richard William Hill's review of the piece notes that "the media description of the work might accurately read: 'light moving on water.'"[34] The early scenes in the video show an industrial beach near land belonging to the Musqueam First Nation. If one looks closely, a sewage pipe is visible on the horizon of the beach; the sound in the video is from jets departing Vancouver International Airport.[35] Thus, a formerly pristine stretch of water is marked by a sewage-treatment plant and the sounds of international travel. As the camera scans the beach, it comes to a stack of drift timber, and suddenly the wood bursts into yellow and orange flames. In Venice, where the video is projected onto a water screen, the fire is rendered almost crystalline as it flickers through the water.[36] The camera rests for a while on the flames. Then it moves to Belmore, who appears in the icy cold water of the Pacific. She's distraught and struggling, trying to fill a large battered red bucket. Eventually, the scene shifts and Belmore's thrashing has stopped. For a while she is still, meditative, and sitting in the frigid water, and then she rises and starts to walk up the beach, carrying the bucket, directly towards the camera. Richard William Hill saw the piece in Venice and comments on what happens next:

> With a startlingly loud and primal grunt (several audience members actually flinch) she tosses the contents of the bucket toward the screen. The liquid that leaves the bucket is no longer transparent water however, but is now dark, almost black, as it sails toward the audience. It doesn't quite reach you, of course, but hits a transparent screen between the artist and the camera where it splatters out in ropy red tendrils. It's blood.

As I look at a production still from the performance (Figure 6.1 and cover), what strikes me about Belmore, as I see her through this sea of blood, is that it looks like *she's* been assaulted. In this image, her face is blurred through the red screen, almost as if it has been smashed in a fight. In another, her head is partially turned, her eyes closed. Indeed, it seems that Belmore and the bloodied screen are as one – while the beach and water in the background belong to a different horizon, one that fades in gentle tones of grey and green, in stark contrast to the foreground image. Two other production stills show her silhouetted against a red horizon.

I want to reflect on *Fountain* in light of Michael Taussig's analysis of public secrets and what he calls "defacement," or the labour of the negative. I focus on defacement as Belmore herself is disfigured by the performance, even as the audience in Venice also recoils from the assault of the red-black liquid. Further, in Belmore's silhouette against a red horizon, we see a single figure against a catastrophic background, so that the landscape itself is despoiled in a reference that seems apocalyptic in nature. In Taussig's analysis, when something is defaced, from a human body to a public object, the very hideousness of the act arouses a strange surplus negative energy from within the defaced thing itself. To see this kind of public wounding is to witness a certain kind of desecration – through which, he argues, that same object or person is made sacred.[37] Defacement, then, can concern the effort to recoup negative energy and purposefully redeploy it as a form of critique that offers to tell a "truth" (Plate 10). But this truth is not simply the unmasking

Figure 6.1 Production still from *Fountain*. Rebecca Belmore: "When I think of an apocalypse in Aboriginal terms, I think of the experience of colonization. The attempt to destroy a whole world-view ... In the video the artist and the viewer stand on either side of a sheet of blood and we are seeing each other through it." Courtesy of Rebecca Belmore; image provided by Belkin Art Gallery

of a secret, just as defacement does not necessarily destroy a secret; rather, this defacement is a revelation that might "do justice to a secret."[38]

I suggest that Belmore's *Fountain* is a deliberate and tactical attempt to use the labour of the negative to do justice to a public secret. The energies are elemental: fire, water, but most of all blood. We view the artist through a screen of blood, and it is the heaving of blood towards the screen that causes the audience to flinch and recoil. And perhaps this is not surprising, for the cultural meanings associated with blood signal significant dangers: as a harbinger of death as well as a giver of life, and as the preferred substance for sacrifice. Blood has also been represented as a kind of truth serum. For example, in George Eliot's mid-nineteenth-century tale, *The Lifted Veil*, a woman on the verge of death is temporarily revived by a timely transfusion of blood, only to voice ugly truths that effect the fall of her mistress.[39] I suggest that the labour of the negative elaborated in *Fountain* draws on all these associations and more. Belmore comments: "When I think of an apocalypse in Aboriginal terms, I think of the experience of colonization. The attempt to destroy a whole world-view ... In the video the artist and the viewer stand on either side of a sheet of blood and we are seeing each other through it." [40] Certainly this quality of "seeing" – looking through and at a disfigured image – re-enacts a public wounding.

Yet Belmore's work is also about water. Entitled *Fountain,* the video was shot by the Pacific Ocean in Vancouver, exhibited in a city of fountains, and projected onto water. As well, the "movement of light on water" combined with the painterly feel of the blood on the screen provide a remarkable sense of fluidity and beauty. In this sense Belmore is not only reflecting on the past and the present but also referencing urgent hopes for a future. For water is a key factor in the next round of global power struggles. While Canada has a great deal of the world's water resources, the question of its distribution is already in dispute. If one of the last great waves of predatory European capitalism was built on the acquisition of the Americas, resulting in the catastrophic genocide of Indigenous peoples – then the next global contest may be about water. This race for control over access to fresh water will no doubt profoundly challenge the nationalist boundaries established through the last wave of imperial conquest. Belmore speaks to this troubled context through artwork that draws connections between the previous global contests and the upcoming ones: "I hope that a transformative connection is made as the viewer and I face each other across this screen, where water changes into blood, blood into water and history into art." [41] As Martin notes, the Venice Biennale is located in the country of Christopher Columbus, and water has been a frequent conduit for European worldviews. [42] As the first Indigenous woman to represent Canada at the prestigious Venice Biennale, Belmore reflects on this complicated legacy of blood, water, and European colonialism: "I think this whole idea of myself as an Ojibwe woman coming to Venice and bringing back a work that is a fountain [she pauses to find the right words] ... is like throwing it back at you." [43]

I suggest Belmore is using defacement as Taussig describes it, to burn up the "husk of the beautiful outer appearance of the secret as it enters the realm of ideas." [44] Thus, her work draws on a particular economy of signs and works metaphorically to unleash other energies for reading those signs differently in the present. As Belmore herself says, "The piece moves from fire to water to blood. My intent is to link our bodies to the essential elements necessary to life. To embrace a moment where we can acknowledge how we are all connected and implicated in history." [45]

The *Oxford Companion to Medicine* tells us that the most frequent reference to blood is to its ability to reanimate those who are wounded or virtually dead. These references range from ancient Italy, where the Romans drank the blood of fallen gladiators to assimilate their vitality; to studies in the late 1800s that explore the function of blood in treating anemia; to the contemporary technologies for blood transfusion.[46] We now like to think of the exchange of blood as a hazard-free procedure, yet we also know risks remain. In *Fountain,* Belmore is engaging the risk of "looking back" through blood: back on a racist colonial legacy that continues in the present day and forward through the labour of the negative, through defacement. This is how she invites us to enter – by looking through blood, water, and memory, for reanimation.

Notes

Preface

1 Erin O'Keefe, "Brand Olympics: Canada's New Patriotism Is Resoundingly Brand Agnostic," 19 February 2010, available at http://www.interbrand.ca/blog/post/2010/02/19/Brand-Olympics-Canadas-New-Patriotism-is-resoundingly-brand-agnostic.aspx.

2 Mullkam Samint, "The 2010 Vancouver Winter Games and Canadian Patriotism," Vancouver Ethiopian Blog, 25 February 2010, available at http://vancouverethiopian.wordpress.com/2010/02/25/the-2010-vancouver-winter-games-and-canadian-patriotism/.

3 John Honderich, "Olympics Were an Explosion of Passion and Patriotism," 3 March 2010, available at http://olympics.thestar.com/2010/article/774708–olympics-were-an-explosion-of-passion-and-patriotism.

4 Ibid.

5 Margaret Atwood, "A Second Chance or a Boot in the Face? Two Protests, Seemingly Miles Apart, Were about the Kind of Country We Want to Live in," *Globe and Mail*, 6 July 2010. For a letter signed by over fifteen hundred citizens that provides a detailed critique, see http://rabble.ca/blogs/bloggers/judes/2010/07/toronto-call-no-more-police-state-tactics.

6 For the use of the flag at the peaceful protest at Queen and Spadina, protesting the G20 and the mass arrest of protesters on 26 June 2010, see http://www.youtube.com/watch?v=seoObXNYtg4andNR=1. For singing of the national anthem at the same Queen and Spadina protest, see http://www.youtube.com/watch?v=Heb9BXjYcII. For examples of police breaches of protesters' rights to peaceful protest and abuses while in prison, see http://toronto.mediacoop.ca/video/torontonians-gather-police-hq-condemn-abuses/4020. For Canada Day protest, see http://www2.macleans.ca/2010/07/02/g20-protesters-rally-on-canada-day/.

7 I want to clarify that many of the organizers of the G20 protests, specifically those in groups like "No One Is Illegal," do not think that Canada is a "benign" nation. However, clearly others who joined these protests did, and *Maclean's* magazine, in highlighting these images, reinscribed this notion.

8 Jessica Earle, "The Olympics a Crash Course on Canadian Patriotism," 1 March 2010, available at http://edmonton.ctv.ca/servlet/an/local/CTVNews/20100301/EDM_olypride_100301/20100301?hub=EdmontonHome.

9 I use the term "Indigenous" to refer to all peoples whose ancestors lived in the region now called Canada prior to colonization and who are working to retain control over some or all of their own social, economic, cultural, and political institutions. When I refer to a specific group – for example, Anishinaabek or Iroquois people – I refer to them as such. This usage is consistent with international Indigenous social movements (and the United Nations and the International Labour Organization), which are working to make connections between experiences of colonization across current national borders. As this book articulates a critique of colonial states as inevitably exclusionary, I choose a term that works both within and beyond the nation. The choice of "Indigenous" seems particularly important given that the current Canadian government has adopted the term "Aboriginal" for the Department of Aboriginal Affairs (formerly the Department of Indian Affairs), whose responsibility it is to administer the Indian Act. For further discussion of the use of this term, see Sanders, "Indigenous People," 4-13.

10 For a critique of the representation of Indigenous people in the opening ceremony of the Olympics, see Toban Black, "An Aboriginal Olympics?" 15 February 2010, available at http://contexts.org/socimages/?s=Olympics%2C+canada.

11 For information on the Aboriginal march, the first demonstration mobilized to protest the G20 in Toronto, see schedule for Thursday, 24 June 2010, available at http://g20.torontomobilize.org/schedule.

12 Fun and Games Sidebar, *Globe and Mail*, 6 March 2010, F5.

13 Mike Myers, quoted in David L. Pike, "Across the Great Divide: Canadian Popular Cinema in the 21st Century," *Bright Lights Film Journal* 56 (May 2007), available at http://www.brightlightsfilm.com/56/canada.htm.

14 Patrick Brethour, "The Year Canada Grew Up," *Globe and Mail*, 1 July 2010.

15 "The Reality of First Nations: Fact Sheet," Assembly of First Nations, available at http://www.afn.ca/article.asp?id=764. This situation is caused, as I argue later, by systemic racism. See http://action.web.ca/home/narcc/issues.shtml?cat_name= Aboriginal/AboriginalandAA_EX_Session=1872d9ba12bb0bc960330fe3b8bf97aa.

16 Quoted in Saul, *Fair Country*, 303.

17 Maria Campbell, in Griffiths and Campbell, *Book of Jessica*, 96.

18 Alexander, *Pedagogies of Crossing*, 268.

19 Bhabha, "The World and the Home," 445-55, 454.

20 Gandhi, *Affective Communities*, 4.

21 The Canadian pianist Glenn Gould (1932-82) was known for his vigour and clarity in performing contrapuntal music. See "Glenn Gould," Microsoft Encarta Online Encyclopedia 2007, available at http://encarta.msn.com, Microsoft Corporation, 1997-2007.

22 Brogan, *Cultural Haunting*.

Chapter 1: Introduction

1 Maria Campbell, in Griffiths and Campbell, *Book of Jessica*, 96.

2 Miller, *Shingwauk's Vision*, starts an analysis of the residential school system in Canada through memorializing the specific history of the Shingwauk Residential School.

3 Chute, *Legacy of Shingwaukonse*, 110.

4 Ibid., 111.

5 Ibid., 112-23, 131-36.

6 Ibid., 124-30.

7 Stefani, *Ten Good Years*.

8 For conversations that led me to think about the hospitality of ghosts and about my responses, I want to thank Shohini Ghosh.

9 Brogan, *Cultural Haunting*, 19.

10 Caruth, "Interview," in Caruth, *Trauma*, 130.

11 Lawrence, "Rewriting Histories"; Freeman, "*Toronto Has No History!*".

12 Taussig, *Defacement*, 50.

13 Ibid.

14 Personal communication from Susanne Luhmann to the author, February 2006.

15 Brogan, *Cultural Haunting*, 10.

16 Derrida, *Specters of Marx*, 176.

17 Taussig, *Defacement*, 160.

18 Ibid., 159.

19 Ibid., 51.

20 I borrow this phrase from the workshop at which I presented a manuscript version of this book. This was at the Canadian Association for Cultural Studies national conference, "What's the Matter? Cultural Studies and the Question of Urgency," University of Alberta, Edmonton, 25-28 October 2007.

21 Quoted in Taussig, *Defacement*, 2.

22 Kennedy, *Oxford Encyclopedia of Theatre and Performance*, at http://www.oxfordreference.com.catalogue.library.brocku.ca:80/views/ENTRY.html?subview=Mainandentry=t177.e1503.

23 Buse and Scott, *Ghosts*, 4.

24 Bergland, *National Uncanny*, 8-9.

25 Gordon, *Ghostly Matters*, 5-6.

26 Freud, *Uncanny*.

27 Gelder and Jacobs, "Postcolonial Ghost Story," in Buse and Scott, *Ghosts*, 179-99.

28 Kristeva, *Strangers to Ourselves*, 182.

29 Gordon, *Ghostly Matters*, 18, 22.

30 Campbell, *Halfbreed*.

31 Episkenew, *Taking Back Our Spirits*, 69-86.

32 Turcotte, "Fearful Calligraphy," 124.

33 Turner, *Imagining Culture*, 4.

34 Edwards, *Gothic Canada*, xxii.

35 Goldman and Saul, "Talking with Ghosts," 645.

36 Eddy and Schreuder, "Introduction," in Eddy and Schreuder, *Rise of Colonial Nationalism*, 3.
37 Thobani, *Exalted Subjects*, 38, emphasis in original.
38 Stoler, "Making Empire Respectable," 345.
39 Mawani, *Colonial Proximities*, 4-5.
40 See also Carter, *The Importance of Being Monogamous*, and Perry, *On the Edge of Empire*.
41 Quoted in Gittings, *Canadian National Cinema*, 8-9.
42 Mawani, *Colonial Proximities*, 21.
43 The literature on the impact of these epidemics in Canada includes: Johnston, "Epidemics"; Decker, "Tracing"; Harris, "Voices of Smallpox." On the impact of eugenics, see McLaren, *Our Own Master Race*. On armed conflict, see Lawrence, "Rewriting Histories." On biological warfare, see Elizabeth A. Fenn, "Biological Warfare in Eighteenth-Century North America: Beyond Jeffery Amherst," *Journal of American History* 86, 4 (2000), available at http://www.historycooperative.org/cgi-bin/justtop.cgi?act=justtopandurl=http://www.historycooperative.org/journals/jah/86.4/fenn.html.
44 Lawrence, *Real Indians*, esp. 25-104.
45 Miller, *Reflections*, esp. 107-70.
46 On the residential school experience, see Milloy, *A National Crime*; and Miller, *Shingwauk's Vision*.
47 Stasiulis and Jhappan, "Fractious Politics," 115-16.
48 United Nations, Department of Economic and Social Affairs, Division for Social Policy and Development, Secretariat of the Permanent Forum on Aboriginal Issues, International Expert Group meeting on the Millennium Development Goals, Aboriginal Participation and Good Governance (New York, 11-13 January 2006), available at http://www.un.org/esa/socdev/unpfii/documents/workshop_MDG_chartrand.doc.
49 Adapted from "The Reality for First Nations in Canada," Fact Sheet, Assembly of First Nations, http://afn.ca/article.asp?id=764.
50 Coalition for the Advancement of Aboriginal Studies, *Learning about Walking in Beauty: Placing Aboriginal Perspectives in Canadian Classrooms*, available at http://www.crr.ca/Load.do?section=26andsubSection=38andid=316andtype=2 – 60k.
51 White, *Tropics of Discourse*, 184-85.
52 Quoted in Billig, *Banal Nationalism*, 38.
53 Billig, *Banal Nationalism*, 42.
54 Quoted in Billig, *Banal Nationalism*, 42.
55 Billig, *Banal Nationalism*, 6-8.
56 Ibid., 16-17.
57 Mackey, *House of Difference*.
58 This territory has been explored in different ways by Francis, *Imaginary Indian*; and Goldie, *Fear and Temptation*.
59 Deloria, *Playing Indian*, 191.

60 Barber, *Canadian Oxford Dictionary*, 1055.

61 Ibid., 1606.

62 Mackey, *House of Difference*, 1-2.

63 For example, see Dawson, *Mountie*; and Francis, *Imaginary Indian*.

64 Slotkin, *Regeneration through Violence*.

65 Nichols, *Indians*.

66 Personal communication with the author.

67 Rod Mickleburgh, "2010 Winter Games, Based on Aboriginal Myths, Olympic Mascots a Hit with Children," *Globe and Mail*, 28 November 2007. See also Peter Kennedy and Grant Kerr, "Inukshuk to Be Logo of Vancouver Games: BC Graphic Artist Was Inspired by Inuit Landmark Used for Navigation," *Globe and Mail*, 25 April 2005.

68 Razack, *Dark Threats*, 9-14.

69 Quoted in Otter, *Philosophy of Railways*, 20-22.

70 Gordon Lightfoot, "Canadian Railroad Trilogy," *The Way I Feel* (UA Records, UAS 6587, Mono, AL 3587, 1967).

71 Atwood, *Survival*, 34.

72 McGregor, *Wacousta Syndrome*, 21.

73 Rukszto, "Minute by Minute," 111, 144. See also Day, *Multiculturalism*.

74 Bill Curry, "Multiculturalism Debate Proves Divisive: 'Them' and 'Us' Split Spreading Nationwide, Federal Officials Warn," *Globe and Mail*, 19 October 2007.

75 The "reasonable accommodation" debate broke out in 2006 when the small town of Hérouxville, Quebec, adopted a city bylaw that banned the stoning of women and, other than on Hallowe'en, the covering of faces. Hérouxville has only one person from a racial minority – a young boy adopted by a local family. Many critics have suggested that this bylaw emerges from a blatantly anti-immigrant, and specifically anti-Muslim, siege mentality, a sentiment that gained credibility when a provincial commission mandated to investigate reasonable accommodation in Quebec prompted an outpouring of exactly these sentiments. Yet it is important to remember that these views have remarkable credibility in more places than Quebec. Indeed, at the start of the reasonable accommodation debate, Sheema Khan noted that "Hérouxville was not an aberration, but the canary in a mineshaft." See Sheema Khan, "Can We Put the Racism Genie Back in the Bottle?" *Globe and Mail*, 7 April 2007.

76 Tariq Amin-Khan et al., "Justifying the Need for the 'War on Terror,'" *Rabble News*, 5 April 2006.

77 Now, however, less from the "wilderness" and more from various unruly "others."

78 Dyer, *White*, 223.

79 Lloyd, "Race under Representation," 64.

80 Ibid., 70.

81 Frankenberg, *White Women*, 191.

82 Dyer, *White*. As Dyer reminds us, in the nineteenth century "all of creation was connected in a hierarchy that proceeded from the lowest to the highest, the latter being

God. Black people were placed only just above the apes ... White men [sic] were placed at the highest point of earthly creation, linked via the angels to God ... [But] it is not spirituality or soul that is held to distinguish whites, but what we might call 'spirit': get up and go, aspiration, awareness of the highest reaches of intellectual comprehension and aesthetic refinement. Above all the white spirit could both master and transcend the white body, while the non-white soul was a prey to the promptings and fallibilities of the body. A hard, lean body, a dieted or trained one ... tight rather than loose movement, tidiness in domestic arrangement and eating manners ... abstinence or at any rate planning in relation to appetites, all of these are the ways the white body and its handling display the fact of the spirit within. But that spirit itself cannot be seen" (22-23). Thus the emphasis in white religious, racial, and civilizational discourses on enterprise, aspiration, and bodily transcendence has meant that the body is thought of as a base and potentially evil handmaiden to the spirit as it is overtly identified with a lack of self-control, idleness, gluttony, and sexuality. And this dichotomy is particularly powerful in relation to white women, of course, for white ideology has always emphasized the importance of heterosexuality and the responsibility of white women to reproduce the race. And while it required men to fight against sexual desires, it also suggested that respectable white women didn't have any (27-30).

83 Anderson, "Introduction to Part Two," in Jessup, *Antimodernism*, 98.
84 Quoted in McKay, "Handicrafts," in Jessup, *Antimodernism*, 117.
85 Goldberg, *Racist Cultures*.
86 Scott, *Gender and the Politics of History*, 6.
87 This Foucauldian notion is summarized in Hall, *White*, 23.
88 Bhabha, "Interrogating Identity."
89 Massumi, "Navigating Movements," 221.
90 Ibid., 220.
91 Quoted in Mercer, *Welcome to the Jungle*, 64.
92 Shohat and Stam, *Unthinking Eurocentrism*, 352.
93 Ibid., 355.
94 Muñoz, *Disidentifications*, 12.
95 Gagnon, *Other Conundrums*, 22.
96 Muñoz, *Disidentifications*, 128.
97 Gandhi, *Affective Communities*, 29.
98 Ibid., 31.
99 Kapferer and Kapferer, "Monumentalizing Identity," 96.
100 Taussig, *Defacement*, 59.

Chapter 2: The Strange Career of the Beaver

1 Like many of these beaver images, Bell Canada's "hoser" beavers have generated extremely mixed responses, ranging from rating near the top of the "most loved" advertising characters to scoring high on a Leger Marketing survey for the most annoying advertisements. See Keith McArthur, "Annoying but Successful: Whither the

Beavers?" *Globe and Mail*, 23 April 2007, available at http://ctv2.theglobeandmail. com/servlet/story/RTGAM.20070423.wrbeavers23/business.

2 The book resulted from the first Canadian exhibit to investigate the iconography of the beaver, sponsored by the Musée régional de la Côte-Nord, in Sept-Îles, Québec, in 1994.

3 Gagnon, *Images*. Gagnon's book is the primary text informing the subsequent discussion. As the book is not available in English, all citations from it were translated into English by my colleague and friend Yolande Mennie.

4 Gagnon, *Images*, 76.

5 Ibid., 76-77.

6 Ibid., 82.

7 Schulte and Müller-Schwarze, "Understanding," 111.

8 Including the famous 1715 "A New and Exact Map of the Dominions of the King of Great Britain on ye Continent of North America" by Dutch geographer Herman Moll, which was reproduced in six editions.

9 Gagnon, *Images*, 90.

10 Ibid., 95.

11 Quoted in Gagnon, *Images*, 96.

12 Ibid., 97.

13 Bovet, "Maleness," 122. To quote Bovet: "The presence of this organ in male beavers, which never functions as a female uterus does, is just one example of a condition called *intersexuality*, which is well documented in a number of mammalian species, and produces masculinized females as well as feminized males" (122). The uterus-like structure does not prevent beavers from reproducing. Bovet's notes provide a list of the scientific literature on this matter. I want to thank Bovet for his generous response to my earlier article on this topic.

14 Bovet, "Beavers," 123.

15 Gagnon, *Images*, 103-4.

16 Ibid., 117-18.

17 Vibert, *Traders' Tales*, 117.

18 Ibid.; and Warkentin, *Canadian Exploration Literature*, 9.

19 Vibert, *Traders' Tales*, 118.

20 Ibid. Traders were especially critical of Aboriginal people when they chose to satisfy their own requirements for subsistence rather than to stockpile beaver for trade. See Black-Rogers, "Varieties," 364.

21 For some discussion of the complexity and ambivalence of European attitudes towards Aboriginal peoples in North and South America, see Berkhofer, *White Man's Indian*; Honour, *New Golden Land*; Pratt, *Imperial Eyes*; Marshall and Williams, *Great Map*.

22 Indeed, in Adam Smith's four-stage theory of human development, the hunting and gathering mode of life occupies the most rudimentary position. See Vibert, "Real Men," 5.

23 Vibert, "Real Men," 4.

24 Nadeau, *Fur Nation*, 30-31.
25 Crean, "Hats," 378-79.
26 Quoted in Hunt, *Governance*, 85.
27 Grant, "Revenge," 37.
28 Quoted in Carter, *Men and the Emergence*, 140.
29 Amphlett, *Hats*, 106-7, emphasis added. For more analysis of "effeminacy" and its link to a critique of luxury, see Hunt, *Governance*, 78-89; Shapiro, "Sex"; Kimmel, "Lord and Master"; and Carter, *Men and the Emergence*, 124-62.
30 Quoted in Hunt, *Governance*, 52, 229.
31 Davis, *Fashion*, 38.
32 Ibid., 38-39.
33 Callaway, "Dressing for Dinner," 242.
34 Vibert, *Traders' Tales*, 248.
35 Quoted in Vibert, *Traders' Tales*, 252.
36 Vibert, *Traders' Tales*, 252.
37 Quoted in McClintock, *Imperial Leather*, 224.
38 Davis, *Fashion*, 38-39.
39 McClintock, *Imperial Leather*, 184.
40 Ibid., 188.
41 The HBC charter required that the Company give two elk skins and two black beaver pelts to the Canadian monarch or his/her heirs whenever they visited an area that was formerly Rupert's Land. The ceremony was first conducted with the Prince of Wales (the future Edward VIII) in 1927; then with King George VI in 1939; and last with George VI's daughter, Queen Elizabeth II, in 1959 and 1970. On the last such visit, the pelts were given in the form of two live beavers, which the Queen donated to the Winnipeg Zoo. However, when the Company permanently moved its headquarters to Canada, the HBC charter was amended to remove the rent obligation. Each of the four "rent ceremonies" took place in or around Winnipeg. See Mark Kearney and Randy Ray, "Royals Not Pelted Anymore," *Toronto Star*, 11 June 1995.
42 Rich, "Pro Pelle Cutem," 15.
43 Ibid., 13.
44 Ibid., 12; McClintock, *Imperial Leather*, 210.
45 McClintock, *Imperial Leather*, 210.
46 Ibid., 210-11.
47 Fleming, "Beaver Tales," 10.
48 Ibid.
49 McClintock, *Imperial Leather*, 226.
50 Specifically, 398 cartoons in the caricature collection use the beaver image.
51 Poole, *Nation and Identity*, 16.
52 Other variations also occur, but these two examples demonstrate the range of possibilities.
53 Mackey, *House of Difference*, 19-22.

54 The only exception I found to this was a cartoon by John Larter published in the *Toronto Star* on 7 August 1986 entitled "View of the World from Ontario." In the foreground it features two Aboriginal trappers who are tanning a beaver skin, while anti-trapping protesters emerge over the hillside. The caption depicts a conversation between the two trappers and reads: "So far the white man has killed off our lakes, our rivers, our forests, our wildlife, our fish ... I wonder what's next?" This caricature does present a sympathetic portrayal of Aboriginal people, and the beaver is aligned with them rather than with the white protesters.

55 Mosse, *Nationalism and Sexuality*, 4.

56 Rawson, *Wicked Words*, 8-10. For example, up until that time, words like "arse" were frequently heard in Queen Anne's court (1702).

57 Mosse, *Nationalism and Sexuality*, 4.

58 Ibid., 5.

59 Ibid., 151.

60 Valverde, *Age of Light,* 59.

61 Examples of these legal battles include decisions that overturned the bans against James Joyce's *Ulysses* (admitted to the United States in 1933 and into Canada in 1949) and D.H. Lawrence's *Lady Chatterley's Lover* (decriminalized in 1959 in the United States; 1960 in the United Kingdom; and 1962 in Canada). See Rawson, *Wicked Words*, 10.

62 Thorne, *Bloomsbury Dictionary*, 32.

63 Henke, *Gutter Life and Language*, 21-22.

64 Rawson, *Wicked Words*, 39.

65 Thorne, *Bloomsbury Dictionary*, 32.

66 Partridge, *Dictionary of Slang*, 1:41.

67 Rawson, *Wicked Words*, 39.

68 Ibid.

69 Van Kirk, *Many Tender Ties*, 146.

70 Green, "Pochahontas Perplex." For an analysis of specifically Canadian narratives, see Goldie, *Fear and Temptation*, esp. 63-84. Narratives about Aboriginal women have a complex arc, which each of these authors addresses in more detail. Representations range from the pure and non-sexual Indian princess or maiden who often succors her white male partner over and against her own people, with Pocahontas as the most well-known example of this genre; to the more crudely sexual images of Indian squaws who, in a parody of the song "Little Red Wing," "lays on her back in a cowboy shack, and lets cowboys poke her in the crack" (Green, "Pochahontas Perplex," 19). Goldie sums up that, even in the "positive" literary representations, "whether she remains the distant [and pure] image or becomes the reality of miscegenation, she must die, must become the past, in order for the white to progress towards the future and move beyond the limitations of his sexual – or at least romantic – temptation and achieve possession of the land" (Goldie, *Fear and Temptation*, 73). On the women in the Downtown Eastside, see Neville, "Rebecca Belmore."

71 True Patriot Love was the first exhibit by a living woman artist sponsored by the National Gallery.

72 As Kass Banning notes, there were many "firsts" in Wieland's contributions to the art scene. One of them was her incorporation of social and political content into re-imagining a number of classically Canadian narratives in pieces such as *Laura Secord Saves Upper Canada*, *Montcalm's Last Letter* and *Confederasprea*. See Banning, "Mummification of Mommy," 153.

73 Rabinovitz, "Issues," 40.

74 McPherson, "Wieland," 21.

75 Banning, "Mummification of Mommy," 154.

76 Crean, "Notes," 64.

77 McPherson, "Wieland," 25.

78 Moray, "Wilderness," 43.

79 Bordo, "Jack Pine."

80 Quoted in Moray, "Wilderness," 44.

81 Wieland's paintings first began to show the influence of pop art in 1963, during her period living in New York City. However, the artist kept her distance from this movement, saying: "I was terrified of the art scene, and something in me resisted becoming part of it. I didn't know what I wanted, but I kept doing what I felt I had to ... I just took what I could from it without losing sight of something in myself – something that would never be developed if I were to become part of a movement." Later, however, Wieland was influenced by Oldenburg's soft sculpture, first exhibited at the Green Gallery in New York in 1962. See Fleming, "Joyce Wieland."

82 For a fuller analysis of this material, see Pratt, "Affairs with Bears."

83 Pratt, quoted in Verduyn, *Lifelines*, 130. There is a further connection with the myth of Rhapisunt, in which a woman sleeps with a bear, gives birth to cubs, and then becomes a Bear Mother. And this narrative calls up the cult of the Bear goddess of Brauron, in which adolescent girls were allowed the run of the forest and behaved like tomboys, neither washing nor caring for themselves but, rather, living in the rough like bear cubs.

84 Verduyn, *Lifelines*, 117, 233.

85 This narrative is strikingly similar to a number of contemporary novels from Canada, Australia, and New Zealand (including Margaret Lawrence's *The Diviners*), in which a female protagonist's search for individuation and indigenization is associated with sexual contact with a Métis, Aboriginal, or Maori man. In these contexts, Terry Goldie notes that the Aboriginal male seems to signify a twin set of dangers and desires – namely, the fear of a raw and potentially violent sexual primitivism together with the lure of erotic pleasure – and contact with these figures brings the women closer to a "free" existence in nature. See Goldie, *Fear and Temptation*.

86 Joe Hermer supplied this turn of phrase.

87 Coburn, "Artist's Statement," 34.

88 Mosse, *Nationalism and Sexuality*, 91-92.

89 Ibid., 105.
90 Kang, "Autobiographical Stagings."
91 Yoon, "Artist's Statement," 30.
92 Personal interview with Jin-me Yoon, 11 January 2003.
93 Ibid.
94 The former Museum of Man in Ottawa and the Royal Ontario Museum in Toronto provide Canadian examples.
95 Haraway, "Teddy Bear Patriarchy," 24.
96 Ibid., 36.
97 Ibid., 52.
98 Personal interview with Jin-me Yoon.
99 Monika Kin Gagnon in conversation with Jin-me Yoon, in Radul, *Jin-me Yoon*, 64.
100 Ibid., 60.
101 Personal interview with Jin-me Yoon.
102 Ibid.
103 Gagan, "Relevance," 37.
104 Quoted in Lafleur, "Resting," 222. Massey was the first Canadian-born governor general of Canada, and he held this office from 1952 to 1959.
105 Lafleur, "Resting," 222.
106 Quoted in Rony, *Third Eye*, 101.
107 Quoted in Townsend-Gault, "Hot Dogs," 127.
108 Townsend-Gault, "Hot Dogs," 120.
109 Personal interview with Rebecca Belmore, 26 January 2003.
110 Ibid.
111 Ibid.
112 Ibid.
113 Deborah Fulsang, "Baby, It's Cold Outside," in *Globe and Mail*, 4 January 2003. See also Bill Cunningham "On the Street: Warm Front," *New York Times*, 12 January 2003; and Adria Vasil "Pelt Patrol: Trolling Queen for Furs to Gum up," in *NOW Magazine*, 9-15 January 2003, 15.
114 See, for example, Deidre Kelly, "Stealth Fur," *Globe and Mail*, 23 November 2002.
115 Muñoz, *Disidentifications*, 128.
116 Haraway, *Primate Visions*, 9.

Chapter 3: Things Not Named

1 Kirby, "Steamy Scenes," 25-27.
2 Gordon Lightfoot, "Canadian Railroad Trilogy," *The Way I Feel*, UA Records, UAS 6587, Mono, AL 3587, 1967.
3 Quoted from Willa Cather in Somerville, "Scientific Racism," 246.
4 Marnie Fleming, "Preface and Acknowledgements," in Flemming, *Track Records*, 9.
5 Innis, *Fur Trade*, 6. See also Innis, *History*; Innis, "Transportation as a Factor"; and Innis, "Transportation in the Canadian Economy."

6 Otter, *Philosophy of Railways*, 15.

7 Ibid., 22.

8 Harris, *Resettlement*, 184.

9 Quoted in Owram, *Promise of Eden*, 102.

10 Owram, *Promise of Eden*, 104.

11 Ibid., 113.

12 Department of Agriculture slogan, quoted in Owram, *Promise of Eden*, 112.

13 Canadian Pacific Railway booklet, *Plain Facts from Farmers in the Canadian North West* (1885), CP Archives X1064 (RG.I.A. 8202), 4.

14 Owram, *Promise of Eden*, 165.

15 Jones, "It's All Likes They Tell You," 110.

16 Quoted in Owram, *Promise of Eden*, 183.

17 Canadian Pacific Railway booklet, *Plain Facts* (1885).

18 Quoted in Dempsey, "Fearsome Fire Wagon," in Dempsey, *CPR West*, 65.

19 Hart, "See This World," 151-52.

20 Quoted in Hart, "See This World," 156-57.

21 Ibid., 157.

22 For an extended analysis of the "mosaic" metaphor, see Day, *Multiculturalism*, 146-76.

23 The head tax was first instituted by the government of British Columbia (1884) and then the federal government (1886) to discourage Chinese immigration to Canada. The tax rose from $50 when first instituted to $500 before the Exclusion Act, 1923. When Hoy arrived it was $100.

24 Moosang, *First Son*, 111-15.

25 Ibid., 147.

26 Quoted in Roy, "Choice between Evils," 17.

27 John Cartwright, the president of the Toronto and York Regional Labour Council. See http://www.whsc.on.ca/Publications/atthesource/summer2003/inrecognition.pdf.

28 Moosang, *First Son*, 141-42.

29 See Mawani, *Colonial Proximities*, and Perry, *On the Edge of Empire*.

30 For further analysis of the intersection of state racism and cross-racial encounters, see Mawani, *Colonial Proximities*.

31 Berton, *National Dream*; Berton, *Last Spike*, 92.

32 Berton, *National Dream*; Berton, *Last Spike*, 206.

33 Moy, "Political Economy," 60. Moy highlights House of Commons debates from 1923, which document that, between 1885 and 1923, the Canadian state extracted taxes (over and above the Head Tax) that totalled over $22 million. Further, Lai reminds us that, in the 1870s, after coal and fur, opium was British Columbia's third largest export to the United States. The import, manufacture, and use of opium was legal in Canada until 1908. See Lai, "Chinese Opium Trade."

34 Indeed, representatives of the CPR and of the other primary industries of the west all agreed that their financial viability was actually dependent on Chinese labourers. See Moy, *Political Economy*, 42-54.

35 I borrow this phrase from Dening, *Performances*, 103-27.

36 Waugh, "Good, Clean Fung."

37 Richard Fung, interview with the author, 18 August 1999.

38 Unlike Hoy's images, this photo suggests an era before 1912 when Chinese men would still have been wearing the long braid and tonsure. Moosang notes that, before 1912, under the Qing Dynasty, men in China were expected to wear their hair in a long braid that hung from the centre of the back of the head and to shave (or tonsure) their foreheads. See Moosang, *First Son*, 119.

39 Steven, "Art of Calculated Risk," 30-31.

40 Ibid., 33.

41 Richard Fung, interview with the author, 7 March 2000.

42 These two artists are part of a broader-based black London arts scene that began flourishing in the 1980s. These artists use a broad range of media technologies and visual formats to reinvigorate an artistic examination of identity, culture, and history. See Powell, *Black Art*, 223.

43 Xing, *Asian America*, 161-62.

44 Richard Fung, interview with the author, March 2000.

45 Quoted in Xing, *Asian America*, 162.

46 Scott, "Experience," 24.

47 Halperin, *Saint*, 105.

48 Lai, "Prison."

49 David Chuenyan Lai took the photographs of Chinese men's writing on "the wall," and these were the images used by Fung in the dramatized sequences in *Dirty Laundry*. Reproductions can be seen in the article cited above.

50 These lines are an amalgamation of two actual "poems" found in the "prison" referred to above. See Lai, "Prison," 18-19.

51 Lai, "Prison," 16-19.

52 Caruth, "Introduction," in Caruth, *Trauma*, 5.

53 Foucault, *History of Sexuality*, 101.

54 Richard Fung, interview with the author, 7 March 2000.

55 Quoted in McClintock, *Imperial Leather*, 300.

56 Barber, *Canadian Oxford Dictionary*, 1540, 1544.

57 Lai, "Prison," 19.

58 Steven, "Art of Calculated Risk," 33.

59 Royal Commission on Chinese Immigration, *Report*, v.

60 While some historians would place the development of white racial formation somewhat earlier, I am persuaded that the late nineteenth century constituted a crucial moment in the development of changed notions of race in Canada. First, following on the work of Laura Stoler, my analysis assumes that definitions of Euro-Canadian and Chinese masculinity were not simply pre-formed in their respective metropoles and exported to the Canadian west. Instead, I suggest that British Columbia's polyglot settler community required a radical rethinking of colonial authority. Second, as Anne McClintock discusses, the development of "commodity racism" played a

crucial role. To expand: "If, after the 1850s, scientific racism saturated anthropo-logical, scientific and medical journals, travel writing and novels, these cultural forms were still relatively class-bound and inaccessible to most Victorians, who had neither the means nor the education to read such material. Imperial kitsch as con-sumer spectacle, by contrast, could package, market and distribute evolutionary ra-cism on a hitherto unimagined scale" (McClintock, *Imperial Leather*, 209). For further analysis, see McClintock, "Soft-Soaping Empire," 207-31.

61 The references in the lyrics refer to the following countries: Lily = Wales; Thistle = Scotland; Shamrock = Ireland; Rose = England. While it is possible that the "lily" could also refer to French Canada, it seems clear that, in the context of this ditty, the intended referent is the four groups that composed the motherland of "Great Britain."

62 An excellent starting place for examining the meanings associated with gender and sex in European contexts is Duberman et al., *Hidden from History*. See the sections on the nineteenth and early twentieth centuries. For an analysis of the western fron-tier, see Chapman, "An Oscar Wilde Type"; Williams, "Seafarers"; Jacobs et al., *Two-Spirit People;* Chapman, "Male Homosexuality"; and Perry, *On the Edge of Empire*.

63 Ingram, "Returning to the Scene." See also interview with Richard Fung on Rex ver-sus Singh, Gayatri Bajpai, "Exclusive Interview with Richard Fung | Sense of Wonder" in Schema Magazine, available at http://www.schemamag.ca/indepth/2010/05/richard-fung-is-a-toronto-based.php

64 Danysk, "Bachelor's Paradise." Danysk explains that the term "to batch" entered the Prairie lexicon with ease, indicating the social acceptablility of labouring men with-out women.

65 Ibid., 160.

66 For analysis of the difficult construction of Christian marriage norms in the Canadian west, see Carter, *The Importance of Being Monogamous*.

67 Pon, "Like a Chinese Puzzle."

68 Bederman, *Manliness and Civilization*, 25.

69 As Marianna Valverde and Madge Pon note, white fears of Chinese masculinity were marked by a distinct contradiction. Chinese men were thought of as too "timid" and "unmuscular" to engage in the aggressive sexual entrapment of white women. Nevertheless, they could still be conceptualized as a threat due to their ability to "lure" white women into opium dens where they would be easy prey to sexual dan-ger. See Pon, "Like a Chinese Puzzle"; Valverde, *Age of Light*, 110-11.

70 Shah, *Contagious Divides*, 19.

71 Said, *Orientalism*.

72 Quoted in Muñoz, *Disidentifications*, 12.

73 "Triads" is a vernacular term for Chinese criminal gangs.

Chapter 4: Banff National Park

1 Quote from Paul Lavoie, chairman and CEO of Toronto's Taxi Advertising and Design, in Keith McArthur, "Tourism Ads to Shun Mounties and Moose," *Globe and Mail*, 12 May 2005.

2 McArthur, "Tourism Ads."

3 Opinion polls and surveys from Statistics Canada suggest that national parks represent an important image of Canadianness. Indeed, after medicare, the Bill of Rights, and the flag, parks are the most widely recognized symbol of national identity. Bruce Kirkby, "Our National Parks Are the Envy of the World," *Globe and Mail*, 18 March 2011, http://www.theglobeandmail.com/.

4 In response to my earlier writing on the Lesbian National Parks and Services, some readers have interpreted my analysis as a criticism of Shawna Dempsey and Lorri Millan and their work. I want to clarify that I am not critical, but instead appreciate the artists' courage and smarts in this project. It is only because the project works so well as comedy that it is effective for the deconstructive reading I propose here. In my view, not all artistic projects have to take up "race" directly in order to be useful for *reading* race as a set of historically constructed viewing practices.

5 Quoted in Hummel, *Endangered Spaces*, 15-16.

6 Jasen, *Wild Things*.

7 Quoted in Hart, *Selling of Canada*, 39.

8 Advertisement for Rimrock Resort Hotel in Banff, Alberta. The ad is undated, but the Rimrock Banff opened in 1993.

9 Berland, "Fire and Flame," 13. Yellowstone continues to attract Canadian interest. Most recently, Noranda Minerals gained authorization to set up a large gold and silver mine just three kilometres outside Yellowstone, creating a potential reservoir of toxic waste over the watershed that feeds the park. See Runte, *National Parks*, xii.

10 Interestingly, the artist Paul Kane, the Canadian equivalent to George Catlin, was first inspired to paint the Aboriginal cultures through hearing Catlin speak in Piccadilly, England, in 1842. See Eaton and Urbanek, *Paul Kane's Great Nor-West*, 7.

11 Quoted in Weber, "I Would Ask," 15-18 (emphasis in original). The first Canadian commissioner of National Parks, J.B. Harkin, also mentions the role of Judge Cornelius Hedges of Montana, who organized the campaign to actually set aside Yellowstone as a park through an act of Congress in 1872.

12 Harkin, *Origins and Meaning*. Harkin began his term as commissioner in 1911.

13 Anderson, *Imagined Communities*, 163-85.

14 Hermer, *Regulating Eden*.

15 For information on the impact of national parks on Aboriginal people in the United States, see Keller and Turek, *American Indians*. For information on European empires in Africa, see Neumann, *Imposing Wilderness*.

16 Cronon, "Trouble with Wilderness," 36.

17 In both Canada and the United States, the western frontier was represented as "free land." This discourse was foundational to legal claims of entitlement that prepared the way for European settlement. In many other respects, however, Canadian discourse about the frontier has been markedly different from that of the United States. For further analysis, see Cross, *Turner Thesis*; Francis, "Wasteland to Utopia."

18 McNeil, "Social Darwinism."

19 Indian and Northern Affairs reports that, in September 2003, Minister Robert Nault, along with Chief Adrian Stimson Sr. of Siksika Nation, officially announced the settlement of a historic claim dating back to 1910, when approximately 5,068 hectares of reserve lands were allegedly surrendered by the Siksika Nation. The settlement for the surface rights of the lands provided the Siksika with approximately $82 million in compensation for the damages and losses suffered as a result of the surrender. The amount is significant because, historically, former reserve lands in southern Alberta have been productive agricultural lands. The entire compensation package will be placed in trust to ensure that future generations of Siksika Nation members benefit from the settlement. See http://www.ainc-inac.gc.ca/ab/ayr04/ayrty7_e.html.

Regarding the contested aspects of Treaty 7, see Snow, *These Mountains*, 18-29; and Treaty 7 Elders et al., *True Spirit*. Essentially, Snow argues that, while the federal government wanted legal title to the entire North-West Territories, the Stoney people saw the treaties as strictly peace treaties and understood that they would continue to have access to their traditional hunting territory. In addition, he suggests that the person who interpreted on behalf of the Stoney, Reverend John McDougall, had a vested interest on the side of the government as he wanted to establish a more permanent agricultural reserve at Morely.

20 Boody, "Architecture of Tourism," 18.

21 Berland, "Fire and Flame," 14, emphasis in original.

22 Laurie Meijer Drees argues that Stoney people used the Banff Indian Days celebration as an opportunity for social interaction and the assertion of their cultural identity. She concludes that "government policies did not necessarily reflect popular attitudes towards Indians in Canada; instead, it shows that White society was fascinated with what it perceived to be Indian culture, and that Native people in this period had a central and active role in the creation of their own destinies and public history." My own review of the representational strategies used in the Banff Indian Days brochures from 1925 to 1967 suggests that, as this event came under the direction of white entrepreneurs (who used it to bolster the image of Banff as a spectacularized "wild west"), the images of Indianness became more generic and stereotypical. See Drees, "Indians' Bygone Past," 8. In 1978, the Stoney refused to participate any longer in this event, resulting in its cancellation. However, in 2004, Stoney members decided to restart Banff Indian Days under their own management, and they are working towards ensuring that a revitalized celebration has a primarily spiritual focus. Interview with Annette Johnston, Cultural Interpreter with the Stoney Nation, 24 August 2005.

23 Bradford, "Useful Institution," 88.

24 From an early twentieth-century advertisement by Tobin Arms Manufacturing Company, who promoted hunting as a form of recreation that would, it promised, bring its customers back to being the "original animal man." See Jasen, *Wild Things*, 105.

25 Jasen, *Wild Things*, 105. For further analysis of the early twentieth-century crisis in masculinity and the developing popularity of wilderness holidays, see Rotundo, *American Manhood*, 247-62.

26 Moss, *Manliness and Militarism*, 123.

27 Ibid., 124.

28 Tompkins, *West of Everything*, 187. Internationally, this role was played by the Society for the Preservation of the Fauna of the Empire.

29 Jasen, *Wild Things*, 120.

30 Quoted in Jasen, *Wild Things*, 109.

31 Pamphlet entitled *Banff the Beautiful*, 1890s-1910.

32 Quoted in Marty, *Grand and Fabulous Notion*, 41.

33 Quoted in Jasen, *Wild Things*, 108.

34 Between 1885, when Rocky Mountain Park was first established, and 1909, when a federal order-in-council first approved monies for employing park wardens, the North-West Mounted Police monitored the interior of Alberta, reporting on the movement of wildlife and apprehending poachers. See Foster, *Working for Wildlife*, 27-73.

35 Burns with Schintz, *Guardians of the Wild*, 8.

36 Sandilands, "Where the Mountain Men," 149.

37 I want to thank Catriona Sandilands, whose article, cited above, prompted my thinking in this area.

38 Foster, *Working for Wildlife*, 28-30. Stewart held this office from 1887 to 1896.

39 Burns with Schintz, *Guardians of the Wild*, 15..

40 Ibid., 16.

41 Ibid.

42 Ibid.

43 Ibid., 15.

44 Ibid., 17.

45 Sandilands, "Where the Mountain Men," 148.

46 First instituted by the Department of Indian Affairs under Hayter Reed in 1885.

47 Drees, "Making Banff," 57-68.

48 There was a "lively debate" about the use of traps, guns, poison, and dogs to hunt these animals, and Burns describes it in detail. See Burns with Schintz, *Guardians of the Wild*, 22-24.

49 Ibid., 24.

50 Ibid., 88-89.

51 Ibid., 81.

52 Ibid., 84-95.

53 Ibid., 101.

54 Ibid., 107.

55 Ibid., 98-107.

56 In 1870, nearly half the Indigenous people on the Stoney reserve died in the small-pox epidemic, and the Spanish Flu (1918) also took a disproportionate toll. See Drees, "Making Banff," 66-68. In addition, the government's continual focus on "economizing" on supplies sent to Aboriginal communities sometimes meant that people were destitute to the point of starvation. See, among others, Titley, *Narrow Vision*; Shewell, *Enough*.

57 Personal communication with Brenda Holder from Mahikan Trails (Aboriginal-run guiding operation), Jasper, Alberta, 6 June 2010.

58 Dobak, "Killing the Canadian Buffalo."

59 Marte, "Foodmaps," 261-62.

60 Sobal, "Men."

61 Owram, *Promise of Eden*, 113.

62 Quoted in Julier, "Hiding Gender," 175.

63 For the implications of this in Canadian wilderness painting, see Bordo, "Jack Pine."

64 Walker, *Inside/Outside*, 166.

65 Martha Wilson, quoted in Dubin, *Arresting Images*, 154.

66 Maclear, *Beclouded Visions*, 24.

67 As is clear in earlier sections of this chapter, national park staff members are actually called wardens. In the second half of this chapter I switch to using the term "rangers" in concert with the Lesbian National Parks and Services Rangers.

68 Walter, *Private Investigators*, 45.

69 For further reading on early experiments in performance art, see Goldberg, *Performance*.

70 Quoted in Dubin, *Arresting Images*, 153.

71 Lynne Fernie, interview with the author, 7 October 1998.

72 Quoted in Dubin, *Arresting Images*, 154.

73 Dempsey and Millan re-performed the piece at the Michigan Women's Music Festival in August 1999, at the Winnipeg Gay and Lesbian Pride Day parade in the summer of 1998, and in Australia in 2000. Recently, they have published *Handbook of the Junior Lesbian Ranger*. The handbook and crests are available from Lesbian National Parks and Services International Headquarters, 485 Wardlaw Avenue, Winnipeg, Manitoba, Canada, R3L 0L9, or you can e-mail them at finger@escape.ca. To view their website go to http://www.fingerinthedyke.ca.

74 See also Wollen et al., *On the Passage*.

75 Maclear, "Accidental Witness," 9.

76 Kathryn Walter, "Lesbian National Parks and Services: Scenario," in Walter, *Private Investigators*, 46.

77 Walter, *Private Investigators*, 46.

78 Shawna Dempsey, interview with the author, 4 December 1999.

79 Lorri Millan, interview with the author, 13 January 2000.

80 Ibid.

81 Maclear, "Accidental Witness," 16.

82 Butler, *Bodies That Matter*.

83 Ibid., *Gender Trouble*, 31.

84 Quoted in Armitage, "Gendering Conquest," 187.

85 Parks Canada, *Annual Report to the Canadian Human Rights Commission, Terms of Settlement of Demuth*, 1 April 1999 to 31 March 2000 (Ottawa: Parks Canada, 2000), app. A. For American figures, which are slightly better, see Dornsife, "Women," 32-33, 46, 57.

86 Hermer, *Regulating Eden*, 37; Chase, *Playing God*, 245.

87 Dornsife, "Women," 32.

88 Adkins, "Sexual Work," 215-16.

89 Ibid., 216.

90 While domestic service in the Canadian hotel industry is, in general, deeply racially segregated, this is not the case in Banff. Here most domestic service in hotels and non-professional work throughout the park is performed by young white workers paid at minimum wage for short-term contracts.

91 Eagle Scout Rally for Family Foundation distributes *Suffer the Children*. Their mission is outlined on their website: "We are a few good men, all Christian Eagle Scouts. Our BELIEF is that character matters. Our MISSION is to prevent our nation's most precious resource, its youth, from the physical health risks and emotional ravages of the homosexual lifestyle. Our MESSAGE is simple, *DON'T GO THERE!!!*" While this organization seems extreme, the video did circulate in Toronto in the early 1990s. Further, the fears promoted in this video and similar literature continue to have a profound effect in schools across the country. In most jurisdictions, equity policies *still* do not allow education about lesbian, gay, bisexual, and transgender lives in public schools.

92 For an analysis of the debates regarding "proselytization" at the former Toronto Board of Education, see Campey et al., "Opening."

93 Judith Butler examines a similar rhetorical strategy in her article "Contagious Word: Paranoia and 'Homosexuality' in the Military," in Butler, *Excitable Speech*, 103-26.

94 Alberta was one of the last provinces to enact legislation to protect lesbian and gay citizens and only did so when forced to by the Supreme Court.

95 Millan, interview with the author.

96 Baines, "Overlapping/Contesting Representations," 67.

97 The primary objection brought by conservative lobby groups against school boards considering the inclusion of sexual orientation in their human rights policy is that anti-heterosexism educators will "recruit" youth into a homosexual lifestyle. Thus, in Toronto, parents worried that queer educators would proselytize other students. See Campey et al., "Opening," n. 90.

98 Despite the increase in visitors from Asia, as of the late 1980s the tourist population of Banff remains primarily white. The largest groups that visit Banff are Canadians, Americans, Britons, and Japanese. See Hock and Sisco, *Local Interpretations*, 66.

99 Quoted in Dyer, "White," 45-46.

100 Dyer, *White*, 51. Dyer elaborates: "The importance of the process of boundary establishment and maintenance has long been recognized in discussions of stereotyping and representation. This process is functional for dominant groups, but through it the capacity to set boundaries becomes a characteristic attribute of such groups, endlessly reproduced in ritual, costume, language and, in cinema, *mise-en-scène*."

101 Maclear, "Eyewitness Account," in Walters, *Private Investigators*, 56.

102 Maclear, *Beclouded Visions*, 10 (emphasis in original). Here Maclear is estimating the number of Chinese workers who died in the construction of the Canadian Pacific Railway. Historical reconstructions of this figure are extremely difficult to confirm as local media at the time often did not record the deaths of Chinese workers and there are few "official" records.

103 Maclear, *Beclouded Visions*, 12.

104 Putnam et al., *Place Names*, 56.

105 The Foundation to Commemorate Chinese Railroad Workers in Canada erected a $150,000 monument in Toronto next to the SkyDome in 1989 to commemorate the seventeen thousand Chinese men who laboured to construct the railway and the four thousand estimated to have died at this task. See Joel Baglole, "Wreath Laid for Railway Workers: 17,000 Chinese Were 'Pioneers,'" *Toronto Star*, 3 July 1999.

106 Quoted in Lippard, *Lure of the Local*, 289.

107 For the implications of this in Canadian wilderness painting, see Bordo, "Jack Pine."

Chapter 5: Playing Indian

1 Carr, *Inventing*, 106.

2 Trachtenberg, *Shades of Hiawatha*, 52.

3 Curator's Statement, Clarence Boyer, "Hiawatha: Archival Photographs," Art Gallery of Algoma, February 2005, 1.

4 "Hiawatha at the Toronto Exhibition," *Sault Daily Star*, 25 August 1937.

5 Foreman, *Indians Abroad*, 166-73; personal correspondence from W. Eisenbichler, associate director, Sault Ste. Marie Public Library, 13 July 1992.

6 Brydon, "Hiawatha Meets," 90.

7 Carr, *Inventing*, 125.

8 McNally, "Indian Passion Play," 110.

9 Ibid.

10 Schoolcraft's primary source was his wife, Jane Johnston, who was the daughter of John Johnston and Susan Ojeeg (who was the daughter of the famous Chief Waub Ojeeg of La Pointe). Jane and her family provided Schoolcraft with many contacts with other prominent people in the Sault region. See Massie, "Supplementary Introduction." Schoolcraft's earliest ethnological text is the *Algic Researches* (1839), and he later published *Historical and Statistical Information Respecting ... the Indian Tribes of the United States* (1851-57).

11 However, Hiawatha did not work alone. He actually converted to the cause of Deganawida, another culture hero who made it his mission to end the wars among Mohawk, Seneca, Oneida, and others. But Deganawida had a speech impediment,

and so Hiawatha, as his interpreter, went from tribe to tribe persuading the chiefs to stop the bloodshed and to join a great council at Onondaga – from which the great League of the Iroquois was born. See Kretch, "Alan Trachtenberg."

12 Carr, *Inventing*, 127.

13 Bercovitch, *Cambridge History*, 215-16.

14 Quoted in Bercovitch, *Cambridge History*, 194.

15 Brydon, "Hiawatha Meets," 128.

16 Phillips, *Trading Identities*, x.

17 Brydon, "Hiawatha Meets," 31.

18 Betty and Lana Grawbarger, interview with author, 11 November 2005. The Grawbargers are descendents of Chief Shingwaukonse. Janet Chute, who has written a history of the Garden River Anishinaabe, confirms that Schoolcraft's assistants consulted with Shingwaukonse. See Janet Chute, *Legacy of Shingwaukonse*, 144.

19 It is possible that Armstrong organized Kabaosa's visit to Boston as a prelude to visiting Longfellow's family. See Brydon, "Hiawatha Meets," 40.

20 "Hiawatha at the Toronto Exhibition: Cast of 34 Players in Colorful Dramatic Pictures of the Algoma Wilds: Will Run Nightly for the Duration of the Exhibition – How the Play Originated – First Performed in 1900," *Sault Daily Star*, 25 August 1937.

21 Chute, *Legacy of Shingwaukonse*, 144.

22 Phillips, *Trading Identities*, 24-25.

23 Brydon, "Hiawatha Meets," 36.

24 Wilson, *Missionary Work*, 166.

25 Edgar, "Hiawatha," 690. William Edgar's 1904 review and analysis of the performance highlights how Armstrong consulted with Garden River cast members in developing the script of the play, reviewing sections of the poem and "verifying and correcting" the narrative while "obtaining the Indian version of the story."

26 When the troupe performed in Toronto, the island stage was located on Lake Ontario; and when the performances were overseas or in the United States, a simulated island and lake were constructed for the performance. See "Sault of Yesteryear," *Sault Star*, 9 August 1973.

27 John Erskine Pine was the grandson of Chief Shingwaukonse.

28 Betty and Lana Grawbarger, interview with author.

29 Yeigh, "Drama of Hiawatha," 208.

30 Betty and Lana Grawbarger, interview. 5.

31 Jean Pine, Alice Corbiere and Joe Corbiere, interview with author, 7 August 2008.

32 Personal interview with Jean Pine and Angela Neveau, 17 November 2005.

33 Ibid., 1.

34 Betty and Lana Grawbarger, interview with author. Further information on the Midewiwin comes from a recent article in the *Canadian Historical Review*: "Commonly called the Great Medicine Society or Medicine Dance in the English language, the Midewiwin functioned to promote a balanced life, often achieved through healing practices, sacred teachings, and narratives, with the assistance of

manidoog (spirits, gods, *manitou*). Historically, the Midewiwin also created and sustained an ethno-cultural identity for the Anishinaabe." See Neylan, "Preserving the Sacred."

35 My analysis here has been influenced by Kasfir, "African Art."

36 Clarence Boyer, interview with author, 4 October 2005.

37 See Devens, *Countering Colonization*.

38 In the photo of the performance at the Toronto Exhibition in 1937, thirteen of the thirty-one performers are women.

39 Alan Trachtenberg describes a series of performances that ran from 1881 to 1911, in which "Indian" students performed staged readings of "Scenes from Hiawatha" at Carnegie Hall in New York as well as other theatres and summer resorts in New England. See Trachtenberg, *Shades of Hiawatha*, 89.

40 Quoted in Petrone, *First Peoples*, 60.

41 In my interview with Betty and Lana Grawbarger, they presented testimony regarding Betty's years at the school in the 1930s and the experience of her father in the early 1900s.

42 Betty and Lana Grawbarger, interview with author, 7.

43 Trachtenberg, *Shades of Hiawatha*, 92-97.

44 Quoted in Trachtenberg, *Shades of Hiawatha*, 95.

45 Ibid.

46 Edgar, "Hiawatha," 691.

47 Yeigh, "Drama of Hiawatha," 217.

48 Edgar, "Hiawatha," 693.

49 My reflections on loss are influenced by Behar's "Death and Memory."

50 Rosaldo, *Culture and Truth*.

51 Interview with Pine and Neveau.

52 Tilley, "Hayter Reed," 135. The "dances" referred to in Section 149 of the Indian Act are the Sun Dance and the Rain Dance, both central to the ceremonial cycle of the Saulteaux, Cree, and Dakota.

53 Here my analysis is indebted to McMaster, *Portraits*.

54 These novels were available from Chapter's Bookstore in Ottawa in the spring of 2000.

55 Here my analysis in indebted to Ryan, *Trickster Shift*, 3-12.

56 Personal communication from Kent Monkman to the author, 2003.

57 Ibid.

58 Including Stan McKay, the director of a centre for Aboriginal studies in Winnipeg.

59 Mason, *Travels*, 56-59.

60 The HBC governor Sir George Simpson supported the accusations against Evans and worked to have him removed from the community, but it seems that the primary person responsible for instigating the allegations of sexual misconduct was William Mason, a junior white missionary in Norway House. The evidence that stands in favour of Evans includes the fact that the schoolgirls who made the original accusations

against him retracted them in writing and said that their stories had been solicited by Mason. Further, many First Nations and European residents spoke in Evans' defence at his trial. Two other points are also relevant: first, two years earlier Evans caught Mason sexually harassing his own daughter; second, after Evans' death, Mason took full credit for inventing the Cree syllabics when the first Cree Bible was printed in England (Mason, *Travels*, 64, 68-69). While all this suggests Evans' innocence, one other account is less clear. See Hutchinson, "James Evans' Last Year."

61 Personal communication from Kent Monkman to the author, 2003. For further information on Monkman's work, see http://www.kentmonkman.com.

62 Teitelbaum, "Mourners Cry," 35.

63 Hubbard, *Artist*.

64 Driscoll, *All That Is Glorious*, 8-9.

65 Personal interview with Kent Monkman, 3 June 2003.

66 See Mawani, *Colonial Proximities*; Perry, *On the Edge of Empire*; Carter, *The Importance of Being Monogamous*.

67 Interview with Kent Monkman, 3 June 2003.

68 Ibid., October 2003.

69 Ibid.

70 Quoted in Swanson, "Noble Savage," 5.

71 Quoted in Hill, "Drag Racing," 25.

72 Interview with Kent Monkman, October 2003.

73 Smith, *Decolonizing Methodologies*.

Chapter 6: Conclusion

1 de Certeau, *Practice of Everyday Life*, 108.

2 Derrida, *Spectres of Marx*, 176.

3 Gordon, *Ghostly Matters*, 18, 22.

4 Kaplan, "Magical Power," 183-99.

5 Massumi, "Navigating Movements," 223.

6 Wu, *On Metaphoring*, 40.

7 Wilby, "Witch's Familiar," 284.

8 Ibid., 289.

9 Ibid., 291-94.

10 Bergland, *National Uncanny*, 8-9.

11 Pels, "Introduction," 35.

12 Stasiulis and Jhappan, "Fractious Politics," 117.

13 Michael Valpy, *Globe and Mail*, 1 July 2004.

14 Bannerji, *Dark Side*; Day, *Multiculturalism*; Mackey, *House of Difference*; Razack, *Race*; Razack, *Dark Threats*.

15 Text of Jean Chrétien's farewell speech, 2003, quoted in Leung, "Usable Pasts," 168.

16 Leung, "Usable Pasts," 170-71.

17 Walcott, *Black Like Who*, 36-37, 39, 118. See also Nelson, *Razing Africville*.

18 Marc Frenette and René Morissette, "Earnings of Immigrant Workers and Canadian-Born Workers, 1980-2000," in *The Daily*, an online bulletin from Statistics Canada, 8 October 2003, http://www.statcan.gc.ca/daily-quotidien/031008/dq031008a-eng.htm.

19 Ibid. These increasing disparities have emerged despite the fact that the educational attainment of recent immigrant women increased faster than that of their Canadian-born counterparts. For instance, in 1980, 15 percent of immigrant women had a university degree. The corresponding number in 2000 was 38 percent. Meanwhile, the share of Canadian-born women with a degree has only progressed from 10 percent to 22 percent.

20 Anna Mehler Paperny, "Jobless Rate up for Toronto Immigrants: Rate Drops for Native-Born Residents," *Globe and Mail*, 4 December 2010.

21 The Reality for First Nations in Canada. Fact Sheet from the Assembly of First Nations, available at http://www.afn.ca/article.asp?id=764.

22 Andrew Siggner, "Study: Aboriginal People Living in Metropolitan Areas," from *The Daily*, an online bulletin from Statistics Canada, 23 June 2005, http://www.statcan.ca/Daily/English/050623/d050623b.htm.

23 Abu-Laban and Gabriel, *Selling Diversity*, 122.

24 Ibid., 124.

25 Sharma, *Home Economics*.

26 Galabuzi, *Canada's Economic Apartheid*.

27 Alexander, *Pedagogies of Crossing*, 190.

28 Lawrence and Dua, "Decolonizing Antiracism," 126.

29 Sharma and Wright, "Decolonizing Resistance." See also Henderson and Wakeham, "Colonial Reckoning."

30 Massumi, "Navigating Movements," 218.

31 Quoted in Smith, "Native American Feminism," 131.

32 Watson and Belmore, "Interview," 24-41, 24.

33 Ibid., 26.

34 Hill, "Built on Running Water," 50.

35 Martin, "Waters of Venice," 52.

36 Megan Williams, "Painting the Town Red: Rebecca Belmore's Splashy Debut at Venice Biennale," 10 June 2005, available at http://www.cbc.ca/arts/artdesign/belmore.html.

37 Taussig, *Defacement*, 1-2.

38 Crichlow, "Stan Douglas," 12.

39 Kim Pelis, "Blood Transfusion," in *The Oxford Companion to Medicine*, available at *Oxford Reference Online*, http://www.oxfordreference.com.catalogue.library.brocku.ca:80/views/ENTRY.html?subview=Mainandentry=t185.e68.

40 Watson and Belmore, "Interview," 27.

41 Ibid., 28.

42 Martin, "Waters of Venice," 50.

43 Williams, "Painting."

44 Taussig, *Defacement*, 2.
45 Watson and Belmore, "Interview," 27.
46 Pelis, "Blood Transfusion."

Bibliography

Abu-Laban, Yasmeen, and Christina Gabriel. *Selling Diversity: Immigration, Multiculturalism, Employment Equity, and Globalization.* Toronto: University of Toronto Press, 2002.

Adkins, Lisa. "Sexual Work and the Employment of Women in the Service Industries." In *Gender and Bureaucracy,* ed. Mike Savage and Anne Witz, 207-28. Cambridge, MA: Blackwell, 1992.

Alexander, M. Jacqui. *Pedagogies of Crossing: Meditations on Feminism, Sexual Politics, Memory, and the Sacred.* Durham, NC: Duke University Press, 2005.

Alfred, Taiaiake. *Wasáse: Indigenous Pathways of Action and Freedom.* Peterborough, ON: Broadview Press, 2005.

Althusser, Louis. *Essays on Ideology.* London and New York: Verso: 1970.

Amphlett, Hilda. *Hats: A History of Fashion in Headwear.* London: Richard Sadler, 1974.

Anderson, Benedict. *Imagined Communities: Reflections on the Origin and Spread of Nationalism.* London: Verso, 1991.

–. "Introduction to Part Two: Staging Antimodernism in the Age of High Capitalist Nationalism." In *Antimodernism and Artistic Experience: Policing the Boundaries of Modernity,* ed. Lynda Jessup, 97-103. Toronto: University of Toronto Press, 2001.

Anderson, Kay J. *Vancouver's Chinatown: Racial Discourse in Canada, 1875-1980.* Montreal and Kingston: McGill-Queen's University Press, 1991.

Armitage, Susan. "Gendering Conquest." Review essay on Polly Welts Kaufman, "National Parks and the Women's Voice." *Journal of Women's History* 3 (Autumn 1997): 186-92

Atwood, Margaret. *Strange Things: The Malevolent North in Canadian Literature.* Oxford: Clarendon Press, 1995.

–. *Survival: A Thematic Guide to Canadian Literature.* Toronto: Anansi Press, 1972.

Augaitis, Daina, and Sylvie Gilbert. "Between Views and Points of View." In *Between Views,* curated by Daina Augaitis and Sylvie Gilbert, 2-7. Banff, AB: Banff Centre for the Arts, 1991.

Backhouse, Constance. *Colour-Coded: A Legal History of Racism in Canada, 1900-1950.* Toronto: University of Toronto Press, 1999.

Baines, Holly. "Overlapping/Contesting Representations: Tourism and Native Indian Canadians." MA thesis, University of Toronto, 1995.

Bannerji, Hamani. *The Dark Side of the Nation: Essays on Multiculturalism, Nationalism and Gender.* Toronto: Canadian Scholars Press, 2000.

Banning, Kass. "The Mummification of Mommy: Joyce Wieland as the AGO's First Living Other." In *Sightlines: Reading Contemporary Canadian Art,* ed. Jessica Bradley and Lesley Johnstone, 153-67. Montreal: Artextes Editions, 1994.

Barber, Katherine, ed., *The Canadian Oxford Dictionary.* Toronto, Oxford, New York: Oxford University Press, 1998.

Baron, Ava, ed. *Work Engendered: Toward a New History of American Labour.* Ithaca, NY: Cornell University Press, 1991.

Bederman, Gail. *Manliness and Civilization: A Cultural History of Gender and Race in the United States, 1880-1917.* Chicago: University of Chicago Press, 1995.

–. "'Civilization,' the Decline of Middle-Class Manliness, and Ida B. Wells' Anti-Lynching Campaign (1892-94)." *Radical History Review* 52 (1992): 5-30.

Behar, Ruth. "Death and Memory: From Santa María del Monte to Miami Beach." In *The Vulnerable Observer: Anthropology That Breaks Your Heart,* 34-89. Boston: Beacon Press, 1996.

Bercovitch, Sacvan, ed. *The Cambridge History of American Literature.* Vol. 2: *1820-1865.* Cambridge: Cambridge University Press, 1995.

Berger, Carl. *The Sense of Power: Studies in the Ideas of Canadian Imperialism, 1867-1914.* Toronto: University of Toronto Press, 1970.

Bergland, Renee L. *The National Uncanny: Indian Ghosts and American Subjects.* Hanover, NH: University Press of New England, 2000.

Berkhofer, Robert F., Jr. *The White Man's Indian: Images of the American Indian from Columbus to the Present.* New York: Alfred A. Knopf, 1978.

Berland, Jody. "Fire and Flame, Lightning and Landscape: Tourism and Nature in Banff, Alberta." In *Between Views,* curated by Daina Augaitis and Sylvie Gilbert, 12-17. Banff, AB: Banff Centre for the Arts, 1991.

Berton, Pierre. *The Great Railway Illustrated.* Toronto: McClelland and Stewart, 1972.

–. *The Last Spike: The Great Railway, 1881-1885.* Toronto: McClelland and Stewart, 1974.

–. *The National Dream: The Great Railway, 1871-1881.* Toronto: McClelland and Stewart, 1970.

Bhabha, Homi. "DissemiNation: Time, Narrative, and the Margins of the Modern Nation." In *Nation and Narration,* ed. Homi Bhabha, 1-7. New York: Routledge, 1990.

–. "Interrogating Identity: The Post-Colonial Prerogative." In *Anatomy of Racism,* ed. D.T. Goldberg, 183-209. Minneapolis: University of Minnesota Press, 1993.

–. "Introduction: Narrating the Nation." In *Nation and Narration,* ed. Homi Bhabha, 1-7. New York: Routledge, 1990.

–. "The World and the Home." In *Dangerous Liaisons: Gender, Nation and Postcolonial Perspectives,* ed. Anne McClintock, Aamir Mufti, and Ella Shohat, 445-55. Minneapolis: University of Minnesota Press, 1997.

Billig, Michael. *Banal Nationalism.* London: Sage, 1995.

Black, Francis L. "Why Did They Die?" *Science* 258 (December 1992): 739-40.

Black-Rogers, Mary. "Varieties of 'Starving': Semantics and Survival in the Subartic Fur Trade, 1750-1850." *Ethnohistory* 33, 4 (1986): 353-83.

Boody, Trevor. "The Architecture of Tourism: Banff Boulderized." *Canadian Architect* 42, 1 (1997): 18-19.

Bordo, Jonathan. "Jack Pine: Wilderness Sublime or the Erasure of the Aboriginal Presence from the Landscape." *Journal of Canadian Studies* 27, 4 (1992-93): 98-128.

Bovet, Jacques. "The Maleness of Male Beavers: A Response to Margot Francis." *Journal of Historical Sociology* 18, 1-2 (2005): 122-23.

Bradford, Tolly. "A Useful Institution: William Twin, 'Indianness', and Banff National Park, c. 1860-1940." *Native Studies Review* 16, 2 (2005): 77-98.

Bristow, Joseph. *Empire Boys: Adventures in a Man's World.* London and New York: HarperCollinsAcademic, 1991.

Brogan, Kathleen. *Cultural Haunting: Ghosts and Ethnicity in Recent American Literature.* Charlottesville: University Press of Virginia, 1998.

Brydon, Sherry. "Hiawatha Meets the Gitche Gumme Indians: The Visualization of Indians in Turn of the Century Hiawatha Pageant Plays." MA thesis, Carleton University, 1993.

Burns, Robert J., with Mike Schintz. *Guardians of the Wild: A History of the Warden Service of Canada's National Parks.* Calgary: University of Calgary Press, 2000.

Buse, Peter, and Andrew Scott, eds. *Ghosts: Deconstruction, Psychoanalysis, History.* London: Macmillan, 1999.

Butler, Judith. *Bodies that Matter: On the Discursive Limits of "Sex."* New York and London: Routledge, 1993.

–. *Excitable Speech: A Politics of the Performative.* New York and London: Routledge, 1997.

–. *Gender Trouble: Feminism and the Subversion of Identity.* New York and London: Routledge, 1990.

Callaway, Helen. "Dressing for Dinner in the Bush: Rituals of Self-Definition and British Imperial Authority." In *Dress and Gender: Making and Meaning in Cultural Contexts,* ed. Ruth Barnes and Joanne B. Eicher, 232-47. New York and Oxford: BERG, 1992.

Calloway, Colin G., ed. *The World Turned Upside Down: Indian Voices from Early America.* Boston and New York: Bedford Books of St. Martin's Press, 1994.

Campbell, Maria. *Halfbreed.* Toronto: McClelland and Stewart, 1973.

Campbell, Maria, and Linda Griffiths. *The Book of Jessica: A Theatrical Transformation.* Toronto: Coach House Press, 1989.

Campey, John, Tim McCaskell, John Miller, and Vanessa Russell. "Opening the Classroom Closet: Dealing with Sexual Orientation at the Toronto Board of Education." In *Sex in Schools: Canadian Education and Sexual Regulation,* ed.

Susan Prentice, 82-100. Toronto: Our Schools/Our Selves Education Foundation, 1994.

Carr, Helen. *Inventing the American Primitive: Politics, Gender and the Representation of Native American Literary Traditions, 1789-1936.* New York: New York University Press, 1996.

Carter, Philip. *Men and the Emergence of Polite Society: Britain, 1660-1800.* London and New York: Longman, an imprint of Pearson Education, 2001.

Carter, Sarah. *The Importance of Being Monogamous: Marriage and Nation-Building in Western Canada to 1915.* Edmonton: University of Alberta Press/Athabasca University Press, 2008.

Caruth, Cathy, ed. *Trauma: Explorations in Memory.* Baltimore: Johns Hopkins University Press, 1995.

–. "An Interview with Robert Jay Lifton." In Caruth, *Trauma.*

–. "Introduction." In Caruth, *Trauma.*

Case, Sue-Ellen. *Split-Britches: Lesbian Practice/Feminist Performance.* London and New York: Routledge, 1996.

–. "Towards a Butch-Femme Aesthetic." In *Making a Spectacle: Feminist Essays on Contemporary Women's Theater,* ed. Lynda Hart, 282-99. Michigan: University of Michigan Press, 1989.

Cavanaugh, Catherine. "'No Place for a Woman': Engendering Western Canadian Settlement." *Western Historical Quarterly* 28 (1997): 493-518.

Chan, Anthony. *Gold Mountain: A History of the Chinese Communities in the New World.* Vancouver: New Star Books, 1983.

Chapman, Terry L. "Male Homosexuality: Legal Restraints and Social Attitudes in Western Canada, 1890-1920." In *Law and Justice in a New Land: Essays in Western Canadian Legal History,* ed. Louis Knafla, 277-92. Toronto: Carswell, 1986.

–. "'An Oscar Wilde Type': 'The Abominable Crime of Buggery' in Western Canada, 1890-1920." *Criminal Justice History* 4 (1983): 97-118.

Chase, A. *Playing God in Yellowstone.* San Francisco: Sierra Club, 1986.

Chauncey, George. "Christian Brotherhood or Sexual Perversion? Homosexual Identities and the Construction of Sexual Boundaries in the World War I Era." In Duberman, *Hidden from History,* 294-317.

Childs, Elizabeth C. "The Colonial Lens: Gauguin, Primitivism, and Photography in the Fin de siècle." In *Anti-Modernism and Artistic Experience: Policing the Boundaries of Modernity,* ed. Lynda Jessup, 50-69. Toronto: University of Toronto Press, 2001.

Churchill, Ward. *A Little Matter of Genocide: Holocaust and Denial in the Americas 1492 to the Present.* Winnipeg: Arbeiter Ring Publishing, 1998.

Chute, Janet. *The Legacy of Shingwaukonse: A Century of Native Leadership.* Toronto: University of Toronto Press, 1998.

Citron, Michelle. *Home Movies and Other Necessary Fictions.* Minneapolis: University of Minnesota Press, 1999.

Clifford, James. "Of Other Peoples: Beyond the 'Salvage' Paradigm." In *Discussions in Contemporary Culture,* ed. Hal Foster, 120-30. Dia Art Foundation, Number One, Seattle: Bay Press, 1987.

Coburn, Wendy. "Artist's Statement." In Diamond and Fleming, *Beaver Tales,* 34.

Crean, J.F. "Hats and the Fur Trade." *Canadian Journal of Economics and Political Science* 28, 3 (1962): 378-79.

Crean, Susan M. "Notes from the Language of Emotion." *Canadian Art* 4 (Spring 1987): 64-65.

Creese, Gillian. "Class, Ethnicity, and Conflict: The Case of the Chinese and Japanese Immigrants, 1880-1923." In *Workers, Capital, and the State in British Columbia: Selected Papers,* ed. Rennie Warburton and David Coburn, 55-85. Vancouver: UBC Press, 1988.

Crichlow, Warren. "Stan Douglas and the Aesthetic Critique of Urban Decline." *Cultural Studies – Critical Methodologies* 3, 1 (2003): 8-21.

Cronon, William. "The Trouble with Wilderness: Or, Getting Back to the Wrong Nature." In *Out of the Woods: Essays in Environmental History,* ed. Char Miller and Hal Rothman, 28-50. Pittsburgh: University of Pittsburgh Press, 1997.

Cross, Michael S., ed. *The Turner Thesis and the Canadas: The Debate on the Impact of the Canadian Environment.* Toronto: Copp Clark, 1970.

Danysk, Cecilia. "'A Bachelor's Paradise': Homesteaders, Hired Hands, and the Construction of Masculinity, 1880-1930." In *Making Western Canada: Essays on European Colonization and Settlement,* ed. Catherine Cavanaugh and Jeremy Mouat, 154-85. Toronto: Garamond Press, 1996.

Davis, Fred. *Fashion, Culture, and Identity.* Chicago: University of Chicago Press, 1992.

Dawson, Michael. The *Mountie: From Dime Novel to Disney.* Toronto: Between the Lines, 1998.

Day, Richard. *Multiculturalism and the History of Canadian Diversity.* Toronto: University of Toronto Press, 2000.

de Certeau, Michel. *The Practice of Everyday Life.* Trans. Steven Rendall. Berkeley: University of California Press, 1984.

Decker, Jody F. "Depopulation of the Northern Plains Natives." *Social Sciences and Medicine* 33, 4 (1991): 381-96.

–. "Tracing Historical Diffusion Patterns: The Case of the 1780-1782 Smallpox Epidemic among the Indians of Western Canada." *Native Studies Review* 4, 1-2 (1988): 1-24.

Dehli, Kari. "Creating a Dense and Intelligent Community: Local State Formation in Early 19th Century Upper Canada." *Journal of Historical Sociology* 3, 2 (1990): 109-32.

Deloria, Philip. *Playing Indian.* New Haven: Yale University Press, 1998.

Demsey, Hugh A., ed. *The CPR West: The Iron Road and the Making of a Nation.* Vancouver: Douglas and McIntyre, 1984.

–. "The Fearsome Fire Wagon." In Dempsey, *CPR West,* 55-70.

Denevan, William. "Native American Populations in 1492: Recent Research and Revised Hemispheric Estimate." In *The Native Population in the Americas in 1492*. 2nd ed., ed. William Denevan, xvii-xxxviii. Madison: University of Wisconsin Press, 1992.

Dening, Gred. *Performances.* Chicago: University of Chicago Press, 1996.

Derrida, Jacques. *Spectres of Marx.* New York: Routledge, 1994.

Devens, Carol. *Countering Colonization: Native American Women and Great Lakes Missions, 1630-1900.* Berkeley: University of California Press, 1992.

Diamond, Reid, and Marnie Fleming. *Beaver Tails* (catalogue). Toronto: Oakville Galleries, 2000.

Dobak, William A. "Killing the Canadian Buffalo, 1821-1881." *Western Historical Quarterly* 27, 1 (1996): 33-52.

Dolan, Jill. "The Discourse of Feminisms: The Spectator and Representation." In *The Routledge Reader in Gender and Performance*, ed. Lizbeth Goodman and Jane de Gray, 289-92. London and New York: Routledge, 1998.

Dornsife, Carolyn Jane. "Women in Nontraditional Employment: Gender Differences in the Job Satisfaction of National Park Rangers." PhD diss., University of Oregon, 1989.

Drees, Laurie Meijer. "'Indians' Bygone Past': The Banff Indian Days, 1902-1945." *Past Imperfect* 2 (1993): 7-28.

–. "Making Banff a Wild West: Norman Luxton, Indians and Banff Tourism, 1902-1945." MA thesis, University of Calgary, 1991.

Drinnon, Richard. *Facing West: The Metaphysics of Indian-Hating and Empire-Building.* Minneapolis: University of Minnesota Press, 1980.

Driscoll, John. *All That Is Glorious around Us: Paintings from the Hudson River School.* Ithaca, NY: Cornell University Press, 1997.

Dua, Enakshi. "'Race' and Governmentality: The Racialization of Canadian Citizenship Practices." In *Making Normal: Social Regulation in Canada,* ed. Deborah Brock. Toronto: Nelson, 2003.

Duberman, Martin, Martha Vicinus, and George Chauncey, eds. *Hidden from History: Reclaiming the Gay and Lesbian Past.* New York: Meridian, 1989.

Dubin, Steven C. *Arresting Images: Impolitic Art and Uncivil Actions.* London and New York: Routledge, 1992.

Durham, Jimmie. "Geronimo." In *Partial Recall: With Essays on Photographs of Native North Americans,* ed. Lucy Lippard, 55-58. New York: New York Press, 1992.

Dyer, Richard. *White.* London and New York: Routledge, 1997.

–. "White." *Screen* 29, 4 (1988): 44-65.

Eaton, Diane, and Sheila Urbanek. *Paul Kane's Great Nor-West.* Vancouver: UBC Press, 1995.

Eddy, John, and Deryck Schreuder, eds. *The Rise of Colonial Nationalism: Australia, New Zealand, Canada and South Africa First Assert Their Nationalities, 1880-1914.* Sydney: Allen and Unwin, 1988.

Edgar, William. "'Hiawatha,' as the Anishinaabeys Interpret It." *American Monthly Review of Reviews* 5, 30 (1904): 689-93.

Edwards, Justin. *Gothic Canada: Reading the Spectre of a National Literature.* Edmonton: University of Alberta Press, 2005.

Eisenstein, Sergei. *Film Form: Essays in Film Theory.* Trans. and ed. Jay Leyda. San Diego: Harcourt Brace Jovanovich, 1949.

Episkenew, Jo-Ann. *Taking Back Our Spirits: Aboriginal Literature, Public Policy, and Healing.* Winnipeg: University of Manitoba Press, 2009.

Evans, Jessica. "Introduction: Nation and Representation." In *Representing the Nation: A Reader, Histories, Heritage and Museums,* ed. David Boswell and Jessica Evans, 1-9. London and New York: Routledge, in association with the Open University, 1999.

Felman, Shoshana, and Dori Laub, eds. *Testimony: Crises of Witnessing in Literature, Psychoanalysis, and History.* New York: Routledge, 1992.

Fleming, Marnie. "Beaver Tales: Traits and Traditions." In Diamond and Fleming, *Beaver Tales,* 7-12.

–. "Joyce Wieland: A Perspective." In *Joyce Wieland,* ed. Philip Monk, 17-116. Toronto: Key Porter Books, 1987.

–, ed. *Track Records: Trains and Contemporary Photography.* Oakville: Oakville Galleries in collaboration with the Canadian Museum of Contemporary Photography, 1997.

Foreman, Carolyn T. *Indians Abroad: 1493-1938.* Norman: University of Oklahoma Press, 1943.

Foster, Janet. *Working for Wildlife: The Beginning of Preservation in Canada.* Toronto: University of Toronto Press, 1978.

Foucault, Michel. *The History of Sexuality.* Vol. 1. New York: Random House, 1980.

–. "Nietzsche, Genealogy, History." In *The Foucault Reader,* ed. Paul Rabinow, 76-100. New York: Pantheon Books, 1984.

–. "Truth and Power." In *Power/Knowledge: Selected Interviews and Other Writings, 1972-1977,* ed. Colin Gordon, 109-33. New York: Pantheon Books, 1980.

–. "Two Lectures." In *Power/Knowledge: Selected Interviews and Other Writings, 1972-1977,* ed. Colin Gordon, 78-108. New York: Pantheon Books, 1980

Francis, Daniel. *The Imaginary Indian: The Image of the Indian in Canadian Culture.* Vancouver: Arsenal Pulp Press, 1997.

Francis, R. Douglas. "From Wasteland to Utopia: Changing Images of the Canadian West in the Nineteenth Century." *Great Plains Quarterly* 7, 3 (1987): 179-81.

Frankenberg, Ruth. *White Women, Race Matters: The Social Construction of Whiteness.* London: Routledge, 1993.

Freeman, Victoria. *Distant Relations: How My Ancestors Colonized North America.* Toronto: McClelland and Stewart, 2002.

–. "'Toronto Has No History!' Indigeneity, Settler Colonialism and Historical Memory in Canada's Largest City." PhD diss., University of Toronto, 2010.

Freud, Sigmund. *The Uncanny.* Ed. Adam Phillips, trans. David Mclintock. Introduction by Hugh Haughton. New York: Penguin Classics, 1982.

Frye, Northrop. "The Mythos of Winter: Irony and Satire." In *Satire: Modern Essays in Criticism,* ed. Ronald Paulson, 233-48. Englewood Cliffs, NJ: Prentice-Hall, 1971.

Fung, Richard. *Dirty Laundry,* video recording, Toronto: Vtape, 1996.

Gagan, David P. "The Relevance of 'Canada First.'" *Journal of Canadian Studies* 5, 4 (1970): 36-44.

Gagnon, François-Marc. *Images du castor canadien: XVIe-XVIIe siècles.* Sillery, QC: Les Éditions du Septentrion, 1994.

Gagnon, Monika Kin. *Other Conundrums: Race, Culture, and Canadian Art.* Vancouver/Kamloops: Arsenal Pulp Press/Artspeak Gallery, Kamloops Art Gallery, 2000.

Galabuzi, Grace-Edward. *Canada's Economic Apartheid: The Social Exclusion of Racialized Groups in the New Century.* Toronto: Canadian Scholars Press, 2006.

Gandhi, Leela. *Affective Communities: Anticolonial Thought, Fin-De-Siecle Radicalism, and the Politics of Friendship.* Durham, NC: Duke University Press, 2006.

Gelder, Ken, and Jane M. Jacobs. "The Postcolonial Ghost Story." In Buse and Scott, *Ghosts,* 179-99.

Gibbon, John Murray. *Canadian Mosaic: The Making of a Northern Nation.* Toronto: McClelland and Stewart, 1938.

Gittings, Christopher. *Canadian National Cinema.* London: Routledge, 2002.

–, ed. *Imperialism and Gender: Constructions of Masculinity.* Hebden Bridge, UK: Dangaroo Press, 1996.

Goldberg, David Theo. *Racist Cultures.* Cambridge, MA: Blackwell, 1993.

Goldberg, Roselee. *Performance: Live Art 1909 to the Present.* London: Thames and Hudson, 1979.

Goldie, Terry. *Fear and Temptation: The Image of the Indigene in Canadian, Australian, and New Zealand Literatures.* Montreal: McGill-Queen's University Press, 1989.

Goldman, Marlene, and Joanne Saul. "Talking with Ghosts: Haunting in Canadian Cultural Production." *University of Toronto Quarterly* 75, 2 (2005): 645.

Gordon, Avery. *Ghostly Matters: Haunting and the Sociological Imagination.* Minneapolis: University of Minnesota Press, 1997.

Grant, Hugh. "Revenge of the Paris Hat: The European Craze for Wearing Headgear Had a Profound Effect on Canadian History." *The Beaver* 68, 6 (December 1988/January 1989): 37-44.

Green, Rayna. "The Pochahontas Perplex: The Image of Indian Women in American Culture." In *Unequal Sisters,* ed. Ellen Dubois and Vicki Ruiz, 15-21. New York: Routledge, 1990.

Griffiths, Alison. "Science and Spectacle: Native American Representation in Early Cinema." In *Dressing in Feathers: The Construction of the Indian in American Popular Culture,* ed. S. Elizabeth Bird, 79-95. Boulder, CO: Westview Press, 1996.

Griffiths Linda, and Maria Campbell. *The Book of Jessica: A Theatrical Transformation.* Toronto: Coach House Press, 1989.

Hall, Catherine. *White, Male and Middle-Class: Explorations in Feminism and History.* New York: Routledge, 1992.

Halperin, David M. *Saint Foucault: Towards a Gay Hagiography.* New York and Oxford: Oxford University Press, 1995.

Haraway, Donna. *Primate Visions: Gender, Race, and Nature in the World of Modern Science.* New York and London: Routledge, 1989.

–. "Teddy Bear Patriarchy: Taxidermy in the Garden of Eden, New York City, 1908-1936." *Social Text: Theory/Culture/Ideology* 11 (1984-85): 20-64.

Harkin, J.B. *The Origins and Meaning of the National Parks of Canada.* Extracts from the papers of the late Jas. B. Harkin, first commissioner of the National Parks of Canada. Distributed by National Parks Branch, Department of Northern Affairs and National Resources, 1957.

Harris, Cole. *The Resettlement of British Columbia: Essays on Colonialism and Geographical Change.* Vancouver: UBC Press, 1998

–. "Voices of Smallpox around the Straight of Georgia." In Harris, *Resettlement*, 3-30.

Hart, E.J. "See This World before the Next: Tourism and the CPR." In Dempsey, *CPR West*, 151-70.

–. *The Selling of Canada: The CPR and the Beginning of Canadian Tourism.* Banff: Alpine Publishing Company, 1983.

Henderson, Jennifer, and Pauline Wakeham. "Colonial Reckoning, National Reconciliation? Aboriginal Peoples and the Culture of Redress in Canada." *ESC: English Studies in Canada* 35, 1 (2009): 1-26.

Henke, James T. *Gutter Life and Language in the Early "Street" Literature of England: A Glossary of Terms and Topics, Chiefly of the Sixteenth and Seventeenth centuries.* West Cornwall, CT: Locust Hill Press, 1988.

Henry, Frances, and Carol Tator. *The Colour of Democracy: Racism in Canadian Society.* 3rd ed. Toronto: Nelson, 2006.

Hermer, Joe. *Regulating Eden: The Nature of Order in North American Parks.* Toronto: University of Toronto Press, 2002.

Hill, Richard William. "Built on Running Water: Rebecca Belmore's Fountain." 51st Venice Biennale, 10-16 June 2005. *FUSE* 29, 1 (2006): 49-51.

–. "Drag Racing: Dressing Up (and Messing Up) White in Contemporary First Nations Art." *FUSE* 23, 4 (2000): 18-27.

Hinsch, Bret. *Passions of the Cut Sleeve: The Male Homosexual Tradition in China.* Berkeley: University of California Press, 1990.

Hobsbawm, Eric. "Mass-Producing Traditions: Europe, 1870-1914." In *The Invention of Tradition,* ed. Eric Hobsbawm and Terrance Ranger, 263-307. Cambridge: Cambridge University Press, 1983.

Hock, Louis, and Elizabeth Sisco. *Local Interpretations.* Banff, AB: Banff Centre for the Arts, 1991.

Honour, Hugh. *The New Golden Land: European Images of America from the Discoveries to the Present Time.* New York: Pantheon Books, 1975.

Hubbard, R.H., ed. *The Artist and the Land: Canadian Landscape Painting, 1670-1930.* Madison: University of Wisconsin Press, 1973.

Hummel, Monte, ed. *Endangered Spaces: The Future for Canada's Wilderness.* Toronto: Key Porter Books, 1989.

Hunt, Alan. *Governance of the Consuming Passions: A History of Sumptuary Law.* New York: St. Martin's Press, 1996.

Hutchinson, Gerald M. "James Evans' Last Year." *Journal of the Canadian Church Historical Society* 19, 1-2 (1977): 42-56.

Ingram, Gordon Brent. "Returning to the Scene of the Crime: Uses of Trial Dossiers on Consensual Male Homosexuality for Urban Research, with Examples from Twentieth-Century British Columbia." *GLQ: A Journal of Lesbian and Gay Studies* 10, 1 (2003): 77-110.

Innis, Harold. *The Fur Trade in Canada: An Introduction to Canadian Economic History.* Toronto: University of Toronto Press, 1999.

–. *A History of the Canadian Pacific Railway.* Toronto: University of Toronto Press, 1971.

–. "Transportation in the Canadian Economy." In *Essays in Canadian Economic History,* ed. Mary Q. Innis, 220-32. Toronto: University of Toronto Press, 1956.

–. "Transportation as a Factor in Canadian Economic History." In *Essays in Canadian Economic History,* ed. Mary Q. Innis, 62-77. Toronto: University of Toronto Press, 1956.

Jacobs, Sue-Ellen, Wesley Thomas, and Sabine Lang, eds. *Two-Spirit People: Aboriginal American Gender Identity, Sexuality and Spirituality.* Urbana and Chicago: University of Illinois Press, 1997.

Jasen, Patricia. *Wild Things: Nature, Culture, and Tourism in Ontario, 1790-1914.* Toronto: University of Toronto Press, 1995.

Jessup, Lynda, ed. *Antimodernism and Artistic Experience: Policing the Boundaries of Modernity.* Toronto: University of Toronto Press, 2001.

Johnston, Susan. "Epidemics: The Forgotten Factor in Seventeenth-Century Native Warfare in the St. Lawrence Region." In *Native Peoples, Native Lands: Canadian Indians, Inuit and Metis,* ed. Bruce Alden Cox, 14-31. Ottawa: Carleton University Press, 1987.

Jones, David C. "'It's All Likes They Tell You': Immigrants, Hosts and the CPR." In Dempsey, *CPR West,* 107-24.

Julier, Alice P. "Hiding Gender and Race in the Discourse of Commercial Food Consumption." In *From Betty Crocker to Feminist Food Studies: Critical Perspectives on Women and Food,* ed. Arlene Voski Avakian and Barbara Haber, 163-84. Amherst and Boston: University of Massachusetts Press, 2005.

Kang, Hyun Yi. "The Autobiographical Stagings of Jin-me Yoon." In Radul, *Jin-me Yoon,* 23-44.

Kapferer, Bruce, and Judith Kapferer. "Monumentalizing Identity: The Discursive Practices of Hegemony in Australia." In *Streams of Cultural Capital*, ed. David Palumbo-Liu and Hans Ulrich Gumbrecht, 79-96. Stanford: Stanford University Press, 1997.

Kaplan, Martha. "The Magical Power of the (Printed) Word in Fiji." In *Magic and Modernity: Interfaces of Revelation and Concealment*, ed. Peter Pels and Birgit Meyer, 183-99. Stanford: Stanford University Press, 2003.

Kasfir, Sidney Littlefield. "African Art and Authenticity." *African Arts* 25, 2 (1992): 40-60.

Katz, Johnathan Ned. *The Invention of Heterosexuality*. New York: A Dutton Book, Penguin Group, 1995.

Kaufman, Polly Welts. *National Parks and the Woman's Voice: A History*. Albuquerque: University of New Mexico Press, 1996.

Keller, Robert H., and Michael F. Turek. *American Indians and National Parks*. Tucson: University of Arizona Press, 1998.

Kennedy, Dennis, ed. *The Oxford Encyclopedia of Theatre and Performance*. Oxford: Oxford University Press, 2003.

Kimmel, Michael S. "From Lord and Master to Cuckold and Fop: Masculinity in Seventeenth-Century England." *University of Dayton Review* 18, 2 (1986-87): 93-107.

Kinsman, Gary. *The Regulation of Desire: Homo and Hetero Sexualities*. Montreal: Black Rose Books, 1996.

Kirby, Lynne. "Steamy Scenes and Dream Machines." In *Track Records: Trains and Contemporary Photography*, ed. Marnie Fleming, 25-27. Oakville, ON: Oakville Galleries in collaboration with the Canadian Museum of Contemporary Photography, 1997.

Klotman, Phyllis R., and Janet K. Cutler. *Struggles for Representation: African American Documentary Film and Video*. Bloomington: Indiana University Press, 1999.

Kretch III, Shepard. "Alan Trachtenberg, Shades of Hiawatha: Staging Indians, Making Americans. New York: Hill and Wang, 2004." Book review. *Journal of Social History* 39, 2 (2005): 550-51.

Kristeva, Julia. *Strangers to Ourselves*. New York: Columbia University Press, 1991.

Lafleur, Brenda. "'Resting' in History: Translating the Art of Jin-me Yoon." In *Generations and Geographies in the Visual Arts: Feminist Readings*, ed. Griselda Pollock, 217-27. London and New York: Routledge, 1996.

Lai, David Chuenyan. "Chinese Opium Trade and Manufacture in British Columbia, 1858-1908." *Journal of the West* 38, 3 (1999): 21-26.

–. "A 'Prison' for Chinese Immigrants." *Asianadian: An Asian Canadian Magazine* 2 (1980): 16-19

Lawrence, Bonita. *Real Indians and Others: Mixed-Blood Urban Native Peoples and Aboriginal Nationhood*. Vancouver: UBC Press, 2004.

–. "Rewriting Histories of the Land: Colonization and Indigenous Resistance in Eastern Canada." In *Race, Space and the Law: Unmapping a White Settler Society,* ed. Sherene Razack, 21-46. Toronto: Between the Lines, 2002.

Lawrence, Bonita, and Ena Dua. "Decolonizing Antiracism." *Social Justice* 32, 4 (2005): 120-43.

Lawson, Murray G. *Fur: A Study in English Mercantilism.* Toronto: University of Toronto Press, 1943.

Leung, Carrianne K.Y. "Usable Pasts, Staging Belongings: Articulating a 'Heritage' of Multiculturalism in Canada." *Studies in Ethnicity and Nationalism* 2, 2 (2006): 162-79.

Lippard, Lucy R. *The Lure of the Local: Senses of Place in a Multicentered Society.* New York: The New Press, 1997.

–, ed. *Partial Recall: Photographs of Native North Americans.* New York: The New Press, 1992.

Lloyd, David. "Race under Representation." *Oxford Literary Review* 13, 1-2 (1991): 62-94.

Lowe, Lisa. "Break the Frame." In *Like Mangoes in July: The Work of Richard Fung,* ed. Helen Lee and Kerri Sakamoto, 78-79. Toronto: Insomniac Press and Images Festival, 2002.

MacCannel, Dean. *The Tourist: A New Theory of the Leisure Class.* New York: Schocken Books, 1976.

Mackey, Eva. *The House of Difference: Cultural Politics and National Identity in Canada.* London and New York: Routledge, 1999.

Maclear, Kyo. *Beclouded Visions: Hiroshima-Nagasaki and the Art of Witness.* Albany: State University of New York Press, 1999.

–. "The Accidental Witness." In Walter, *Private Investigators,* 9-16.

Marchetti, Gina. "Still Looking: Negotiating Race, Sex and History in Dirty Laundry." In *Like Mangoes in July: The Work of Richard Fung,* ed. Helen Lee and Kerri Sakamoto, 80-88. Toronto: Insomniac Press and Images Festival, 2002.

Marshall, P.J., and Glyndwr Williams, *The Great Map of Mankind: Perceptions of New Worlds in the Age of Enlightenment.* Cambridge: Harvard University Press, 1982.

Marte, Lidia. "Foodmaps: Tracing Boundaries of 'Home' through Food Relations." *Food and Foodways* 15, 3 (2007): 261-89.

Martin, Lee-Ann. "The Waters of Venice: Rebecca Belmore at the 51st Biennale." *Canadian Art* 22, 2 (2005) 48-53.

Marty, Sid. A *Grand and Fabulous Notion: The First Century of Canada's Parks.* Toronto: NC Press, 1944.

Mason, Roger Burford. *Travels in the Shining Island: The Story of James Evans and the Invention of the Cree Syllabary Alphabet.* Toronto: Natural Heritage Books, 1996.

Massie, Larry B. "Supplementary Introduction" to Henry R. Schoolcraft, *The Hiawatha Legends: North American Indian Lore,* 14-15. Gwinn, MI: Avery Color

Studios, 1984. (Reproduced from the original by J.B. Lippincott and Co., Philadelphia and Trubner and Co., London, 1856.)

Massumi, Brian. "Navigating Movements: A Conversation with Brian Massumi." In *Hope: New Philosophies for Change*, ed. Mary Zournazi, 210-42. Australia: Pluto Press, 2002.

Mawani, Renisa. *Colonial Proximities: Crossracial Encounters and Juridical Truths in British Columbia, 1871-1921*. Vancouver: UBC Press, 2009.

McClintock, Anne. *Imperial Leather: Race, Gender and Sexuality in the Colonial Contest*. New York and London: Routledge, 1995.

–. "Soft-Soaping Empire: Commodity Racism and Imperial Advertising." In McClintock, *Imperial Leather*, 207-31.

McGregor, Gaile. *The Wacousta Syndrome: Explorations in the Canadian Langscape*. Toronto: University of Toronto Press, 1985.

McKay, Ian. "Handicrafts and the Logic of 'Commercial Antimodernism': The Nova Scotia Case." In Jessup, *Antimodernism*, 117-29.

–. *The Quest of the Folk: Antimodernism and Cultural Selection in Twentieth-Century Nova Scotia*. Montreal and Kingston: McGill-Queen's University Press, 1994.

McLaren, Angus. *Our Own Master Race: Eugenics in Canada, 1885-1945*. Toronto: Oxford University Press, 1990.

McMaster, Gerald. "Colonial Alchemy: Reading the Boarding School Experience." In *Partial Recall: With Essays on Photographs of Native North Americans*, ed. Lucy Lippard, 77-87. New York: The New Press, 1992.

–. *Portraits from the Dancing Grounds*. Ottawa: The Ottawa Art Gallery, 11 July-8 September 1996.

McNally, Michael D. "The Indian Passion Play: Contesting the Real Indian in Song of Hiawatha Pageants, 1901-1965." *American Quarterly* 58, 1 (2006): 105-36.

McNeil, Kent. "Social Darwinism and Judicial Conceptions of Indian Title in Canada in the 1880s." *Journal of the West* 38, 1 (1999): 68-76.

McPherson, Hugo. "Wieland: An Epiphany of North." *artscanada* 158-59 (August/ September 1971): 17-27.

Melosi, Martin V. "Equity, Eco-racism, and Environmental History." In *Out of the Woods: Essays in Environmental History*, ed. Char Miller and Hal Rothman, 194-211. Pittsburgh: University of Pittsburg Press, 1997.

Mercer, Kobena. *Welcome to the Jungle: New Positions in Black Cultural Studies*. New York and London: Routledge, 1994.

Miller, J.R. *Reflections on Native-Newcomer Relations: Selected Essays*. Toronto: University of Toronto Press, 2004.

–. *Shingwauk's Vision: A History of Native Residential Schools*. Toronto: University of Toronto Press, 1996.

Milloy, John. *A National Crime: The Canadian Government and the Residential School System, 1879 to 1986*. Winnipeg: University of Manitoba Press, 1999.

Monkman, Kent. http://www.kentmonkman.com

Moosang, Faith. *First Son: Portraits by C.D. Hoy.* Vancouver: Presentation House Gallery and Arsenal Pulp Press, 1999.

Moray, Gerta. "Wilderness, Modernity and Aboriginality in the Paintings of Emily Carr." *Journal of Canadian Studies* 33, 2 (1998): 43-65.

Morgensen, Scott. "Settler Homonationalism: Theorizing Settler Colonialism within Queer Modernities. In "Sexuality, Nationality, Indigeneity," special issue, ed. D. Justice, M. Rifkin, and B. Schneider, *GLQ* 16, 1-2 (2010): 105-31.

Moss, Mark. *Manliness and Militarism: Educating Young Boys in Ontario for War.* Canadian Social History Series, ed. Gregory S. Kealey. Don Mills, ON: Oxford University Press, 2001.

Mosse, George L. *Nationalism and Sexuality: Respectability and Abnormal Sexuality in Modern Europe.* New York: Howard Fertig, 1985.

Moy, Frank Kunyin. "The Political Economy of Chinese Labour in Canada, 1858-1923." MA thesis, York University, 1970.

Mufti, Aamir, and Ella Shohat. "Introduction." In *Dangerous Liaisons: Gender, Nation, and Postcolonial Perspectives,* ed. Anne McClintock, Aamir Mufti, and Ella Shohat, 1-12. Minneapolis: University of Minnesota Press, 1997.

Muñoz, José Esteban. *Disidentifications: Queers of Colour and the Performance of Politics.* Minneapolis: University of Minnesota Press, 1999.

Nadeau, Chantal. *Fur Nation: From the Beaver to Brigitte Bardot.* London and New York: Routledge, Taylor and Francis Group, 2001.

Nelson, Jennifer. *Razing Africville: A Geography of Racism.* Toronto: University of Toronto Press, 2008.

Neumann, R.P. *Imposing Wilderness: Struggles over Livelihood and Nature Preservation in Africa.* Berkeley: University of California Press, 1999.

Neville, Charo. "Rebecca Belmore: Vigil and The Named and the Unnamed, 2002." *West Coast Line 53* 41, 1 (2007): 52-57

Neylan, Susan. "Preserving the Sacred: Historical Perspectives on the Anishinaabe Midewiwin." *Canadian Historical Review* 85, 3 (2004): 576-78.

Nichols, Roger L. *Indians in the United States and Canada: A Comparative History.* Lincoln: University of Nebraska Press, 1998.

Osborne, Brian S. "The Iconography of Nationhood in Canadian Art." In *The Iconography of Landscape: Essays on the Symbolic Representation, Design and Use of Past Environments,* ed. Denis Cosgrove and Stephen Daniels, 162-78. Cambridge: Cambridge University Press, 1988.

Otter, A.A. Den. *The Philosophy of Railways: The Transcontinental Railway Idea in British North America.* Toronto: University of Toronto Press, 1997.

Owram, Doug. *Promise of Eden: The Canadian Expansionist Movement and the Idea of the West, 1856-1900.* Toronto: University of Toronto Press, 1992.

Partridge, Eric. *A Dictionary of Slang and Unconventional English.* Vol. 1. London: Routledge and Kegan, 1961.

Pêcheux, Michel. *Language, Semantics and Ideology: Stating the Obvious.* Trans. Harbans Nagpal. London and Basingstoke: Macmillan, 1982.

Pels, Peter. "Introduction: Magic and Modernity." In *Magic and Modernity: Interfaces of Revelation and Concealment,* ed. Birgit Meyer and Peter Pels, 1-38. Stanford: Stanford University Press, 2003.

Perry, Adele. *On the Edge of Empire: Gender, Race, and the Making of British Columbia, 1849-1871.* Toronto: University of Toronto Press, 2001.

–. "'Oh I'm Just Sick of the Faces of Men': Gender Imbalance, Race, Sexuality, and Sociability in Nineteenth-Century British Columbia." *BC Studies* 105-06 (Spring/ Summer 1995): 27-43.

Petrone, Penny. *First Peoples, First Voices.* Toronto: University of Toronto Press, 1984.

Phillips, Ruth B. *Trading Identities: The Souvenir in Native North American Art from the Northeast, 1700-1900.* Seattle/Montreal: University of Washington Press/ McGill-Queen's University Press, 1998.

Pon, Madge. "Like a Chinese Puzzle: The Construction of Chinese Masculinity in Jack Canuck." In *Gender and History in Canada,* ed. Joy Parr and Mark Rosenfeld, 88-100. Toronto: Copp Clark, 1996.

Poole, Ross. *Nation and Identity.* London and New York: Routledge, 1999.

Powell, Richard J. *Black Art and Culture in the 20th Century.* London: Thames and Hudson, 1997.

Pratt, Annis. "Affairs with Bears: Some Notes towards Feminist Archetypal Hypotheses for Canadian Literature." In *Gynocritics/La Gynocritique: Feminist Approaches to Writing by Canadian and Québécois Women/Approches Féministes à l'écriture des Canadiennes et Québécoises,* ed. Barbara Godard, 157-78. Toronto: ECW Press, 1987.

Pratt, Mary Louise. *Imperial Eyes: Travel Writing and Transculturation.* London and New York: Routledge, 1992.

Putnam, William Lowell, Glen Boles, and Roger Laurilla. *Place Names of the Canadian Alps.* Revelstoke, BC: Footprint Publishing, 1990.

Rabinovitz, Lauren. "Issues of Feminist Aesthetics: Judy Chicago and Joyce Wieland." *Women's Art Journal* 1, 2 (1982): 38-41.

Radul, Judy, curator. *Jin-me Yoon: Between Departure and Arrival* (catalogue). Vancouver: Western Front Exhibitions Program, 1997.

Ramenofsky, Ann F. *Vectors of Death: The Archaeology of European Contact.* Albuquerque: University of New Mexico Press, 1987.

Rawson, Hugh. *Wicked Words: A Treasury of Curses, Insults, Put-Downs, and Other Formerly Unprintable Terms from Anglo-Saxon Times to the Present.* New York: Crown Publishers, 1989.

Razack, Sherene. *Dark Threats and White Knights: The Somalia Affair, Peacekeeping, and the New Imperialism.* Toronto: University of Toronto Press, 2004.

–. *Looking White People in the Eye: Gender, Race, and Culture in Courtrooms and Classrooms.* Toronto: University of Toronto Press, 1998.

Razack, Sherene, ed., *Race, Space and the Law: Unmapping a White Settler Society.* Toronto: Between the Lines, 2002.

Rich, E.E. *The History of the Hudson's Bay Company.* Vol. 2: *1670-1870.* London: Hudson's Bay Record Society, 1959.

–. "Pro Pelle Cutem." *The Beaver* 268 (Spring 1958): 15.

Rony, Fatimah Tobing. *The Third Eye: Race, Cinema, and Ethnographic Spectacle.* Durham, NC: Duke University Press, 1996.

Rosaldo, Renato. *Culture and Truth: The Remaking of Social Analysis.* Boston: Beacon Press, 1989.

Rothman, Hal K. "'Powder Aplenty for Native and Guest Alike': From Community to Corporate Control." In *Devil's Bargains: Tourism in the Twentieth-Century American West,* 252-86. Kansas: University Press of Kansas, 1998.

Rotundo, Anthony. *American Manhood: Transformations in Masculinity from the Revolution to the Modern Era.* New York: Basic Books, 1993.

Roy, Patricia E. *A White Man's Province: British Columbia's Politicians and Chinese and Japanese Immigrants, 1858-1914.* Vancouver: UBC Press, 1989.

–. "A Choice between Evils: The Chinese and the Construction of the Canadian Pacific Railway in British Columbia." In Dempsey, *CPR West,* 13-34.

Royal Commission on Chinese Immigration. *Report of the Royal Commission on Chinese Immigration: Report and Evidence.* Ottawa: Government Printer, 1885.

Rukszto, Katarzyna. "Minute by Minute: Canadian History Reimagined for Television Audiences." PhD diss., York University, 2003

Runte, Alfred. *National Parks: The American Experience.* Lincoln: University of Nebraska Press, 1987.

Ryan, Allan J. *The Trickster Shift: Humour and Irony in Contemporary Native Art.* Vancouver/Seattle: UBC Press/University of Washington Press, 1999.

Said, Edward. *Orientalism.* New York: Vintage Books, 1979.

Sanders, Douglas E. "Indigenous People: Issues of Definition." *International Journal of Cultural Property* 8, 1 (1999): 4-13.

Sandilands, Catriona. "Where the Mountain Men Meet the Lesbian Rangers: Gender, Nation, and Nature in the Rocky Mountain National Parks." In *This Elusive Land: Women and the Canadian Environment,* ed. Melody Hessing, Rebecca Raglon, and Catriona Sandilands, 142-68. Vancouver: UBC Press, 2005.

Saul, John Ralston. *A Fair Country: Telling Truths about Canada.* Toronto: Viking Canada, 2008.

Schama, Simon. *Landscape and Memory.* Toronto: Random House, 1995.

Schneider, Rebecca. *The Explicit Body in Performance.* London and New York: Routledge, 1997.

Schulte, Bruce A., and Dietland Müller-Schwarze. "Understanding North American Beaver Behavior as an Aid to Management." In *Beaver Protection, Management, and Utilization in Europe and North America,* ed. Peter E. Busher and Ryszard M. Dziciolowski, 109-28. New York: Kluwer Academic/Plenum Publishers, 1999.

Scott, Joan. "Experience." In *Feminists Theorize the Political,* ed. Judith Butler and Joan W. Scott, 22-40. New York and London: Routledge, 1992.

–. *Gender and the Politics of History.* New York: Columbia University Press, 1988.

Sedgwick, Eve Kosofsky. "How to Bring Up Your Kids Gay." In *Fear of a Queer Planet: Queer Politics and Social Theory,* ed. Michael Warner, 69-81. Minneapolis: University of Minnesota Press, 1993.

Shah, Nayan. *Contagious Divides: Epidemics and Race in San Francisco's Chinatown.* Berkeley and Los Angeles: University of California Press. 2001.

Shapiro, Susan. "Gender and Fashion in Medieval and Early Modern Britain." *Journal of Popular Culture* 20, 4 (1987): 113-28.

Sharma, Nandita. *Home Economics: Nationalism and the Making of "Migrant Workers" in Canada.* Toronto: University of Toronto Press, 2006.

Sharma, Nandita, and Cynthia Wright. "Decolonizing Resistance, Challenging Colonial States." *Social Justice* 35, 3 (2009): 120-38.

Shewell, Hugh. *Enough to Keep Them Alive, 1873-1965.* Toronto: University of Toronto Press, 2004.

Shields, Rob. *Places on the Margin: Alternative Geographies of Modernity.* London and New York: Routledge, 1991.

Shohat, Ella, and Robert Stam. *Unthinking Eurocentrism: Multiculturalism and the Media.* London and New York: Routledge, 1994.

Sinha, Mrinalini. *Colonial Masculinity: The "Manly Englishman" and the "Effeminate Bengali" in the Late Nineteenth Century.* Manchester: Manchester University Press, 1995.

Slotkin, Richard. *Regeneration through Violence: The Mythology of the American Frontier, 1600-1860.* Middletown, CT: Wesleyan University Press, 1973.

Smith, Andrea. "Native American Feminism, Sovereignty, and Social Change." *Feminist Studies* 31, 1 (2005): 116-32.

Smith, Linda Tuhiwai. *Decolonizing Methodologies: Research and Indigenous Peoples.* London/Dunedin: Zed Books/University of Otago Press, 1999.

Smith, Paul Chaat. "Ghost in the Machine." *Aperture* 139 (1995) 6-9.

Snow, John. *These Mountains Are Our Sacred Places: The Story of the Stoney Indians.* Toronto: Samuel Steven, 1977.

Sobal, Jeffry. "Men, Meat, and Marriage: Models of Masculinity." *Food and Foodways* 13 (2005): 135-58.

Somerville, Siobhan. "Scientific Racism and the Emergence of the Homosexual Body." In *Queer Studies: A Lesbian, Gay, Bisexual, and Transgender Anthology,* ed. B. Beemyn and M. Eliason, 241-61. New York: Haworth Press, 1998.

Stasiulis, Daiva, and Radha Jhappan. "The Fractious Politics of a Settler Society: Canada." In *Unsettling Settler Societies: Articulations of Gender, Race, Ethnicity and Class,* ed. Daiva Stasiulis and Nira Yuval-Davis, 95-131. London: Sage, 1995.

–. "Introduction: Beyond Dichotomies – Gender, Race, Ethnicity and Class in Settler Societies." In *Unsettling Settler Societies: Articulations of Gender, Race, Ethnicity and Class,* ed. Daiva Stasiulis and Nira Yuval-Davis, 1-38. London: Sage, 1995.

Stefani, Alice Rose. *Ten Good Years.* Fairfield, CA: First Books Library, 2001.

Steven, Peter. "The Art of Calculated Risk: Richard Fung's Dirty Laundry." *POV* 29 (1996): 30-33.

Stoler, Ann Laura. "Carnal Knowledge and Imperial Power: Gender, Race, and Morality in Colonial Asia." In *Gender at the Crossroads of Knowledge: Feminist Anthropology in the Postmodern Era*, ed. Micaela di Leonardo, 51-101. Berkeley: University of California Press, 1991.

–. "Making Empire Respectable: The Politics of Race and Sexual Morality in Twentieth-Century Colonial Cultures." In *Dangerous Liaisons: Gender, Nation and Post-Colonial Perspectives*, ed. Anne McClintock, Aamir Mufti, and Ella Shohat, 344-73. Minneapolis: University of Minnesota Press, 1997.

Sturken, Marita, and Lisa Cartwright. *Practices of Looking: An Introduction to Visual Culture*. Oxford, New York: Oxford University Press, 2001.

Sugars, Cynthia. "Postcolonial Pedagogy and the Impossibility of Teaching: Outside in the (Canadian Literature) Classroom." In *Home-Work: Postocolonialism, Pedagogy, and Canadian Literature*, ed. Cynthia Sugars, 1-34. Ottawa: University of Ottawa Press, 2004.

Swanson, Kerry. "The Noble Savage Was a Drag Queen: Hybridity and Transformation in Kent Monkman's Performance and Visual Art Interventions." *Sexualities and Politics in the Americas* 2, 2 (2005): 1-19.

Taussig, Michael. *Defacement: Public Secrecy and the Labour of the Negative*. Stanford: Stanford University Press, 1999.

Teitelbaum, Matthew. "The Mourners Cry." In *The Art of Betty Goodwin*, ed. Jessica Bradley and Matthew Teitelbaum, 7-35. Vancouver/Toronto: Douglas and McIntyre/The Art Gallery of Ontario, 1998.

Thobani, Sunera. *Exalted Subjects: Studies in the Making of Race and Nation in Canada*. Toronto: University of Toronto Press, 2007.

Thompson, E.P. *The Making of the English Working Class*. London: Victor Gollancz, 1963.

–. *Wigs and Hunters: The Origin of the Black Act*. London: Allen Lane, 1975.

Thorne, Tony. *Bloomsbury Dictionary of Contemporary Slang*. London: Bloomsbury Publishers, 1990.

Thornton, Russell. *American Indian Holocaust and Survival: A Population History since 1492*. Norman: University of Oklahoma Press, 1987.

Tilley, Brian. "Hayter Reed and Indian Administration in the West." In *Swords into Ploughshares: War and Agriculture in Western Canada*, ed. R.C. Macleod, 109-28. Edmonton: University of Alberta Press, 1993.

Titley, Brian. *A Narrow Vision: Duncan Campbell Scott and the Administration of Indian Affairs in Canada*. Vancouver: UBC Press, 1986.

Tompkins, Jane. *West of Everything: The Inner Life of Westerns*. New York and Oxford: Oxford University Press, 1992.

Townsend-Gault, Charlotte. "Hot Dogs, a Ball Gown, Adobe, and Words: The Modes and Materials of Identity." In *Native American Art in the Twentieth Century:*

Makers, Meanings, Histories, ed. W. Jackson Rushing III, 113-33. London and New York: Routledge, 1999.

Trachtenberg, Alan. *Shades of Hiawatha: Staging Indians, Making Americans, 1880-1930.* New York: Hill and Wang, 2004.

Treaty 7 Elders and Tribal Council with Walter Hildebrandt, Sarah Carter, and Dorothy First Rider. *The True Spirit and Original Intent of Treaty 7.* Montreal and Kingston: McGill-Queen's University Press, 1996.

Turcotte, G. "'A Fearful Calligraphy': De/scribing the Uncanny Nation in Joy Kogawa's *Obasan.*" In *Reconfigurations: Canadian Literatures and Postcolonial Identities/ Littératures canadiennes et identités postcoloniales,* ed. M. Maufort and F. Bellarsi, 123-43. Brussels: Peter Lang, Bruxelles, 2002.

Turner, Margaret. *Imagining Culture: New World Narrative and the Writing of Canada.* Montreal and Kingston: McGill-Queen's University Press, 1995.

Ubelaker, Douglas H. "North American Indian Population Size: Changing Perspectives." In *Disease and Demography in the Americas,* ed. J. W. Verano and D. H. Ubelaker, 169-78. Washington, DC: Smithsonian Institution Press, 1992.

Valverde, Marianna. *The Age of Light, Soap, and Water: Moral Reform in English Canada, 1885-1925.* Toronto: McClelland and Stewart, 1991.

Van Kirk, Sylvia. *"Many Tender Ties": Women in Fur-Trade Society in Western Canada, 1670-1870.* Winnipeg: Watson and Dwyer, 1980.

Verduyn, Christl. *Lifelines: Marion Engel's Writings.* Montreal and Kingston: McGill-Queen's University Press, 1995.

Vibert, Elizabeth. "Real Men Hunt Buffalo: Masculinity, Race and Class in British Fur Traders' Narratives." *Gender and History* 8, 1 (1996): 4-21.

–. *Traders' Tales: Narratives of Cultural Encounters in the Columbia Plateau, 1807-1846.* Norman: University of Oklahoma Press, 1997.

Voisey, Paul. "The 'Votes for Women' Movement." In *The Best from Alberta History,* ed. Hugh Dempsey, 166-83. Saskatoon, SK: Western Producer Prairie Books, 1981.

Walcott, Rinaldo. *Black Like Who? Writing/Black/Canada.* Toronto: Insomniac Press, 1997.

–. "'Who Is She and What Is She to You?': Mary Ann Shad Cary and the (Im)possibility of Black/Canadian Studies." In *Rude: Contemporary Black Canadian Cultural Criticism,* ed. Rinaldo Walcott, 27-48. Toronto: Insomniac Press, 2000.

Walker, R.B.J. *Inside/Outside: International Relations as Political Theory.* Cambridge: Cambridge University Press, 1993.

Walter, Kathryn, ed. *Private Investigators: Undercover in Public Space.* Banff, AB: Banff Centre Press, 1999.

Ward, Peter. *White Canada Forever: Popular Attitudes and Public Policy towards Orientals in British Columbia.* Montreal: McGill-Queen's University Press, 1978.

Warkentin, Germaine. *Canadian Exploration Literature: An Anthology.* Toronto: Oxford University Press, 1993.

Watson, Scott, and Rebecca Belmore. "Interview." In *Rebecca Belmore: Fountain* (catalogue). Kamloops Art Gallery, Morris and Helen Belkin Art Gallery, University of British Columbia, Canada Pavilion, Venice Biennale, 2005.

Waugh, Thomas. "Good, Clean Fung." In *Screening Asian Americans*, ed. Peter X. Feng, 164-75. Piscataway, NJ: Rutgers University Press, 2001.

Weber, Ronald. "'I Would Ask No Other Monument to My Memory': George Catlin and a Nation's Park." *Journal of the West* 38, 1 (1998): 15-18.

West, Cornel. "The New Cultural Politics of Difference." In *Race, Identity and Representation in Education*, ed. Cameron McCarthy and Warren Crichlow, 11-23. New York: Routledge, 1993.

White, Hayden. *Tropics of Discourse: Essays in Cultural Criticism*. Baltimore: Johns Hopkins University Press, 1978.

Whitelaw, Anne. "'Whiffs of Balsam, Pine, and Spruce': Art Museums and the Production of the Canadian Aesthetic." In *Capital Culture: A Reader on Modernist Legacies, State Institutions, and the Value(s) of Art*, ed. Jody Berland and Shelly Hornstein, 122-37. Montreal and Kingston: McGill-Queen's University Press, 2000.

Wickberg, Edgar, ed. *From China to Canada: A History of the Chinese Communities in Canada*. Toronto: McClelland and Stewart, 1982.

Wilby, Emma. "The Witch's Familiar and the Fairy in Early Modern England and Scotland." *Folklore* 111, 2 (2000): 283-305.

Williams, Walter L. "Seafarers, Cowboys, and Indians: Male Marriage in Fringe Societies on the Anglo-American Frontier." In *The Spirit and the Flesh: Sexual Diversity in American Indian Culture*, 152-74. Boston: Beacon Press, 1986.

Wilson, Rev. E.F. *Missionary Work among the Ojebway Indians*. London: Society for Promoting Christian Knowledge, 1886.

Wollen, Peter, Mark Francis, and Paul-Hervé Parsy, eds. *On the Passage of a Few People through a Rather Brief Moment in Time: The Situationist International 1957-72*. Boston and Paris: The Institute of Contemporary Art in collaboration with the Centre George Pompidou, 1989.

Wu, Kuang-ming. On *Metaphoring: A Cultural Hermeneutic*. Boston: Brill, 2001.

Xing, Jun. *Asian America through the Lens: History, Representations, and Identity*. Walnut Creek: Altamira Press, a division of Sage Publications, 1998.

Yeigh, Frank. "The Drama of Hiawatha, or Mana-bozho: As Played by a Band of Canadian Anishinaabey Indians." *Canadian Magazine* 17, 3 (1901): 207-17.

Yoon, Jin-me. "Artist's Statement." In Diamond and Fleming, *Beaver Tales*, 30.

Index

Numbers in **bold** refer to plates. Numbers in *italics* refer to figures.

pelts, 57, 176n41; social structure, 23-25; and spirit of Canada, **2**, **3**; and women's sexuality, 43-45, 49-51

beaver hats, 26-29, 32-33; styles, *27*, *29*

beaver image: in advertising/commercial culture, 31-35; in art, 46-58; fetishistic, 31-32, 35; in political cartoons, 35-41; in popular culture, 22-26, 174n1; in sexual imaginary, 42-46

Beaver Tales, 49

Bederman, Gail, 91

Behar, Ruth, 190n49

Belmore, Rebecca, **5**, **10**, 55-58, 163-68

Benjamin, Walter, 5, 6, 19

Bergland, Renee L., 6

Berland, Jody, 99

Bhabha, Homi, 18-19, 55

Billig, Michael, xii, 11-12

blood, 165-68

Bobby, Josephine, 74, *75*

Boody, Trevor, 99

Bordo, Jonathan, 48

Bourdieu, Pierre, 11

Bovet, Jacques, 24, 175n13

Boyd, Jerry (or Harry), *73*

Boyer, Clarence, 137-38

Bradford, Tolly, 99-100

Brethour, Patrick, xi

Brogan, Kathleen, 4, 5

Bruce Mines, 1, 2, 3

Buffalo Hunt, 153-54

Buffalo National Park, 106

Buhkwujjenene, Chief, 129

Burns, Robert J., 95, 101, 103-7, 185n48

Butler, Judith, 21, 118

Callaway, Helen, 29

Cameron, Jim, *32*

Campbell, Maria, xii, 1, 7-8

Canada Day protest. *See* protests, G20 Summit

Canada West, 63, *64*

Canada/US relations, 36, *36, 37,* 51

Canadian Charter of Rights and Freedoms (1982), 159

Canadian Magazine, 101, 140

Canadian Multiculturalism Act (1988), 159, 161

Canadian Pacific Archives, 60, 77

Canadian Pacific Railway (CPR), 15; construction, 69, 71, 73, 77-79, 181n34, 188n102, 188n105; in contemporary culture, 59; effect on Indigenous and Métis people, 66-67; and imperial expansion, 62-65, 71, 77, 158; and male homosocial culture, 74, 77; objections to, 61-62; route, 65-66; and tourism, 67-68, 96-97

Canadian Race Relations Foundation, 11

Canadian-Canadians, 40-41, 45-46, 58

Canadianness: benign, ix-x, 11, 13, 14-15, 169n7; contradictions of, 16-17; as fairness, xi-xii; geography of, 1; as goodness, ix-xi; images of, 183n3; and Indigenous activities, 109; norms of, 79

Carlyle, Thomas, 30

Caruth, Cathy, 83

castor canadensis. See beaver

Cather, Willa, 60

Catlin, George, 97, 129, 183n10

Ceci n'est pas une pipe, **8**, 152-53

Chinamen's Peak, 124-25

Chinese-Canadians, *72*; as CPR labourers, 69, 71, 73, 77-79, 181n34 (*see also* bachelors); as CPR labourers, occupational death toll, 71, 73, 124, 188n102, 188n105; detained, 82-85, *84*; history of, 80-81, 92-93 (*see also Dirty Laundry*); as living machines, 78, 79; racialized, 124-25 (*see also* Exclusion Act (1923)); stigmatization

Guérard, Nicolas, **1**, 23

Haraway, Donna, 21, 52, 58
Harkin, James B., 97, 105-6, 183n11
Harper, Stephen, 10
Harris, Cole, 62, 66-67
Hart, E.J., 67-68
haunting: commemoration as, 11, 159;
    cultural, 7-8; involuntary nature of,
    4; of national communities, 156-59;
    power and, 5; and property, 6-7
Head Tax, 69, 77, 90, 180n23, 181n33
Hele, Karl, 132
Heritage Minutes, 15-16
hetero-: femininity, 50, 56-57, 119,
    174n82; masculinity, 9, 16, 79, 96,
    108-10, 153; normativity, 50, 82,
    89-90, 94, 96, 108, 113, 116-18
Hiawatha: culture hero, 130-31,
    189n11; Messiah figure, 137, 140
Hill, Richard William, 164, 165
home, 7, 12, 52-54, 162
homosexuality, 85, 88-92, 122, 152; in
    Alberta, 187n94; as contagion, 121,
    187n91
Hoy, Chow Dong (C.D.), 69-77, 78, 79,
    180n23
Hoy, Joe, 74, 76
Hudson's Bay Company (HBC), 32-33,
    149-50, 176n41

iconography: of Canadianness, 5, 60,
    112; of CPR, 60, 63, 79; of Indian-
    ness, 128-32; of nation building, 60,
    88; of national symbols, 159
identity: Anglo-Canadian, 16-18;
    Canadian, 9, 11-12, 95-96, 162;
    Euro-Canadian, 5, 15-16, 46, 54,
    62-63, 159; national, xii, 60, 183n3;
    Ojibwe, 134; as performative, 144;
    and persona, 164
immigrants: Chinese, 82-88; disen-
    franchisement, 161-62, 192n19;

earnings, 161; as emblems of multi-
    culturalism, 162; non-Anglo-Saxon,
    9-10
Immigration Act (1967), 159
Immigration Building (Victoria), the
    wall, 82-85, *84*, 181n49
immigration policies, 9, 16, 54, 93-94,
    159, 180n23; reasonable accommo-
    dation debate, 16, 173n75. *See also*
    Exclusion Act (1923); Head Tax;
    Immigration Building (Victoria),
    the wall
imperialist nostalgia, 35, 128, 141
Indian Act, 10, 134, 139; 1894 amend-
    ments, 142, 190n52
Indian play, 128, 147-48, 154-55
Indian Scout, **6**; and Champlain monu-
    ment, 144, *145*; and Harlequin
    romances, 146-48
Indianness: images of, 99-100, 142,
    144-47, 184n22; national statuary
    and, 147; sexualized, 147; Toronto
    exhibition, 135-36
Indians. *See* Indigenous peoples
indigenization: of women, 49, 178n85
Indigenous people, *73*, 170n9; as
    backward, 26, 175n20, 175n22; as
    Canadian icons, xi, 14; CPR and,
    65-67, *66*, 68, *70*; as dependants, 3;
    disenfranchised, 10-11; disenfran-
    chisement, 10-11, 159, 161-62;
    economically impoverished, 101-5,
    107; effects of national parks on,
    98-100; erasure of, 48, 49, 95, 109-
    10, 177n54; in fur trade, 45-46;
    inclusion of (*see also* exclusion); as
    intercultural brokers, 45-46, 130;
    labour of, 35, 57; as lazy, 31; poverty
    of, 161; primitivization of, 144-48;
    sexual expression of, 149; sexual-
    ized, 147; as spectacle, 97, 99-100;
    as spectres, 95, 106-7; as token
    Indians, 162

myths: Anishinaabek, 2, 130-32;
    benevolent Mountie, 13; of multi-
    culturalism, 160; of national patri-
    mony, 47-48; of origins, 47, 48, 49,
    98-99; of Rhapisunt, 178n83

Nanabozho. *See* Hiawatha
Nanabush. *See* Hiawatha
narratives: bear, 48-49; Canadianness,
    53; Chinese detainees', 82-85; of
    Chinese detainees, 181n49; of
    colonial authority, 9; European
    traders', 25-26, 175n20; of European
    traders, 30; Indigenous women,
    177n70; mass migration, 83; natural
    history *vs.* Enlightenment, 25;
    patriarchal, 52; poaching, 103-4;
    railway, 60-62; wilderness, 48-49
nation building: assimilation and,
    149-50; Banff vision of, 99; charac-
    ter of, 18-19; museums and, 97;
    racialized and gendered, 45-46;
    trauma of, 4, 5, 6, 11. *See also*
    Canadian Pacific Railway (CPR),
    and western settlement; settlement,
    Asian; settlement, Euro-Canadian
national emblems: as brand, 95-96;
    iconography of, 159; meanings of,
    18; as metaphor, 11; *vs.* national
    literature, 15; *vs.* popular discourse,
    16-17. *See also specific national
    emblems*
National Gallery of Canada, 47, 148,
    178n71
national parks, 97-101, 105-7, 185n48.
    See also specific national parks
national symbols. *See* national emblems
nationalism: banal, 11-12; colonial, 9;
    figures of, 124; gendered and
    racialized, 60-69; images of, ix,
    15-16; secret, xi, xii; shifts in, 159
natural history, 22-25, 51-52
Nault, Robert, 184n19

Neveau, Angela, 141
Nixon, Richard, 36
No One Is Illegal, 169n7
noble Indian, 11, 127, 128-29, 146-47,
    154
Noble Indian, 14
Nolan, Rose, 136
North-West Mounted Police, 66, 87,
    101, 185n34

Ojeeg, Susan, 188n10
Onderdonk, Andrew, 77
open secrets. *See* secrets, open/public
Orbinski, James, xi
Owram, Doug, 62, 65

Park Ranger, The, 95, 107-12
Park Rangers. *See* park wardens
park wardens, 101-7, *102, 105*; gender
    and, 118-19; as icon, 116; and
    Indigenous people, 98-99; reconfig-
    uring, 113. *See also* Lesbian Rangers
patriotism, ix, *x,* xi, 12, 96
Pels, Peter, 157
performance art: as postcard, 51-55,
    112-13, *113*-25, *114*; communal
    participation in, 134-35; double
    coding, 137, 138-39; and labour of
    the negative, 163-68
photography: Chinese *vs.* European
    conventions, 69, 71, *72,* 73-74, 79;
    salvage, 74
Pine, Jean, 134, 135-37
Pine, John Erskine, 134, 189n27
*Plain Facts from Farmers in the
    Canadian North West,* 63, 65, 66
political caricatures, 35-41, 177n54
politics: of art and secrets, 19-21;
    Canada/US, 36, *36, 37*; internal,
    177n54; of language, 170n9; of love
    and friendship, 21; national, *38, 39,
    40, 41*
Pon, Madge, 182n69

Sedgwick, Eve, 92

self-image, Canada, 13-14, 15, 87, 97. *See also* Canadianness; national identity

settlement, Asian, 55. *See also* Chinese-Canadians

settlement, Euro-Canadian, 2, 26-31, 184n17; in Canada *vs.* US, 62-63; CPR and, 62-65, 158-59; effects of, 10; traditions of, 35; western, 71, 74, 77, 90

sexuality: degenerate/deviant, 92, 115, 174n82 (*see also* homosexuality; lesbians); discourse of, 81; in landscape painting, 151-52; norms of, 42, 77, 79 (*see also* hetero-); and power, 19, 148-49; women's, 45, 48-51, 57

sexualization: of Asia, 92; of beaver image, 43-45; of forms of affiliation, 71; of Indianness, 147; of Indigenous people, 147; of railway, 59, 60; of women, 45-46, 50

Shah, Nayan, 80, 86, 92

Sharma, Nandita, 162, 163

Shingwauk Indian Residential School, 1, 139, 171n2

Shingwaukonse, Chief, 2-3, 129, 134, 137, 139, 189n18, 189n27

Shohat, Ella, 20

Sibbald, Howard E., 101, *102*, 103

Siksika Nation, 99, 124, 184n19

silencing, 83-84

Sinclair, Benjamin, 149

Slotkin, Richard, 13

Smith, Donald, 60

social classes: aristocratic, 27-28, 42; and exclusion, 98 (*see also* immigrants; Indigenous people); and language, 42-44; lower, 30, 42, 43; middle, 27, 28, 33, 42-43, 90; of tourists, 96-97, 100-1; working,

6, 86-87 (*see also* Chinese-Canadians)

socio-sexual relationships, 74-77

Song of Hiawatha, 2, 127, 130-32. *See also* Garden River First Nation, *Hiawatha* performances

Souvenirs of the Self (Banff Park Museum), **4**, 19, 51-55

spectres. *See* ghosts

Spence, Thomas, 63-64

Spirit of Canada Eating Beaver, The, **3**, 49-51

Spirit of Canada Suckling the French and English Beavers, The, **2**, 46-49, 50

Stam, Robert, 20

Stasiulis, Daiva, 10

Steinbauer, Henry, 149

Steven, Peter, 85

Stewart, George, 103, 185n38

Stickney, Alpheus, 77

Stimson, Adrian Sr., Chief, 184n19

Stoler, Ann Laura, 9, 182n60

subject without properties, 14-19

subjectivity, 80, 120

survival, 15-16, 83-85

Taussig, Michael, 5, 9, 165, 167

taxidermy, 52, 54-55

Teitelbaum, Matthew, 151

Thobani, Sunera, 9

Thomas, Bear, 142, *145*

Thomas, Jeff, **6**, *14*, 128, 142-48, *145*

Thompson, David, 25

Thompson, E.P., 98

Townsend-Gault, Charlotte, 56

Trachtenberg, Alan, 139, 190n39

Treaty of Washington, 130

Treaty Seven, 99, 101, 184n19

Trudeau, Pierre Elliott, 36, 39, 96

True Patriot Love, 47, 178n71

truth, 6, 85, 165

Turcotte, G., 8
Turner, Margaret, 8
Twelve Angry Crinolines, 55, 56

Uluschak, Edd, 36
United Nations Declaration on the
    Rights of Indigenous Peoples
    (2010), 10
University of Toronto Quarterly, 8-9

Valverde, Marianna, 182n69
Van Horne, William, 77-79, *78*
Van Kirk, Sylvia, 45-46
Verduyn, Christl, 49
Vibert, Elizabeth, 25-26

Wabunosa, 132
Walcott, Rinaldo, 160
Walker, R.B.J., 112
Walter, Kathryn, 113-25
water, 164-67
Watson, Scott, 164
Waugh, Thomas, 80
Webster, Daniel, 61-62
What's the Point?, 144, 146-47
wheat, 63-64
whiteness: of Anglo-Canadian identity,
    16-18, 40-41; of authority, 116-
    17; of Banff, 187n90, 188n98; as
    Canadian ideal, 62-63, 101-4, 108,
    126; as category, 86-87, 124; dis-
    embodiedness of, 17-18; in Heritage
    Minutes, 15-16; imperial, 86-88; as
    innocence, 123-24; of LNPS artists,
    123-24, 125; and nation building,
    45-46; as norm, 79, 96, 174n82; of

wilderness ideal, 97, 100-1, 113. *See
    also* Euro-Canadians; settlement,
    Euro-Canadian
Wieland, Joyce, **2**, 46-49, 50, 58,
    178n81, 178nn71-72
Wilby, Emma, 157
wilderness, 48-49; as brand, 95-96; as
    free land, 98-99, 184n17; as identity,
    95-96; as marketing tool, 67-68;
    railway construction *vs.*, 61-62;
    rethinking, 96-101; as tonic, 100-1,
    185n24; women in, 119-20
Williams, Albert, 134
Williams, Patricia, 6
Wilson, Martha, 112, 114
Winter Olympics (2010), ix, x-xi, 14
women: authority of, 10; immigrant,
    192n19; Indigenous, 45-46, 57,
    177n70; Indigenous artists, 138,
    167, 190n38 (*see also individual
    Indigenous female artists*); as park
    wardens, 118-19; role in nation, 48,
    58, 91-92, 174n82; sexuality of,
    48-49, 49-51; sexualized/inferior,
    45; white, 146, 147
Wright, Cynthia, 163

Xing, Jun, 81

Yeigh, Frank, 140
Yellowstone National Park, 183n9,
    183n11
Yoon, Jin-me, **4**, 19, 51-55

Ziegler, Jean, 163